ONE SIGNAL
PUBLISHERS

ATRIA

ALSO BY STEPHANIE LAND

*Maid*

# class

## A MEMOIR

## Stephanie Land

ONE SIGNAL
PUBLISHERS

ATRIA

NEW YORK | LONDON | TORONTO | SYDNEY | NEW DELHI

This memoir has been pieced together with the help of interviews, notes,
essays, syllabi, social media posts, emails, documents, direct messages,
and my ever-faithful day planner. Some names and identifying characteristics
have been changed. Time and some events have been compressed.
Dialogue has been approximated. Great care has been taken to tell
my truths. This is my story and how I remember it.

ONE SIGNAL
PUBLISHERS

ATRIA

An Imprint of Simon & Schuster, Inc.
1230 Avenue of the Americas
New York, NY 10020

Copyright © 2023 by Stephanie Land

First One Signal Publishers/Atria Books hardcover edition November 2023

ONE SIGNAL PUBLISHERS / ATRIA BOOKS and colophon are
trademarks of Simon & Schuster, Inc.

For information about special discounts for bulk purchases, please contact Simon
& Schuster Special Sales at 1-866-506-1949 or business@simonandschuster.com.

The Simon & Schuster Speakers Bureau can bring authors to your live event. For
more information or to book an event, contact the Simon & Schuster Speakers
Bureau at 1-866-248-3049 or visit our website at www.simonspeakers.com.

Interior design by Joy O'Meara @ Creative Joy Designs

Manufactured in the United States of America

1 3 5 7 9 10 8 6 4 2

Library of Congress Cataloging-in-Publication Data has been applied for.

ISBN 978-1-9821-5139-3
ISBN 978-1-9821-5141-6 (ebook)

*For Coraline*


Years rolled on again, and Wendy had a daughter.
This ought not to be written in ink but in a golden splash.

—*J. M. Barrie*

Sometimes life is hard. Things go wrong.
And in life, and in love, and in business, and in friendship,
and in health and in all the other ways that life can go wrong, and
when things get tough, this is what you should do:
MAKE GOOD ART.

*—Neil Gaiman, University of the Arts,*
*Class of 2012, Commencement Address*

# Contents

# class

# 1

# First Days

My daughter arrived at her first day of kindergarten with a back-pack full of donated supplies. Our morning had been the usual rush to get her hair brushed without too much resistance or screaming, and teeth brushed without me needing to watch, allowing me a moment to take huge gulps of hot coffee while I stared at the day planner lying open on the counter. Now Emilia reached up to hold my hand, eyes fixed on the line of buses across the field. Children ran toward the school, their new backpacks dangling from their elbows, nearly touching the freshly mowed grass. Several broke away in the direction of the large playground that was one of our favorite places to spend summer afternoons. Most of the kids slowed as they reached the asphalt behind the school, crowding together where I assumed there must be a back door to the gymnasium.

As I started to move in that direction, Emilia's small, sweaty hand clutched mine more tightly. I knelt down to look her in the eye and grinned. Emilia had been so excited about her first-day-of-school outfit that she'd worn it to bed. Her babysitter told me about it when I had arrived home at 10 p.m., exhausted after my own first day of classes for my senior year of college. I'd smiled when I saw the outfit she had chosen. It was the same one she'd worn pretty constantly lately, a brightly colored leotard I'd bought her the year before for the preschool she had attended at a gymnastics center. The stretchy material seemed to perfectly fit her determination to never stop moving.

This morning she'd added a maroon zip-up hoodie with gray letters across the front that spelled GRIZ, the mascot for the University of Montana. I had rescued it from a lost-and-found. Those sweatshirts were a dime a dozen in my town.

"You okay?" I asked, resisting the urge to rub her shoulders. She nodded in response. Most of my experience with parenting her was spent alone, so I felt like I knew my kid pretty well. Emilia wasn't the type to want hugs of reassurance. I reached up to try to push her hood down so I could gently smooth her hair. She dodged and I didn't persist, choosing instead to stand up again, watching the kids, some chasing each other and some going back and forth on swings.

Emilia had had a rough few days. She'd spent only a week with her dad this summer and said goodbye to him a few days before. The geographical distance between them had been my doing. Life in close proximity to her dad, Jamie, had become unbearably unhealthy and so I made the difficult decision two years ago to move us more than five hundred miles away to Missoula, Montana. Jamie became abusive soon after I told him that I was pregnant seven years ago, and his cruelty had escalated when I said I wasn't getting an abortion. He took every opportunity since then to tear me down with words and threats of violence, not hiding his joy over my struggles, and expressing resentment and anger for any amount of success I experienced. Our parenting agreement included a paragraph outlining that his time with our daughter was limited due to his history of domestic violence. I had stared at those words, reading them over and over. I'd fought tirelessly for his abuse to be acknowledged by the courts and I still found it hard to trust that I had finally been believed.

Jamie had promised Emilia she could come visit him for a month over the summer, but as usual, he broke as many promises as he made, and then it became my responsibility to break my kid's heart by telling her he wouldn't follow through. Instead of finding child care for that summer, he said his teenage brother (who didn't drive) could fly up and watch Emilia, or maybe his coworker's wife could help out for a few hours a day at her house all the way across town. None of his plans made any sort of logical sense. It was like he thought our kid was already in middle school instead of turning six that summer.

I forced him to tell her himself that he'd shortened her visit to a week because he couldn't find a babysitter, and that she wasn't getting the new bike he'd promised her, either. He didn't call often, but before Emilia's visit all he had talked about was that he planned to teach her how to ride a bike. He promised her a pink bicycle with a basket and one of those doll-size seats you can attach to the back. Emilia drew pictures of it at preschool and between the pages of notes I took in class. Her preschool teacher beamed when Emilia talked about how excited she was. I didn't have the heart to lean over to the teacher and say in a low voice that the father Emilia adored was an emotionally abusive asshole.

After the disappointments at the start of her summer, I tried my best to talk up what we could do instead. That worked, or it seemed to, but she ignored the bike that a housecleaning client had handed down to me. When I asked her if she wanted to try it, she refused, adding that she never wanted to ride a bike ever in her whole life.

Jamie, ironically, lived on Montana Street in Portland, Oregon, in a house he rented with his cousin and a couple of other people. I never knew how many roommates he had or how old they were or where my kid slept at night. This time he said he would get an air mattress for him to sleep on and give her the bed, but I doubted that happened. His preparations for her visit consisted of pulling out two bins of her clothes and toys.

A friend offered to drive me to pick up Emilia from her dad's at the end of her visit since my car wasn't reliable enough for long trips anymore. As we came to a stop in front of Jamie's house, wondering if it was the right one, he opened the front door and walked down first to hand me Emilia's backpack. I jogged across the street to meet him before he could get too close to Sylvie, who sat in the driver's seat with the window down out of curiosity. I didn't want him to smile and wave at her in an effort to charm her, which was his MO. It was another form of his gaslighting, to try to convince the people around me that he was a good guy. Without saying anything, I took the backpack from him and turned to put it on the backseat next to Emilia's booster.

"She's a little upset," he said behind me, loud enough so Sylvie could hear across the street. I didn't want to look at his face. He liked to say things like this. He *liked* to think Emilia didn't want to leave his house, instead of acknowledging the complexities of the situation or protecting her from concepts that were far too adult for her to understand. He *liked* to tell her he didn't know if he would have enough money to see her in six months. He *liked* to tell her that he had to give me "a lot of money" and how that made it hard for him to see her.

Emilia clung to him when he brought her out, her feet hooked together, one hand grasped around her other wrist behind his neck. He made a display of how hard she held on by raising his hands to let go. He laughed, smiling big enough to show his crooked tooth. When I reached for her, she surprised me by immediately putting her arms around my neck, her hands and feet locking together in the same way. We walked across the street like that, Jamie following a few paces before he stopped on the curb in front of his house.

"Bye, Emilia! Daddy loves you!" He said it again when she didn't respond, then I felt her chest quake with sobs, like she couldn't hold them in anymore. I walked around to the other side of the car and held her, feeling her whole body shake with every sound she made in my ear. I burst into tears along with her.

"I'm so sorry," I told her, stroking the back of her head. I didn't know what else to say.

Several minutes passed before I could get Emilia into her booster seat and buckled. When Sylvie started her car and drove off, Emilia put her hand on the window and cried out "Daddy!" over and over until it became a sort of moan.

But Jamie had already gone back inside, never noticing that we took a while to leave, never coming back out to check on her or wave goodbye. It was probably best he didn't. Her first day of kindergarten was in four days and my classes began in two. We had to switch gears whether we were ready to or not.

"Well," I said, pushing myself off the car. The kids on the playground grew in numbers as more ran over from the back of the school to join them. We'd been standing there for about five minutes, watching them chase each other and shout while they played. "I figure we should go see what they have for breakfast!"

Emilia nodded and took a step to walk across the grass with me. Her school offered a free breakfast and lunch to kids who qualified, and even had a program where they'd send home a bag of food in her backpack on Fridays. That form had been easy—just a check in a box next to a question asking if anyone in the household was on food stamps. Applying for the Supplemental Nutrition Assistance Program (SNAP) and receiving food stamps had been a complicated maze since I found out that I was pregnant. "Just" a check next to the word *yes* felt a little too good to be true.

Behind the large brick building I could see the door where most of the kids had funneled in. Her hand squeezed mine again when we entered the gymnasium. On the drive over, I'd had to promise several times that I would sit with her while she ate breakfast. It was a relief to see some other adults doing the same thing, awkwardly perched on the low benches attached to the four rows of tables covering half of the recently polished floor.

Emilia followed a few other kids to a line of tables that had several different breakfast options available. Some of them were in a cellophane pouch kind of thing and had been heated up that way but I couldn't tell what they were. French toast sticks possibly? I was happy to see Emilia choose a personal-size package of cereal, a small carton of milk, and a plastic cup of juice sealed with a foil lid. Next, she held the tray all by herself while she carefully approached the end of the line where a lady was accepting tickets and cash or wrote down a number a kid recited to her. She looked at Emilia and put her hand on her hip.

"And what about you, young lady?"

"I . . ." I started, not knowing what to say. Maybe my forms hadn't been processed. Were we supposed to have tickets? "I filled out a form?"

"Oh," the woman said. "A free meal kid!" I will never know why she felt the need to assert this aloud to a kindergartner and anyone else within earshot. I glanced around us, my face getting hot, but Emilia didn't seem to notice anything. "What's your name, miss?"

"Emilia Land," my daughter said. The woman started to write it down and paused.

"That's E-M-I-L-I-A L-A-N-D," I said, and put my hand on my daughter's back to lead her away. We sat at an empty table, like a couple of new kids. Emilia carefully peeled back the foil on the juice and the top of the plastic container of cereal, but asked for help with the milk. I tried to show her how to do it on her own, and we both laughed because I had a hard time getting it open, too. While she ate, I regretted not bringing my usual to-go cup of coffee poured into an empty jar of Adams crunchy peanut butter—a main staple in my diet since it was covered by Women, Infants, and Children (WIC) checks.

"I remember my first day of kindergarten," I said softly. Emilia looked up at me. Her new haircut made her look like Ramona Quimby. (We'd just finished the series for the second time.) "This is your first day of school in Missoula, Montana! You're gonna be here all the way through high school!" I had tried to explain over the last few months why this had been such a big deal to me. That when I was a kid I had to move around a lot from Washington State to Alaska and back, and how always being the new kid made me feel shy. "You're going to make friends, maybe even today, that you'll have for the rest of your life, Emilia."

"When I go to your school?" She pointed at the "Griz" on her sweatshirt for emphasis, and I tried not to wrinkle my nose, thinking of the drunk football fans who clogged downtown bars on game days.

"If that's what you want," I said. "But you have a long time to figure that out."

She picked up her tray when she was done and carried it to the back door where there were three almost-full trash cans and a table with several stacks of empty trays. After we walked out, Emilia looked at all the boys twice her size chasing each other around on the blacktop, backpacks long forgotten by the wall. She reached her arms up, and I carried her back to the side of the school where we had walked in, setting her down so she could line up with the other kids. A woman stood at the front, holding a sign with a big letter *K* on it, talking and laughing with the teacher standing next to her holding up a sign that had the number one. A tiny blonde girl was crying, and Emilia turned around to look at her. She made a face like she might start crying, too, but then she looked at me and I smiled as big as I could, before the other parents swarmed in closer with cameras and tissues in their hands.

Her teacher walked down the line and talked to each child, then gathered them to her like a hen does with her chicks, and bent down to tell them something the kids all seemed to like. Emilia leaned in and listened, then lined up again like she must have been told to do. She turned and waved and blew me a few kisses and I did the same, wanting to laugh and cry at the same time. I was just so damn proud of us.

Her school supplies had been donated to the gymnastics gym, and I had been so grateful someone called to offer it to us. The donation saved me not only fifty bucks, but the few hours I would have spent searching through the chaotic school supply aisles of Walmart. Instead, we'd been able to make a quick stop to pick out a backpack and some new shoes for school. I marveled for a second at the boots she'd selected herself. She was fully prepared. Well, almost. We still had a couple of weeks to get her medical records. When her school reminded me of that, it dawned on me that she hadn't been sick since we'd moved to Montana. Quite a change from when we lived in Washington, where a trip to the doctor was a monthly occurrence. All of it, all the fighting to move, arguing over visitations, and the transitions coming back home, had come to this moment. We'd done it. I'd done it. It had been my goal to get us somewhere we could live all the way through Emilia's grade-school years—all the way through high school—and here we were. We lived in a place, in a community, where we'd found support and friendship and opportunities and maybe, eventually, something like a chosen family.

Emilia turned and followed the kid in front of her into the building without looking back at me. We'd been through the hard good-byes in day care for several years by then, and I tried not to think about those. I felt like skipping, or hopping over some kind of imaginary milestone. Another parent walked briskly past me and I almost said, *I did it!* before catching myself. Turning around to look at the school again, its yard littered with a couple of forgotten backpacks, I closed my eyes and breathed in and out. I wanted to pause and let the feelings wash through me before rushing home to attack an impossible mountain of homework, laundry, and calls to schedule housecleaning clients. All of this would have to get done within the precious three hours Emilia was in school, before I'd return to this spot to pick her up and hear all about her day.

## 2

# What Happened Last Summer

Jamie had called two weeks before he was supposed to take our kid for the summer. After I saw who it was, I let it ring a couple of times. I stared at the spot on the driver's-side door where the interior had peeled away to reveal the dark orange foam behind it. I'd purposefully arrived fifteen minutes early to pick up Emilia from the gymnastics gym where she went to preschool. I looked forward to that fifteen minutes. It was a precious and rare opportunity to close my eyes and sit in silence.

As lovely as those moments were, I felt a pang of guilt for so desperately looking forward to her spending the summer with her dad. For months I'd been fantasizing about those child-free weeks—

about the extra work I could take on to pay down credit card debt or possibly save some money for inevitable car repairs, and about the extra time I'd have to spend with friends, or maybe go out on a date or two. Most of all, I needed the three-day backpacking trip through the Bob Marshall Wilderness that I'd been planning and training for since the winter months. It wasn't just that I needed a break, though. I needed reassurance that I wasn't alone in raising Emilia. Because I still wasn't ready to accept that I was.

I did find myself wondering if some sort of finality, like Jamie deciding to give up his visitation completely, would be better for Emilia and me. Emilia wouldn't be kept in a place of constant wondering when she would see her dad again. And I would probably shift gears quite a bit as a single mother. Jamie's instability required me to be more stable, more responsible, and to pick up his slack—it was no wonder I craved a break so much, and that the disappointment was so crushing when it was snatched away from me. Maybe it would actually be easier for me if I wasn't expecting to get a break at all.

Through a painstaking number of emails, we'd finally agreed to meet at a halfway point between us the weekend before Memorial Day. It would give me about a week before summer school started, and I had already advertised my cleaning services, scheduling jobs during peak move-out season, when a lot of college kids went home.

For about six months, I had spent two hours every morning before Emilia woke up vacuuming and scrubbing the gym's bathrooms to pay her tuition. While I was gone, I trusted my roommate to listen for Emilia if she tried to do something like sneak ice cream for breakfast (for this and occasional after-school pickups, I gave my roommate a cut on rent). When, only a few months into the school year, I had to tell the gym's owner that I couldn't do it any longer, he thankfully offered me a scholarship before I could try to explain why. I currently had two weeks before my junior year ended, and the three hours it took to clean my Wednesday morning house wore me out after I'd been up late writing a paper. If I'd had to clean the gym as well it would have broken me.

Normally, I didn't answer when Jamie called, and would wait to see if it was important enough to leave a message. He hated that I did this, but I discovered it was easier that way instead of offering him another chance to call me selfish for moving away and going to college. Lately he liked to add that no one would ever love me because of that.

*Fuck it*, I thought, and answered on the fourth ring. "Yeah?"

"I can't take her this summer," he said.

"What do you mean, you can't take her?" I tried not to allow my voice to get high or fast or even loud. "Like you can't pick her up to drive her to your house?"

"No," he said, sounding annoyed already. Then he talked really slow, something he did before he asked if I was stupid. "I can't afford child care. And my mom got a job and can't help out." He had moved from where we met, in Port Townsend, Washington, to Portland a few months after we got to Missoula. His cousin got him a good job as a janitor for a commercial bakery, vouching for him so they would overlook his lack of a high school diploma. He usually headed in at noon and didn't get home until nine. Whenever Emilia went to visit him, he had to fly his mom in from North Carolina to watch her. "It wouldn't make sense for Emilia to come, anyway," he added. "I'd only get to see her a couple of hours a day on the days I have to work." He didn't mention that he worked four days, leaving him the other three days of the week to spend all day with her. I tried not to imagine what Emilia and I could do together if I had three totally free days off every week.

He stopped talking but I couldn't think of a response. Every domino I'd painstakingly set in place for the summer was crashing down. Forget the extra money, forget the extra sleep, forget the precious few evenings I might have to go out with friends, or to go on a hike or climb. Or breathe.

The more immediate and potentially disastrous problem was that it was too late for me to get Emilia into summer camps, especially any that offered a sliding scale. I doubted I could bring her to my summer school literature class, which met from nine to noon five days a week. "Well," I managed to say, "I'm going to need more child support money." I imagined the look on his face in response to this statement. As part of the relocation paperwork for the court to allow us to move to Missoula, I included a new child support agreement where he'd pay almost a hundred and fifty dollars less than he'd been required to pay by the court. I had also promised him that I would never ask for more.

"What I give you isn't enough? You might not realize this, but they take taxes out when you get a *real* paycheck. Us out here in the real world have to work instead of go to college. And we have landlords who increase our rent every year." His voice got louder as he listed off more reasons why he was broke, and I held the phone away from my ear. Eventually he paused, taking a long drag off his cigarette. He must have been on his lunch break at work. I pictured him, a single white male with expendable income and few attachments, while he told me the three hundred dollars he had to pay me each month kept him from living the life he really wanted.

"Summer day camp is two hundred bucks a week here, Jamie. How do you expect me to afford that on my own?"

"Well, I've been telling you to get a full-time job like me." There was a pause in which I could almost hear the wheels turning in his head as it dawned on him that he'd dug himself into a logical hole. He'd just said that even with a full-time job, he couldn't afford child care that summer. How would a full-time job magically enable me to afford it on my own? His voice lost some of its edge. "I guess I can help you out."

I knew better than to trust him enough to accept his offer for whatever he thought "help" might be. My desperation hadn't reached that level. It wasn't that I thought he couldn't afford it: I knew from the frequent vacations he took and the vehicles he drove that he could afford to send me some additional funds for the child care. But if he viewed the money as a favor I'd never hear the end of it. I also knew I couldn't rely on it being consistent. On more than one occasion, he'd dangled the promise of money over my head like a carrot hanging from the end of a stick. I could only get help from him in a way that he'd adhere to if I went through the court system and had someone else decide. Then, of course, I'd have to hear him say I "turned him in" for making more money, but it would be worth it.

"No, it's fine. I'll . . ." I wasn't sure how to finish. What *would* I do? "I'll figure it out." That was usually my only choice when it came to parenting and caring for Emilia. I pressed the button to end the call, resisting the urge to smash my phone to pieces on the dashboard.

Emilia came bouncing up to meet me when I walked into her classroom. "She's been talking about Portland all day," her teacher said, petting my kid's head while she held up another drawing of a bike.

My vision grew blurry with tears that I tried to blink away. "That's great," I said. "Is that a teddy bear in the baby seat?" She skipped along beside me as we made our way to the car. I decided to wait to tell her. Sometimes Jamie needed to get angry and yell at me a bit before he thought situations through in a rational way.

My mind circled for solutions while I vacuumed a lawyer's office later that evening. Then I remembered we had a legal document that a judge had signed in which Jamie agreed to parent for six weeks during the summer. He had once tried to put me in contempt of court for missing his weekend visit. The no-contact order hadn't been lifted yet, so he didn't have a legal leg to stand on, but in this case I did. And maybe I could try the same thing?

On Friday morning, I waited for five minutes outside the court's Family Law Self-Help Center office before it opened. When the administrator arrived, coffee in hand, her gaze went straight to my accordion file folder containing five years' worth of court documents.

After explaining what had happened and asking if I could file for contempt of court for refusing visitation for the summer, the woman barked out a laugh.

"No judge would force a parent to take their child," she said. "It's usually the other way around! They force to give them *back*."

"Right," I said, and looked down. I wasn't there to force him, though, I was there to stick up for my kid. And I guess for me. For some reason I thought the court system might be able to help me, or at least dole out a slap on the wrist. Even a shake of a finger while someone told him to get his shit together and be a father would probably scare him enough to consider more options.

"Does he pay child support?" she asked, and I nodded. "Well, if he has less visitation, then he owes more in support. It's that simple." She turned to walk to the back wall where they kept a row of filing cabinets and returned with a heavy packet that said PARENTING PLAN MODIFICATION on the front. I'd already been through that, but I took the packet anyway. "Get less visitation on paper, then get the child support modified."

Instead of going back home, I drove across town to the child support office to ask if there was another way. I doubted a judge would grant a motion to modify a parenting plan because of one missed summer, especially if Jamie made the case that he had to work. It didn't matter to the court that I had to work, too.

"Your case is out of Washington State," the woman behind the counter told me. "We don't have jurisdiction."

"So I have to call them?"

"No, you have to go through Portland, where the person paying the support lives," she said.

"Then," I began, but decided against saying more. She seemed to be finished with our conversation, and a person was in line behind me. At home I found the number for the office in Portland, and when I finally got someone on the phone, they told me they would mail the packet for a child support modification.

"Just fill that out and mail it to us," she said, "and you'll hear back in six months to a year."

"So I can't do anything?" I asked.

"Ma'am, I just told you what you can do."

"Right," I said. "Thank you."

---

I let Emilia do the dinner dishes, which really meant letting her play with bubbles in the sink. I watched her from our small table, while also looking for a summer day camp with a sliding scale. Emilia gently applied handfuls of bubbles to her cheeks. I felt an ache of love for her big enough to fill my whole chest, but the pressure of suddenly being the only dependable one responsible for her care turned that love into a kind of suffocation, like my body wasn't big enough for both feelings at the same time. Even worse, it triggered a fight-or-flight response, and since I was too tired to fight, all I wanted was to run away.

I'd essentially parented myself since I got my driver's license. Then, when I was twenty-one, my mother resigned her duties for good and took off to Europe, where she met and married her second husband (who is just seven years older than me). Consumed by my own desire to flee, I now worried that I was just like her. But the difference between my mom and me was that she had simply never wanted to be a mom in the first place. I fantasized about leaving the stresses of my life behind, but I never blamed that on Emilia like I felt my mom did with me. My desire was for the overwhelming feelings of desperation, of panic at having nowhere to turn and disaster always breathing down my neck, to end.

A therapist who offered a sliding scale agreed to do a single session with me because it was all I could scrape up the extra funds for. She listened for an hour, then told me I needed to tell a family member about feeling so suffocated by stress that I wanted to disappear. It was such a startling desire that it scared me. I'd struggled with suicidal ideation since I was a teenager, but to run away? I loved my kid. I loved my life. Why did I suddenly feel a thousand urges to get as far away from that as possible? Did I actually *envy* my mom for moving halfway across the world? Out of pure desperation, I picked up my phone to call my dad to ask for help. He couldn't afford to help me financially, so I knew I wouldn't get it from him directly, but I might get him to ask my aunt for some assistance. It was better for the request to come from him. She hated it when people asked her for money, since she was the only person in the family who had any. In my early twenties, she got upset over people not being grateful enough for the gifts she bought for Christmas. Ever since, we each received a few pairs of socks from her instead. In her defense, they *were* nice socks.

I tried my best to explain the situation to my dad, and how I felt like I was drowning from it all. I took a breath, and I asked if he might be able to talk to his sister about paying for Emilia's child care at the gymnastics gym that summer.

"I can probably go back to cleaning the gym to barter partial tuition. And you can remind her that when I borrowed money from her before, I paid her back." I got up and walked into the bedroom so Emilia wouldn't hear. "Dad, please. Please? I don't know what else to do. It's been a rough couple of weeks. I have to work. I can't bring her with me all the time. There's no way she can come to school with me this summer. The money doesn't even have to go to me. She can pay the gym directly. I can give you the phone number if you want." I paused to take a deep breath. My dad let out a sigh. "Dad, I'm . . ." I sniffed involuntarily, feeling a tear fall from the tip of my nose. "I've been kind of sad lately. Um. I got in with this therapist for a single session and she really wanted me to tell you all of this. I kind of can't stop crying sometimes? I'm just really kind of freaking out because it's just me, you know? It's just me and I just . . . there's something deep inside me that really doesn't want to have to live through this anymore." I took a breath and held it in. "And I guess I don't know what to do about that. I just really need some help. I need to know I'm not alone in this anymore."

There was such a long pause that I thought he'd hung up on me. Finally he said, "Gee, Steph, that sounds like a lot." He paused again, long enough for me to let some hope creep in. "Let me give you a call back." Then he hung up.

I looked at my phone in disbelief. My stomach growled as I walked back to our kitchen area, and I briefly considered eating the remains of Emilia's mac and cheese and hot dogs, which were congealing in a plastic Hello Kitty bowl on the table. My phone remained silent and dark.

At work earlier that day I'd tucked fitted sheets into their place over the king-size mattress of one of my regular clients. Her comforter had changed to a lighter weight for summer, blue instead of maroon. In smoothing out the creases, a splotch appeared from one of my tears and I desperately tried to wipe it off. This was a client who was always home, since she worked from an expansive office in the back of the bottom floor. I usually went down there to sheepishly ask if it was okay for me to vacuum as my final task. Horrified, I wiped my face, but the tears wouldn't stop, so I pressed my palms into my cheekbones in a desperate attempt to hold them in. There was no breathing exercise, no consolation, that would fend off this panic. I didn't know how I would make it through the summer without losing our housing. Within weeks we could be homeless—again.

By that time, I had spent years—since I got pregnant and Jamie kicked me out for the first time—living with varying degrees of food and housing insecurity. Emilia, at age five, had lived in fifteen homes, including the ones she spent time at when she went to her dad's. Nothing had any sense of safety or permanence. The possibility of losing the home where my child slept was always at the forefront of my mind and caused a constant, mind-buzzing anxiety attack. Repeatedly, whenever things started to feel secure, the floor would drop out from under me. My life teetered between what I referred to as "a crushing sense of hopelessness" and "a whole new level of exhaustion" without any sort of break between the two. The fight to make rent, eat, and find child care was constant. I never got a break from it.

Maybe there was still time to get a refund on my summer tuition. It was just one literature class, but then I remembered I needed to take it before I could register for the required 300-level Literature Criticism class in the fall, which I had to take before the required Shakespeare class in the spring. Considering to drop the class created a hot flash of anger before it left a searing burn of guilt and shame. Maybe Jamie was right, and my college education was an unnecessary luxury. Most of my classmates were fifteen years younger than me, a single mom who fed her kid with the limited amount I could purchase with food stamps. Who the fuck was I to get a Bachelor of Arts in English? There weren't a lot of jobs for people with degrees in creative writing. Or at least, that's what they told us undergrads, thus rendering my bachelor's degree even more useless, and my dream of obtaining a Master of Fine Arts all the more necessary to achieve. Even now, with loans, grants, and scholarships, there was no way I could pay off the money I had already borrowed. The irony was not lost on me that in order to make enough money to pay off my student loans, I needed to take out more.

Quitting was tempting, because as much as I wanted to be a professional writer, my love for writing terrified me. If I admitted how important writing was to me, if I really went for it, then it could all be taken away. And if I failed, I'd prove right all the friends and family who'd encouraged me to get a two-year degree from a community college so I could step to the front of the line for an administrative assistant job. Once again, my pursuit of higher education and with it the dreams of being a writer, everything I had worked so hard for, seemed like purchasing a fresh-off-the-lot, overpriced car. Sure, I could argue that I needed it to get around, but the fifty-thousand-dollar price tag was extravagant to the point of absurdity.

My computer dinged, and I looked at the window where I'd been chatting with a friend who was well versed in all things Missoula summer camps. "I think the YMCA offers financial aid," she wrote. "I wanna say they have some kind of reserve for emergency situations?"

Between dropping Emilia off at preschool and cleaning another client's house, I stopped by the YMCA to ask about the financial aid, bringing my purple folder with me in case they needed proof of income or expenses or things like utility bills or an envelope that had been mailed to me—the requirements for proof of need never seemed to be the same wherever you went. Instead of the huge packet

I was accustomed to, it was just a couple of pages that took a few minutes to fill out in the lobby. I waited for the girl behind the counter to finish a phone call and she looked at me and smiled, smoothing the top of her hair before she twirled her high ponytail in an effort to keep its single ringlet in place.

"Hi, um, do you know when they usually make decisions on these?" I asked.

The girl started to stumble through an answer to explain why she didn't know, and I said I would call to check tomorrow.

"Thank you," I made sure to add, before I walked back to my car.

My phone rang almost exactly two days later, right after I got to my first house to clean. I expected it to be my dad, and got excited to tell him that I might have figured something out. But it was a local 406 number.

"Hi, Stephanie? I'm here at the YMCA looking at your emergency relief request and I just have a few questions. Do you have a minute?"

"Sure," I said. I didn't have time to pause work while I talked, so I simultaneously reached down to pick up the rug in the entryway to shake it outside.

"We do have space for . . . Is it pronounced Eh-mi-lee-ah?"

"Eh-meel-ya," I said.

"Oh! That's so pretty," she said. "We do have space for Eh-meeeel-ya, so don't worry about that." I audibly sighed with relief. "Our camps go all day, from seven thirty a.m. to five thirty p.m., and the little-kid camp at our lowest on the sliding scale is ninety a week, but some of the other camps are more, like soccer or rock climbing, if you wanted her to do those."

"Okay," I said, then I paused, preparing to thank her and tell her I couldn't afford it. No matter how many times in my life I'd had to say that I couldn't afford something essential, it never got any easier.

I reached for the spray bottle of off-brand glass cleaner that I'd left on top of my tote bag full of clean rags.

"I'm looking at your application here for emergency assistance, though, and could you elaborate a bit on why you need it?"

I took in a breath so big I almost coughed, then tried to explain the situation in a way that didn't sound like I was whining or blaming it on a deadbeat dad. But I started to feel guilty. *This isn't an actual emergency*, I told myself. *Our house didn't burn down. No one's in the hospital. Other people need this more than I do.*

I stopped talking.

"So," she said, after an agonizing pause, "would covering fifty percent of the sliding scale tuition be enough financial aid for you?"

"Forty-five a week times four would be a hundred and eighty, right?"

"Correct," she said.

Mental math was not my strong suit, but I had to do it all the time. Even if I found more clients, I wouldn't be able to go to my summer class in the morning and work enough before I had to pick up Emilia in order to cover that.

"Not really," I said, trying not to mumble.

"What amount could you pay?"

I didn't detect condescension in her tone. She seemed like she sincerely wanted it to work. After a pause, I breathed out and said, "Like, twenty-five bucks a week." I pinched my eyes shut, waiting for her to say no.

"Okay!" she said in a happy tone. "I'll put that in your file so the billing folks will know what to charge you. If there's any mistake, please let the kids at the front desk know and they'll make sure it's corrected. Will she be here all summer?"

This all sounded so wonderful that suspicion creeped into my mind, as if there must be a catch. Maybe they knew I cleaned the other gym and they wanted me to barter there, too. But . . . how could they possibly know that and why did I suspect that they did?

"Uh, yes, she'll be there all summer!" My voice cracked, and I clenched my jaw in an effort to block the emotions from leaking out.

"Do you think she'll want to do those other camps? We're really trying to fill them up."

"What camps? The rock-climbing one? Uh, maybe? We kinda go rock climbing already."

"Oh!" she said. "Then I bet she would love this! We could figure out a reduced rate for that week, too, if it helps."

I couldn't think of the last time anyone had been this helpful. I wanted to tell her that, but stopped myself, not wanting her to know that I needed help all the time. People formed negative opinions when they found out how much assistance you'd accepted, and for how long. By that point I couldn't shake a feeling like I'd overstayed my welcome and needed to move on.

I'd gone someplace else in my mind for a moment, but my surroundings reemerged and I realized I'd stopped working. I checked my watch. "Thank you so much for this. I, um, I need to get back to work." She said of course and we said goodbye. I flipped my phone shut and stared at it for several seconds trying to process what had just happened. I had stopped working long enough that I'd have to go a whole fifteen minutes over my scheduled time for that house, but I didn't care.

"Holy shit," I said out loud, unable to hide a smile. I longed for someone to tell or hug or celebrate with. This was the sad reality of my life: When things were terrible, I was alone. When things were better, I was also alone. My loneliness was so real, so always-present, that it had weight, like something I dragged around behind me. Letting out a breath, I grabbed a rag to wipe the trails of glass cleaner that had rolled down the window on the front door.

———————

Jamie kept calling in the following weeks, but I was too angry to answer.

As I'd predicted, it took about a dozen emails to get him to send me a single check for four hundred bucks to help with the unexpected cost of having Emilia with me. A couple of days after he sent the check, he received court documents from the Missoula County court notifying him that they had granted me a waiver on the two-hundred-dollar fee to move our parenting case from Washington to Montana. He freaked out, sending a long email to tell me that if he were ever to find out that I used the money he sent me for court fees it would be the last amount that I'd receive. He added an "EVER!!!" for emphasis.

I was even angrier when he skipped his video chat with Emilia on her birthday. He missed chances to talk to his daughter often, and Emilia would pretend to talk to him on a toy phone when he didn't show. I had hoped her birthday might be different. I had to tamp down my disgust when he told me that he had a week of vacation time at the end of August over *his* birthday and Emilia could come for a visit then. At least he agreed that instead of meeting halfway, he would drive all the way to Missoula to pick her up. I agreed to somehow get to Portland to pick her up after ten days.

*Maybe I could schedule a few more move-out cleans during that time,* I thought, but I doubted I could because of the short notice and the time of year. Ten days was long enough to miss my kid, but not nearly what I needed to replenish my bank account and myself. Choosing between which one to try for was hard, but extra work would always win.

# 3

## Climbing

Sylvie, the one who had given me the lift to Portland, was a relatively new friend I had met at the climbing gym. A guy who worked there gifted me a membership for the few months we were hanging out and encouraged me to try it. Because I was so nervous, he let me come in with him before they opened so I could practice when the place was empty. I wasn't one to exercise (with the exception of some easy hikes), and I also struggled with chronic pain from what a doctor had once referred to as "severe scoliosis." After a month or so of regular climbing, I took a shower one day and realized I could tilt my head back far enough to feel the spray on top. As I got stronger, the near-constant, burning pain in my back and shoulders started to fade. I could turn my head, lift heavy things without fear of hurting myself, and the long days at work and school didn't leave me unable to get comfortable at night. Suddenly, I could do things that doctors had been telling me since my early teens I would never be able to do.

With less debilitating pain, my quality of life improved enough that the thirty-dollar-a-month membership fee for Emilia and me was worth it. In the summer, I paid nothing because we could climb outside. I spent any sudden, free afternoon due to canceled work or class either hiking Mount Sentinel with a backpack full of rocks or, if the weather wasn't great, I'd climb indoors. My day planner contained scribbles like "3HRS" to represent how long it took me to walk from my front door to the top of Mount Sentinel and back, or "20PUSH, 3PULL" for the number of push-ups and pull-ups that I could do in a row. Climbing rocks, either by foot or with my hands, had become a healthy obsession.

Before Missoula, Emilia and I hadn't experienced feeling part of a community, and the rock climbers, surprisingly, folded us in while always making sure we didn't fall. That summer before my last year of school and Emilia's first was extra magical in a way—especially since climbing seemed like a natural state for her. I watched in awe as she fearlessly traversed her way up a wall at the gym, or to the top of a giant boulder outside.

Sylvie also had kids, including one close to Emilia's age. We'd hung out quite a bit over the last several months because we were both single moms who climbed and usually had our kids with us. We also started going camping together with a group of climbers and our kids on weekends, then started to hang out when we weren't doing either of those things. As much as we had in common, I never thought of her as a close friend. Vulnerability was too risky, and I couldn't allow myself to reach a point where it would be a huge upset if that person didn't show up when I needed them to. But Sylvie was always game for whatever adventure, no matter how big or mundane. She even oddly seemed excited about the road trip to help pick up Emilia from Jamie's place. Most of the people I met through the climbing gym would drop everything and head out to climb rocks if the weather was good, but only a few of them had kids or any conception of what that meant. It was nice to have a friend who also had to make sure there were enough snacks and seat belts and changes of clothes.

During those ten days when Emilia was in Portland, I'd done my first climb with five pitches, snapped a few selfies with my climbing partner, Logan, at three hundred feet up from where we began, and rappelled all the way down. Still, I never did anything too risky by rock-climbing standards. While others climbed thirty feet off the ground without a rope, I stuck to between ten to fifteen. I didn't do many "big" moves, like swinging to grab something or hanging under a ledge. My thought was if I broke my ankle and couldn't work (or worse, drive) . . . I couldn't even imagine how Emilia and I would get through it. Then I had to consider the medical bills—one false move on my part and we'd lose everything all over again. That's why I ended up mostly sitting on the mat by a back wall to watch Sylvie climb, sometimes flirting with cute climber dudes.

Against my better judgment, I started dating a writer named Theodore at the beginning of the summer. We saw each other a couple of times at the climbing gym and I asked a few people who he was. I think he did the same. Then he showed up at a party and I watched him notice me, tell the person who greeted him that he'd talk to him later, and come right over to say hello.

"I think you should go on a real date," he said after a while, squinting at me a little.

"Oh?" I said. "With you?"

"We should go on a real date this weekend," he said, getting up off the table where he had sat down next to me. Our shoulders had pressed into each other a bit while we talked and I hadn't noticed that almost everyone had gone inside the house. I wasn't sure what to say other than yes, but I possibly had a better understanding of what that meant than he did. Having a kid and trying to date felt equivalent to hanging a wedding dress in my closet and bringing it out to show a person when they picked me up for the first time. Men no longer saw me as a lighthearted dating prospect. They looked at me and I could almost see the reflection of white picket fences and family dinners at five thirty in their eyes. To some this could be attractive, but the shitty part was that it wasn't even appealing to me. Not only was I not attracted to a "family man" type, but I wasn't anything near a "family woman." I hated cooking and ate standing at the kitchen counter. My life revolved around work, school, my kid's schedule, and whatever cheap concerts, rock climbing, and hiking I could afford to fit in.

After I picked up Emilia at the YMCA the following Monday and got her buckled in the car, I surprised her by saying we could go to McDonald's playland for dinner. "Surprise" was a bit of a stretch, since it had become a reliable place for me to complete a decent amount of homework. There was usually a free booth, my kid had a great time, and she was contained, entertained, and fed. Most important to me, everyone else was feeding their kids the same shitty food so I didn't have to watch for judgmental side-eyes. Our regular booth was empty but dirty and I was too tired to care, pushing the scattered fries aside to place our tray over the dried ketchup. Emilia knew the rule that she had to eat at least half her food before she got up to play. For each encouragement to take another bite, the guilt clawed at me deeper, knowing her dad would voice his disapproval if she told him about it. Once she ate enough and ran to the plastic equipment to play, I took out my books and notebooks, scattered them among the caked-on ketchup and withered french fries, and stuck my headphones in my ears to block out the renditions of kids singing pop songs that blared through the speakers.

Summer school hadn't been difficult since it was just the one class, but I still needed to absorb myself in Virginia Woolf and William Wordsworth enough to remember details for questions on the upcoming midterm. The thought of a date with Theodore, of explaining my life to him, kept distracting me. I tried to imagine him joining us here, and what he'd think of us.

I'd been a single mother in every sense of the word through most of my kid's six years. Now that Emilia was older and with me nearly full-time, keeping my dating life separate from her required a lot more support if I wanted to see someone on a regular basis or during daylight hours. I wasn't necessarily a single mother by choice, though sometimes I didn't feel like I needed a romantic partner so much as I needed someone to provide backup in parenting. Though I probably wouldn't admit how lonely I was, sitting at that table by myself was enough to bring tears to my eyes.

"Look," Sylvie said after I told her all this later that evening at the climbing gym, "life is short. And you're really hot right now." On Monday nights a large group of us met up because the brewery next door offered six-dollar growler fills during happy hour. "Plus," she said as she got up to walk back to the wall to try the route she'd been working on again, "it's only gonna be so long that you're able to attract hot rock climbers in their late twenties."

"Sylvie," I called after her and she turned to look at me. "I don't even have a regular, dependable custody schedule. Emilia's with me all the time. At least your kids spend weekends with another parent and you get a break. At least you *have* another parent who helps out." I paused and picked at the white tape I'd wrapped around a finger to cover a blister. "And what about Emilia? Shouldn't I be sensitive to her possible involvement? She always gets really attached to the people I date."

"Hey, I get it," she said. "How about if I babysit? It'll be fun. It's just a date."

I wanted to believe that it was just a date, but it never seemed to be. Dating a single mom is different that way, or at least it was for me if I really liked the person. Getting involved with me in an emotionally intimate way meant getting to know my kid, too. By that point, I'd convinced myself that either way, we were doomed.

———

Theodore met me on my front porch that Friday and suggested we go for a walk. Before I could nod, he grabbed my hand to lead me in the direction of a nearby park. We sat under the shade of a tree and I got so nervous that I ended up telling him about my heart being shattered a few months before.

Though I don't think I had ever referred to Evan as a boyfriend out loud, we were serious enough to spend a week backpacking in Utah together over spring break while Emilia stayed with her dad. Serious enough to fill almost an entire Moleskine with poems and notes to each other and things we observed and shared later when we passed the notebook to one another between classes. Evan had sat next to me on our first day of a nonfiction writing workshop at the start of that spring semester. I eyed his messy hair that matched his Carhartt pants, heavy leather boots, and flannel shirt. His hands had grease on them, as if he'd just been working on a car. We were the only two people in clothes with a good amount of dirt on them, presumably because we preferred them that way. He gave me a nod and smiled but it took us a few weeks to have any conversation outside of class. Things progressed quickly after that. He came over in the evenings to read poetry out loud or cook some food with me and my new roommate, a freshman named Kelley.

About ten days after we returned from that Utah trip I found out I was pregnant. Evan paid for the abortion. He held my hand through everything, assuring me we would have a kid together after we graduated. A large part of me knew that was a lie but in that moment I needed to believe it was true. The day after I told him with a good amount of relief that I had stopped bleeding, he asked me to go for a walk after our last class together. He knew my next class started in twenty minutes, but it was like he couldn't wait a minute longer. I grew curious about what was on his mind as we walked to a patch of grass in the shade of a huge tree. There was a dog park nearby and it was so hot the stench of urine and shit blew with the breeze.

"I can't give you what you need," he said. I stared at him, waiting for him to say more. He shrugged, then looked down and picked a blade of grass and ripped it into pieces. I watched it shrink into smaller versions of itself before he tossed it aside and started again on another.

Theodore took my hand when I finished telling him all of this. We sat on the grass next to a creek, and I felt part of my body kind of get sucked into his. He looked at me, leaned in, and kissed my lips, letting them linger for a moment, then stood up without releasing my hand.

"Come on," he said, giving me a half smile that looked a tad mischievous and was fully irresistible. We walked downtown to see a bluegrass band, ordering double Jamesons and PBRs, and danced for a little while. Theo was a bit shorter than me, and stocky like he had been climbing for a long time. He had a smile to match his goofy yet empathetic personality. And he was adorable. Then he suggested that we shimmy ourselves up a building between a fire escape and a brick wall to go make out. I leaped in excitement because it involved three of my favorite things: kissing, being on a rooftop, and climbing. We walked barefoot across the blacktopped roof and peered over the side of the building three stories above the street before we started kissing and couldn't stop.

Theodore walked me home and made sure to ask me out again before giving me a hug and kiss good night.

"Must've been a good date," Sylvie said when I walked in. I followed her gaze to my legs, which still had black smudges on them from the roof.

"Oh, that's . . ." I said, before deciding there was no way to change her mind. Then I smiled really big and added, "He, uh, asked me out again."

"Looks like he'd be silly not to."

Theodore took me to a Widespread Panic concert after a month or so of dating and we planned to spend a rare night together at the place where he was housesitting. I bought a T-shirt when we got there and drank a few beers too fast in the hot sun. Watching several of my favorite songs performed live, even with a new lead singer, was almost too beautiful to bear. These outdoor shows had always been my favorite part of living in Missoula, although it was rare that I could enjoy it. I loved all of it: listening to music outdoors under a big blue sky, then the sun setting on a line of mountains in the distance, dancing with a bunch of strangers who all loved every minute just as much as I did. When the band sang the words *After all that I've been through, you're the only one that matters,* the need to hold Emilia engulfed every part of me. Suddenly I felt my cheeks wet with tears and I failed at hiding it but kept dancing anyway.

"I used to listen to them all the time before we moved here . . . when I cleaned houses a lot," I half-yelled to Theodore before the next song. He smiled like he understood.

We stopped at a grocery store on the way home and he told me he

loved watching me dance around him like a butterfly that was waiting for him to fall in love with me. At his friend's house, we stared at
each other, standing there in the kitchen. I looked around and tried
to imagine living with someone like his friends did, with our books
combined on shelves in the living room and some kind of coffee
apparatus that made more than a single serving. Theodore let out a
soft chuckle and shook his head like he knew I was overthinking the
situation and took me by the hand to the bedroom.

"We should try soaking!" I said.

"What?" he said, pulling away to look at my face. We had been
lying between his friend's sheets for a while, slowly undressing each
other and running our fingers over sensitive places. A look of confusion swept over his face, and then he remembered. "You mean that
Mormon thing?"

At a grad student party, one of the fiction writers told a story
about how he used to hang out with a lot of Mormons in high school.
They had told him some of the things they would do sexually without crossing the line into full-on sex. "Soaking" was, oddly, one of
those methods.

I tugged at Theo's boxers to get them off and he pulled them
down while I did the same with my underwear. Then he lay on top
of me, the full weight of his chest on mine, and looked me directly
in the eyes for consent. He entered me and i sucked in a breath and
got lost in the pleasure for a second. Then he moved out to go deeper
again and I grabbed his butt cheeks with both of my hands. "No!" I
said in a fake harsh whisper. "No moving!" I wanted to laugh but he
started to kiss my neck and everything melted into tingles. I almost
shuddered.

His lips followed my jawline so slowly, by the time they reached
my mouth I bit his bottom lip. He let out a moan and I rocked my
hips to rub against him, feeling us both become more aroused. I'd

never felt anything like it. Like kissing him created uncontrollable pulses and movements while we stayed in one place. When I started to climax, I heard myself say, "Oh my fucking god" before we locked our lips together for a much shorter amount of time than it seemed like it was. I had never felt that kind of connection during sex and I already wanted it again. I wanted nothing but that from now on.

Theodore rested his forehead on my collarbone, his hot breath mixing with the sweat on my chest. "Did we . . . ?" I felt him nod before he turned his head to press his ear to my chest. My left palm was on his back, individual fingertips pressing one at a time, from my first finger to the pinky. I turned my head to the side, away from him, and reached up with my right fingers to tug at my bottom lip, but couldn't hold the laugh in any longer. "We just came at the same time from *soaking*!"

Theodore's chest shook with a chuckle. "Ssshhhh! Don't ruin it," he said with a crack in his voice. I laughed louder.

Then he, too, sat me down one day a few weeks later and told me he couldn't give me what I needed. I was surprised but didn't argue. We'd gone camping together with the weekend Lost Horse climbers group and Emilia had not hidden her excitement about spending time with the two of us together. Every *I'm going with both of you?* was adorable at first, but I glanced over at Theodore and saw that it had started to sink in. It was like, after several weeks of dating me, the kid I usually had around changed from a playmate to a responsibility. Theo and I tried to stay friends after that, but I got too sad and couldn't keep up the happy face to hide it anymore.

More than that, I felt like I'd failed Emilia by allowing this person into her life without any security or a half-veiled promise that they'd stay. This thought surely didn't have any real basis since my kid barely noticed Theodore's absence. She'd been more torn up about our roommate, Kelley, leaving, which, I realized, was much more reasonable and appropriate for her. This was only some guy I hung out with for a while who seemed to make me happy. The expectations were all mine, not hers, but I still felt like an idiot for letting it happen in the first place.

Naturally my solution to that heartache was a vow never to kiss another writer. I swore off fuzzy feelings completely and enjoyed occasional make-out sessions with rock climbers who had no literary aspirations, since they tended to be a noncommittal sort of bunch. This was good, I told myself. It allowed me to keep my heart safe behind a wall thick enough for anyone to have difficulty tearing it down. Including me.

———

Sylvie and I went out to a few bars while Emilia was at her dad's at the end of the summer and before the college students came back to town. I'm pretty sure I was supposed to be her wingman, but I think she became mine most of the time.

The two of us together didn't make much sense, visually speaking. While my height is not what anyone would describe as "tall," Sylvie's was definitely "short." We went out as a mismatched pair: me in my usual faded Carhartt pants and some T-shirt I got at Goodwill, without a stitch of makeup, and Sylvie in some cute shoes to match a tight-fitting outfit that complemented her long hair, huge smile, and personality that more than made up for her size. I envied her social ease and ability to make immediate friends with anyone, but it was just as fun for me to watch her work the dance floor to the bar and back to our table.

We ended up at Al and Vic's. It wasn't my favorite, but Sylvie liked playing pool there. A guy named Daniel had control of the table, and Sylvie had to challenge him by putting quarters under the lip of the table to pay for the next game. Daniel was my height, but a ginger with blue eyes. He flirted in a way that would be showing off if he weren't so bouncy and cute. He came over to talk to us between games and Sylvie found a way to ask if he was into rock climbing. Daniel looked at both of us by letting his eyes meet ours for a few seconds before he looked at the other one. Maybe he was trying to read us to figure out how to answer the question before he snorted and said, "Of course I'm *into* rock climbing." Sylvie kept trying to talk him up but I was the one he leaned in to kiss outside before we said goodbye. I liked him enough to text him my number.

It still surprised me whenever Daniel texted me over the next few weeks after Emilia was back home. Most of his texts said—not asked—to come meet him at the Rhino or wherever he was already playing pool. We left and walked up the street after I got there. He paused to see what was going on at the Badlander, and then beelined for Al and Vic's, where he could dominate most games of eight ball by way of being a shark. This, predictably, didn't always make people the happiest, but it was fun to watch.

# 4

## Economics Learned, Not Taught

Every single aspect of higher education felt like a particularly cruel game, or like I was really getting an advanced degree in irony. A degree had been waved in front of my face like a certificate out of poverty. The fact that the loans sank me further into poverty wasn't lost on me, but they were a means to an end. I kept my eyes focused only ahead. In the process, while some of my classmates had parents who paid their tuition and possibly their living expenses as well, I dug a deeper hole of debt with every semester. When I missed a class, I could calculate the dollar amount that had been wasted by my absence.

The idea of college as a place that young people went to party and make friends was a totally alien concept to me—not that I wouldn't have loved to do those things. But between being years older than everyone else and having to work to feed and clothe and house myself and my kid, it was ludicrous even to long for it. Whether or not any person I passed in the halls liked me was irrelevant. I wasn't there to be liked, I was there to work. Things like recertification paperwork for food stamps and making sure I had a babysitter for my Tuesday evening Montana Writers Live class, which sometimes went until 10 p.m.—those were the things that mattered.

It took about a year at U of M before I felt like I belonged at that college at all, like someone wasn't going to point and stare or tap me on the shoulder and usher me out. But by my senior year, I no longer shyly wandered through halls unsure of where I needed to go. If I decided to get myself a special treat like a burrito roll—refried beans inside of a crusty dinner roll for a dollar fifty—and an Americano, I felt like I was just like everyone else, like I had the right to be there.

At fifteen years old, when I first approached my dad with a pamphlet for college, his response without pausing to look at what I held in my hand was an immediate "How are you going to pay for that?"

I blinked and let the hand holding the information packet fall to my hip. My eyes sank to the floor next to my dad's computer chair. This was why no one ever asked him for anything when he sat there at the end of the month, checkbook out, entering amounts in the computer program he used to balance his account while he opened envelopes and sighed. I mumbled, "I dunno," and sat on the couch next to his desk, knowing I was in for a lecture. I had hoped he'd be excited, maybe even a little proud of me. Instead he walked me through the budget of our family's monthly expenses while I nodded like I understood. My application and information packet for Whitworth College remained unopened on the coffee table.

Both of my parents had pretty good jobs by then. My mom, who was now a social worker for foster children, started college when my little brother began kindergarten. She became the first one in our entire family to have not only a bachelor's degree, but a master's in social work, too. Dad had worked his way up to a project manager position for an electric company in Seattle. I would have understood if they'd talked to me about what to do, if they'd at least offered their help in figuring out how I *would* pay for college. Instead I got another lesson on budgeting.

Their expectations once I got my driver's license had been simple: get a job, move out, take care of myself, and never come back—especially not asking for money. At just ten years old, I was making my own money babysitting kids at my house while my mom was at home. By middle school I spent most of my time outside school babysitting, sometimes full-time as a nanny for the whole summer. In high school, my parents helped me with building my resume and filling out applications for jobs. Dad even bought me a car. It was only worth a thousand bucks or less, but I knew that car had an invisible value. Providing me with a vehicle to get to work was important, not frivolous like an application for a four-year degree at an accredited university would be. I got the sense that not only did work have the greatest value, but I, too, only had value if I was working.

For the remainder of my junior and senior years of high school, I sat next to kids who talked about college tours and ACT study guides and rolled their eyes over their parents bugging them about it. "Where did you apply?" and "Where did you get in?" were favorite topics in those minutes before class while I tried to look deeply engrossed in my book. I never asked how they were going to pay for that, but I wanted to, because up until that conversation with my dad I hadn't wondered how other people could afford to send their kids to college. I assumed parents paid for everything like it was some kind of extended part of raising kids. Like teaching them to drive, you walked around college campuses and did a whole tour before deciding which ones to apply to.

My interest in school waned while my classmates took Advanced Placement classes that would allow them to test out of general education courses their first year of college. They aced tests in anatomy and physics while I struggled to keep up. They took Latin instead of Spanish. They applied to handfuls of schools, speaking of state schools with a deflated tone, using terms like "safety schools" while their friends told them they wouldn't need a fallback. Everyone had to get in somewhere.

Meanwhile, my parents and I didn't go online and fill out a FAFSA, the application for student aid. My mother was fully checked out by that point and my father really didn't seem to want to talk about college, or my dreams, or what I wanted to study. What was important to him was that I knew just how much money it cost him to feed, house, and clothe my brother and me.

This is why it shouldn't have surprised me when my dad never called back after I asked him for help with paying for Emilia's day camp that summer. It would be the last time we ever spoke to each other.

———————

Transferring to Missoula from Skagit Valley College, a community college an hour north of Seattle, hadn't been difficult, but the timing was perhaps not the greatest, since I moved in the middle of the school year. My initial plan was that I could transfer to Missoula's community college, but once I walked around the U of M campus when I visited for a week the summer after Emilia turned four, I knew I needed to take the leap and apply to the university. Going there, ultimately for the creative writing program, had been my dream since before I found out I was pregnant, but it was still one that I questioned if it was affordable to act on. In filling out the application to transfer, I declared sociology as a major to be on some imaginary kind of safe side.

Immediately after Emilia and I arrived in Missoula mid-December, I worked on getting all my paperwork handed in so I could start at U of M the following month for spring semester. I already knew that a lot of my credits didn't transfer, and that was fine since they still counted as electives. I found out I needed an MMR vaccination and that was okay, too, since I could get it at the clinic on campus. But at my first meeting with my guidance counselor, I learned I was not considered a Montana resident—and nonresident tuition was almost triple what it was for a resident.

I wanted to tell her that I had waited six years to sit with her in that windowless office, to relay in painful detail all the things I had to go through to get there. But there was no point in that. Instead I found out that a full Pell Grant, a scholarship, and a maximum amount of loans wouldn't come close to covering half the cost of tuition for one semester as a full-time nonresident student.

"Oh, you won't be able to go full-time," the person in the next office said. His title was "Residency Specialist." "You have to work toward residency."

"But I moved here," I said. "I mean, I moved my four-year-old kid here and all our plants. We're definitely residents, just new ones."

"Yes," he said, "but if all the students who moved here for college from out of state were suddenly residents, or could gain residency while going to school full-time, they'd all pay that lower amount in tuition by their second year."

"Ah," I said, my ears burning with the need to tell him I was different. I had forgotten the part of the game where no one's education mattered more than the money the university could make from your opportunity to soak up all that learning. God forbid they would make it affordable or easy.

He grabbed several pieces of paper out of a bottom drawer in his desk and turned them around so they faced me. My wait for residency wouldn't start ticking down from a year until I had a local license, I registered my car with local plates, and I had a postmarked utility bill with my name and local address on it.

"You can take up to six credits a semester until then," he said, leaning back in his chair. He moved his cheeks to inch his glasses a little bit up the bridge of his nose while he laced his fingers together, resting them on his belly, which was covered by a maroon sweater with a growling bear. *What is it with these people and grizzly bears?* "And you must send me updates, like when you've crossed another item off the list." He looked down at the paper and frowned, then opened his top drawer. "There's usually one of my cards stapled to it . . ." He rustled around a bit more, then reached for the papers in front of me to scribble his name and email address on the top one. "There, you can just email me scanned copies."

"Six credits? That's like two classes." I looked at the second page, where it listed resident and nonresident tuition. Six nonresident credits were the same cost as twelve for a resident.

When I looked up to see if he had a response, I saw he had leaned back in his chair again, expressionless, and I knew our meeting was done.

There seemed to be a skill set required to navigate all of this that I not only lacked, but couldn't have identified or acquired if I had tried. While everyone around me bustled from one building to the next in blowing wind and snow, their heads covered in thick, maroon beanies, I wasn't sure where I needed to go to get a fucking booster for measles, mumps, and rubella. But I had something more important to figure out first: how to pay for day care.

Childcare Resources had its own office in the University Center, which also contained the bookstore, my new credit union (box

checked for residency with that), a store with a huge wall of refriger-
ated beverages, and a cafeteria upstairs. In the center, reaching up toward the glass ceiling, huge tropical trees and plants grew—complete
with a water feature—and apparently had no idea that it was winter.

Outside the child care office were two corkboards full of flyers
for food stamps, Free Student Legal Assistance, and several advertisements for jobs that ranged from dishwashers in the cafeteria upstairs
to a nanny up in a wealthy neighborhood everyone called "The Rattlesnake." Most of the advertisements offering services like babysitting charged as much (or more) an hour as I did to clean houses. I
only had one client so far, with another possible position cleaning an
office building at night, but I wasn't sure how that would work with
my new roommate. I had also recently discovered that the going rate
for a private housecleaner was a lot less in Missoula than it had been
in Washington. I wasn't sure how cobbling together my own clients
would work in the long run if I only got thirty bucks on days I could
work.

At the campus office, they had access to several day care sites considered to be "on campus," and they could also help with applications for grants to pay for them. The good news was that everything
worked on a sliding scale, and it covered the hours I spent in class
or at work. But they didn't include travel time and certainly not the
hours I spent on homework. And the day cares weren't open during
evening hours, when I had a number of classes. This meant that child
care could still cost me up to five hundred a month. I estimated they
would allow me to start with two days a week of child care, but I really needed to enroll for at least three if I wanted to build my housecleaning client list.

This was a maze I had traversed dozens of times. Questioning the
logic was useless, since there simply wasn't any. All government assistance programs operated on the assumption that every person who

walked into their office brought with them the possibility of scamming them in some way. We were asked detailed questions about our assets, what kind of car we drove, or if we had a burial plot—not because the government cared, but to determine if there was money hidden that we didn't disclose. It was ridiculous to imagine that anyone would try to pull a fast one by spending hours at a government assistance office in the middle of the workday so they could possibly leave with a couple hundred bucks a month for food. But this was how I had spent hours and sometimes entire workdays of my life, convincing authorities that I wasn't a criminal. These invasions of privacy caused me to fidget and squirm but I submitted to them, like everything else, because it was another means to an end.

My classes began in January, only one month into my residency. I walked twenty minutes to campus from our downstairs apartment in one of the oldest houses in Missoula, breathing in the crisp air. I couldn't help but smile. From the middle of the pedestrian bridge, I took a picture with my flip phone of the Clark Fork River. The people heading in the same direction as me all looked to be in their early twenties, with their chins tucked into their scarves or the tops of their jackets, hands deep in their pockets, a brand-name backpack facing me as they walked farther ahead. I looked down at my faded Carhartt jacket and old Sorel boots and felt like I always had on the first day of school: a nerdy new kid who didn't know what to wear in order to fit in. If the clothing didn't make me stick out, then being a single mom in my thirties, a life most of my classmates probably couldn't comprehend, definitely would. Just thinking about doing group projects made me take a big breath and hold it.

Not even three steps on campus, and I knew I had to fight for the original reason I applied: to get my Master of Fine Arts in creative writing. In those years, U of M's writing program was still touted as one of the top ten in the country. Before finding out I was pregnant with Emilia, the chance at immersion into this greatness was the only thing I'd ever really wanted. I saw it as my one opportunity to be a writer—a real writer, with a book on the shelf at places like Elliott Bay Book Company in Seattle or weathered paperback copies in used bookstores and free little libraries. It was all I had ever dreamed about since I was ten years old.

Somehow this dream didn't feel like it applied to me anymore. My "place," even as a registered, paying student entering a four-year institution, and a junior with good marks, made it feel like an MFA would not be possible. Like I couldn't afford to dream about it unless I could somehow prove that it would result in a semi-decent job. This type of judgment, this question of if I was part of the "deserving poor," haunted me. Who I had to prove this to or who actually judged me for my choices was never clear, because it felt like everyone most of the time: from what I bought with food stamps to if I went out for coffee with a friend in the middle of the day. The paranoia that I would somehow get caught in a frivolous moment never left me. After several years on government assistance, my value as a member of society no longer seemed to be my education, but rather the low-wage work I would potentially do to make life easier in some way for a person whose family could afford to pay for them to go to college.

Philosophy 101 met on the top floor of Jeannette Rankin Hall (named after the first woman to hold federal office and a former rep-resentative from Montana). It was about a mile-long walk in freezing temperatures to get there, then a hike up three flights of stairs. Most of the seats were filled when I got there on my first day and I thought for a second I was late instead of five minutes early. I decided on a seat in the back corner near the window, anxious to remove my coat and cool off enough for my face to lose its redness. My classmates shuffled their feet as they walked in—most of them without a coat, many of them wearing Ugg boots and sweatpants, like they'd just rolled out of bed. Some of them smiled or nodded at people they recognized—one gave someone a high five—before they flopped and folded into their seats at the same time. I felt alien, like I was someone observing the class, not taking it. When the professor walked in, the only person in the room who looked remotely close to my age, he rolled up his sleeves and I noticed he had a tattoo of a beet on his arm. I liked him immediately.

My other class was Intro to Sociology. It met in the evening in a huge lecture hall and I fought to stay awake through the short films we watched. Emilia still woke up before seven in the morning, and I still stayed up too late for some precious time to myself. Luckily I had enough funds at that moment (and a few connections in town) to hire a babysitter, so I didn't worry about needing to bring Emilia with me. One good thing I discovered about living in a college town was the existence of a large pool of kids in their late teens and early twenties whose eyebrows would go up with interest if you offered to pick up a six-pack for them as part of their pay to sit and watch cartoons with your four-year-old for a few hours. The house we lived in was made up of three other apartments, all full of nineteen-year-old kids thankfully willing to help out from time to time.

---

That college became a sacred place for me. I associated my "writer" self with my presence on campus. Writing, the real writing that mattered, was meant to be done without cartoons blaring in the background and someone asking for pancakes. Looking back, I realize that I really struggled to appear more male: someone unattached to things that could prevent them from writing, and who had an invisible support system in place to keep them there. I thought that in order to succeed as a writer, or even as a hopeful MFA candidate, I needed to have everything so obviously together that I would get invitations to where all the other writers in town went, even if that meant a bar or a party that required child care. The hours of participation in class, off-campus events, and author readings became not only necessary for acceptance as a peer, but what I needed to thrive as a person. All of it fed an insatiably hungry part of me that had quietly dreamed of this for most of my life. That hopeful part of me needed to bulk up, get stronger, and come alive. This dream was what got me through everything—good or terrible—that I needed to do to survive as a single parent who struggled to make ends meet in endless, sometimes impossible ways.

My status as a resident had been official for eight months at the start of my senior year, and the juggling act of work, parenting, and school was well rehearsed. But the constant responsibility of not letting the balls drop to the ground while also jumping through the university's hoops from acceptance to graduation was mentally and physically exhausting. On Tuesday mornings, I dropped Emilia off at kindergarten, then rushed home to clean up a bit, eat, shower, grab several notebooks, and wave to whoever was my roommate at the time if they were home. If I didn't see them, I would send a text making sure they knew to pick up Emilia at the bus stop after school, or find someone who could. My first class, Literary Criticism, met from 11:10 a.m. to 12:30 p.m. After a break that I utilized for homework, I had an Advanced Fiction Workshop at 3:40 p.m. on the third floor of the Liberal Arts Building that ended ten minutes before my Advanced Nonfiction Workshop, which went until 6:30 p.m. My final class on Tuesdays was Montana Writers Live, which met from 7:10 to 10 p.m. in the same room as that first sociology class.

It was odd to drop off my kid at school knowing I wouldn't see her until she woke up the next morning. Well, see her awake. We shared the front room of the apartment, which I imagined had been the main sitting room when the whole house was occupied by one family. It had a huge mantel with a fireplace that hadn't been used in years, a real wood floor, and a big south-facing bay window that had a great view of Mount Sentinel. The downside was temperature regulation: in summer, the sun blazing through the bay window heated the room to ninety degrees and in winter I couldn't keep it over sixty-five, since the floor wasn't insulated. On windy days the curtains moved if it was too soon to install those kits with the clear plastic and double-sided tape that you tighten by blowing on it with a hair dryer on the hottest setting. I had a full-size bed in a corner, a small dresser, and a stand-alone closet on wheels for hanging some clothes with a few shelves big enough for milk crates where I kept socks and smaller stuff. The space allowed only one season's clothes at a time, so I kept my other clothes in a storage area in the basement. In another corner I had a small computer desk and a shelf with a printer, paper, and some textbooks. Emilia had the rest of the room. Cheap shelves made of hollow plastic rods and particleboard were flimsy but did the necessary job of holding bins of miscellaneous tiny plastic shoes and My Little Ponies mixed with naked dolls that were zombie and vampire high school students. She had a table to draw on and a platform bed with enough space under it for a fort. For a while that summer she slept down there in a raft we'd bought to float in the river with a few friends.

My roommate (in addition to Kelley, I had four others over the course of that year) had the only real bedroom on the other side of the apartment. Between us we had a smallish communal living space with another bay window, a futon that I slept on sometimes if Emilia wanted to sleep in my bed, and a huge bookshelf. There was also a kitchen, pieced together by a microwave cart, a medium-size fridge, and an ancient metal, free-standing cupboard with two countertops that dipped down into a single sink. We had occupied this space for almost two years—the longest we'd lived anywhere together—and it was the thirteenth place we'd lived in together since I got pregnant. Sometimes when tourists stopped to read the plaque out front that told the story of when the house was built, we stared at them through the window until they noticed us, then ducked down, hoping they thought they saw a ghost.

Downtown Missoula was just a couple of blocks away from us, and with it came parades and Sunday Streets, when they closed down the main drag for bikes and chalk art. One year they had aerialists—young women hanging by their feet from large strips of silk. Saturday mornings brought two outdoor markets: one packed full of booths selling art, tie-dye dresses, and leather wallets, and another down by the Clark Fork River where vendors sold mostly food. We always made sure to get an egg sandwich from our friend Ethan and I usually let Emilia get a lemonade or a Popsicle. One of the bars downtown had Family Friendly Friday, when you'd find its dance floor overrun by small bare feet dancing to a local band playing kid tunes. Kelley wasn't of drinking age and when she stayed in for the night I would sometimes go out to see a band after putting Emilia to bed, since there was almost never a cover charge and, well, men usually bought me drinks if I wanted them to.

Emilia and I had friends who took her camping now and then or invited her to spend the night. I had rare chances to go out, sleep in, and make a lazy breakfast with Kelley and whomever each of us was dating that month.

Everything about our lives seemed precious and profound at the same time. An unexpected Friday off after I did the kid drop-off in the morning was spent hiking up to the top of a nearby mountain. Those silent moments above every person in town, looking down at our little world that included campus, our house, and Emilia's favorite parks and school—that was my sanctuary.

———————

The first week of my senior year brought homework that included about fifteen textbook pages to read along with Annie Dillard's essay "Total Eclipse," a three-page paper (with at least three citations!) due the following Tuesday in response to "The Rise of English" by Terry Eagleton, three short story "scene shots" (with one scene written out in its entirety) and sixteen copies for the rest of the class to read, a fictional scene written about something found in a police blotter, a 750-word essay also with copies for the class, and I needed to hunt down my copy of Joan Didion's *The White Album*. Summer's ease was over and done, but it fortunately had graced me with a lot to write about.

I completed most of my creative writing assignments as soon as I got them, since they didn't require much concentration on my part. By that point, I had learned how to write fast, usually averaging about a thousand words an hour. In class, I'd take notes as the professor discussed the assignment, jotting down a few ideas on what I could write about, then I would get everything written during my break between my first and second classes. I usually sat with my classmate Reed, who had similar homework. Along with the pleasant company, it was nice to have someone watch my stuff so I could go grab more coffee, and we spent the first few minutes of our work time venting over the inequities we'd noticed between us and our classmates who seemed more financially supported, to put it nicely. Then we'd get to talking about what we were working on, and I discovered how essential that was to the writing process.

Writing and researching academic papers was done at home after Emilia went to bed. Most of these were, to me, part of the game: a certain number of required words in a certain format with an added number of ways I could prove my opinion by showing someone else had the same one. As soon as I printed it out and stapled the pages together, all of it disappeared from my memory. I checked it off my list and moved to the next thing. Sometimes that thing was remembering to make an appointment for Emilia to get a vaccination she needed, asking a friend to babysit on Tuesday night, or making sure I had the proper paperwork to apply for government assistance programs or get recertified for one I had been on for years. Everything I did to keep our life running smoothly or to get me closer to graduation felt necessary but endless, like I wasn't totally sure I would ever escape the grind.

Most of my monthly budget went toward minimum payments for loans and credit cards, and a student loan from fifteen years before, when I did a year of full-time college in Alaska. Because it was a private loan through something called the Alaska Commission on Postsecondary Education, it didn't go into deferment while I was a registered student. The small amount of money I threw at it wasn't as much as they wanted, but it was enough to keep them from calling my relatives to ask them if they knew what a piece of shit I was. My dad's mom had been especially confused as to why someone from Alaska would call to demand information on the whereabouts of her granddaughter who'd just been over for Thanksgiving. Maybe that was why Dad hadn't asked his sister to loan me money. I guess I would never know. All those minimum payments, combined with rent and utilities, added up to an amount that was too often more than I brought in, so the rest would be supplemented with student loans. Every month I estimated how much income I would have, including the three hundred for roommate rent and another three hundred for child support, and tallied up my fixed bills like this:

Rent: $875
Internet: $45
Phone: $70

Netflix: $10
Alaska student loan: $55
Credit union loans: $90
Amazon card: $40
Credit card: $75
Car ins.: $40

---

TOTAL EXPENSES:     $1300.00
TOTAL INCOME:        $972.00

I carried this list of fixed expenses and estimated income with me wherever I went. I scribbled different versions of it in my day planner at the start of each month. I taped it to the wall by my desk at home with dates of when each bill was due. All my school notebooks had these tiny budgets written inside. I would have been incalculably embarrassed if anyone had seen my rather dismal mathematics, but they were vital to my sanity, and to our survival. Those numbers signified the weight of my financial responsibilities, and keeping obsessive track was the only way I didn't regularly spiral into panic. It was a constant dance, and rent always, always came first.

Taking out the maximum amount of student loans looked like a lot on paper, since it was about eight thousand dollars a year, but almost all of that money went to our basic living expenses—rent, internet, phone, and insurance. For my final three years of school, I applied for and accepted the full amount of student loans the government offered. I qualified for the Pell Grant, which came to about fifty-five hundred or so a year, and supplemented my tuition expenses. My scholarship through the Women's Independence Scholarship Program (WISP) brought in another two thousand a semester.

Student loans were split into two categories: subsidized and unsubsidized. Because of my financial need, I qualified for the maximum amount of subsidized loans. Subsidized meant the government would pay the interest the loan accrued while I was in school and for the six-month grace period after graduation—either from undergrad or through grad school and beyond. Unsubsidized loans meant I still accrued interest during school. Some years the interest rates were the same for both, but in others the unsubsidized loan had an interest rate of nearly twice as much. It felt like yet another penalty for being poor. To be honest, I didn't care how the payback of these loans worked—or rather, it wasn't that I didn't care but I knew it didn't matter whether I cared or not. Given the monumental sum, I knew with certainty that I would have that debt for the rest of my life. The loan payments for my BA alone would be about the same as what I currently paid for my share of rent. I could qualify for some relief via lower, income-based payments, but the full loan amount would still accrue interest. This is why by the time some borrowers fully paid off their loans, they could easily have paid double the original amount they'd borrowed.

Several people told me not to pay for graduate school, especially an MFA, but if that was my only ticket to a career in teaching college classes, what choice did I have? Student loan debt seemed like something that everyone—even President Obama—had to pay off eventually. Though the debt was real, it didn't count as heavily toward a debt-to-income ratio as, say, credit card debt. At that point in my college career, I knew my debt was upward of forty thousand, and it would keep me from affording our own house, helping my kids through school, and maybe getting a loan for a car. If I started to think about it, the degree to which I was fucked was overwhelming. But this was *good* debt, I told myself, a *good* investment. Suze fucking Orman told me so, with Oprah nodding in the background. Beyond college, I'd magically qualify for jobs because of a paper that cost me fifty thousand dollars, and then we'd live happily ever after. Sure, that sounded ridiculous, but what other fucking choice did I have?

During the school year I worked less and relied on student loans to fill in the gaps. The amount I made working was our spending money for babysitters, toiletries, gas, or any clothes that Emilia might need. Most of the time, the minimum credit card payments I made were immediately spent again for other necessities or things food stamps didn't cover, such as sponges or paper towels. (A roll of toilet paper was readily available in most public restrooms and fit in my backpack.) When I got the loan money at the beginning of the semester I knew I had to make it stretch as long as possible from September to December and January to April, which came to about a thousand a month. My Pell Grant and scholarship paid for tuition and all the fees they tacked on with that. Luckily, since I'd completed all my core classes like math and science, I could find most of the books I needed in local used bookstores.

Sometimes I would have money left over after rent was paid, enough so that my kid could get some ice cream and I could get a burrito and a five-dollar bottle of wine and maybe eat out once or twice at school. In summer I could fill up my work schedule well enough to pay for everything myself if we didn't have any major surprises, like my car breaking down, but everything was maxed out. It was common for me to only have ten bucks in my bank account and live off peanut butter for the final few days of the month.

Long-term financial planning is for people who aren't living in poverty. I didn't have the time or the energy to calculate how much debt I was in or how much interest I paid every month or how much interest I *would* pay on my student loans for decades into the future. All I cared about was a continued ability to feed, clothe, and house my kid.

# 5

## Solid Gold

One of my favorite professors, Debra Magpie Earling, taught an Advanced Fiction Workshop, and I signed up for that reason alone. Her Storytelling class the previous spring had changed me fundamentally. It had about forty people in it (including Kelley and Reed) and was unique since both undergrads and MFA students took it together. As usual, I hung out in the back at first and didn't say much, but by the end of the semester, I had regular invites to the grad student parties and called several of them friends. At one party in a backyard on the north side of town, a few admitted to assuming I *was* an MFA student. I smiled and said, "Soon! Gotta get my BA first."

Debra's brilliance in teaching resided in her booming, passionate voice whenever she stood in front of us to tell stories both as an example of what our assignment should be and as inspiration for what we could possibly become. It hadn't occurred to me that the storytelling aspect of this class would involve public performance. As a hopeful writer, I had conveniently assumed I would never have to speak to any number that added up to a "crowd" of people.

"I didn't know we'd have to get up in front of everyone," I whispered to Jessica, a fellow undergrad sitting next to me.

"Just make sure you bring a pen with you," she told me.

"Why?"

"It gives your hands something to do so they don't shake as much." Jessica was a much better student than me, or at least a perkier one, and a double major in journalism and English with a creative writing emphasis. She'd been one of the few other students in my first writing workshop the year before who didn't write about one of two subjects: *The Summer Between High School and College* or *My Year Abroad*. I appreciated her for that.

Holding the pen did ease my nerves a little. I also had the reassuring smiles of a few grad students and (if I glanced to my left) Debra's absolutely enraptured expression to get me through. I told them a story about someone hitting my car on the side of a highway with my then three-year-old daughter in the backseat and another about visiting my mom in France. I filled my notebooks with gems Debra doled out to us in class. One day she said, "The stories you choose to tell are the stories that make up who you are." This hit me with such poignancy that I almost didn't want to hand in the story I'd written about being miserable on the flight to Paris to visit my mom for six weeks. An opportunity to travel to France felt like an odd thing to sulk about, and I had focused on that instead of the complexities of how it felt to have your mom move halfway across the world with the expectation that it wouldn't affect you negatively.

For our final presentation, we had to talk about something we were obsessed with—Debra told us a German word for it but I forgot what it was. I knew I would talk about my obsession with writing, which had started when I was ten, and didn't give it that much thought otherwise. At home, a few nights before the day and time I had signed up to present to the class, I went down to the creepy basement area under our apartment and dug out bins full of journals, photo albums, and yearbooks. I still had my diaries with puffy covers and teddy bears and locks to keep my little brother out. For a long time, I had these things on display in my house and proudly referred to them as "My Paper Collection." In an essay for a creative writing class in my early twenties at the University of Alaska Fairbanks, I wrote about them and how they'd be the first thing I would grab if my house ever caught on fire. Now I had to dig them out of a basement. This downright poetic indication of their lower status in my life created an indescribable discomfort in the deepest center of my chest. The last time I had looked at these things, motherhood hadn't yet consumed me. I'd never wanted to believe that the responsibilities of raising a child squashed all the hopes and dreams out of you, but at that moment it sure felt like it.

As I read through those journals and diaries, though, I learned something about my younger self: I had never really been *obsessed* with writing. No, I'd been obsessed with falling in love. Almost every page from the year 1988 on contained some tidbit about a boy I either had a crush on or was heartbroken by. Sometimes, more than one boy. Reading the entries out loud to my roommate, Kelley, and my adorable guitar-playing poet boyfriend, Evan, could not be done without dramatic flair and a small glass of whiskey in my hand. We laughed and I shook my head and let out a lot of sighs. *This is who you are*, the books all seemed to say.

My nervousness on the day of my presentation consumed me, and I asked Debra before class if I could go first. Only Debra knew that I was shaking and desperately trying not to cry. In front of me

I had a table full of journals and diaries and scrapbooks. I picked up several, turning to marked pages, and read passages out loud. Most of them had quotes and lyrics on almost every page (one entire notebook I had filled only with jaded quotes about love). While I read passages, I flipped through a PowerPoint presentation of photos. In my conclusion, after all the talk of family estrangements and relationships not working out, I revealed that the purest form of love I had experienced came from becoming a mother.

"After all those years of living in tiny cabins," I said to the class, "chopping my own wood, and being the dependable friend to call for company on a road trip or to come pick you up at bar time, I fell in love with the act of surrendering to stability."

I flipped the photo shining on the screen behind me to one of Emilia, age three, proudly wearing a ballerina outfit in a studio apartment we had for a while in Mount Vernon, Washington. Then I took in a big breath and read some words I once found in the liner notes of an old Peter Mulvey CD:

> *When, through repetition or exhaustion comes the almost audible click, and you tumble through to where you . . . become just a splash of deep green in the lower left-hand corner of ten thousand mornings.*

I stopped and looked over at Debra, who sat to my left at her desk. She had a faint line on her cheek where a tear had streaked her skin, her mouth open in a stunned expression. Then she started clapping, stopping only to wipe another tear. I looked at my peers and smiled back at them, letting their applause permeate my skin.

———————

Debra offered a one-on-one meeting to everyone in her Storytelling class near the end of spring semester. We met in a coffee shop down the street from my apartment. She was already there when I arrived, and I walked over to the table without sitting down.

"I really need coffee," I said, like a person who desperately had to pee, "but here's my essay."

She was almost through all the pages by the time I returned with my coveted double twelve-ounce Americano with sugar and cream. I had chosen an essay I wrote for my fall semester nonfiction workshop. I still didn't like the title, but "Confessions of the House-keeper" seemed to fit.

I didn't have nicknames for the houses I cleaned in Missoula, partly because there were a lot fewer, and partly because I earned all the work through personal references and interactions. My clients felt like real people to me, and I, in turn, felt like I was an actual human being to them. As a self-employed person, I made less per hour than I had in Washington—just ten to fifteen dollars an hour instead of twenty—but that handful of regular clients were respect-ful, loyal, and we had a sincere, mutual appreciation.

The niceness of the clients aside, the work was still the same. A house with two boys had a room upstairs with a couch and some beanbags and several video game controllers spread out all over the floor. The boys must have been around seven and ten, judging by the size of the pants I folded when they were done in the dryer. Their game room upstairs had a bathroom with a toilet that they never seemed to flush. Once I lifted the lid and saw that it was full of urine the color of a dried orange peel. The smell was worse than an outhouse in July. It took five minutes to clean just the spot between the back of the seat and the tank. In Washington, at a house I called the Sad House, the toilet had been the same. Same with the Chef's House, too, now that I thought of it, and he never flushed, either. How men continued to pee all over their toilets throughout their lives and not care was a mystery I didn't want to solve.

Most of this was in the essay I handed to Debra. When I first presented the same essay to my nonfiction writing class in the fall, none of my classmates had anything to say about it. I thought I might get a few laughs from the crusty urine, but their only response to the essay was silence. The room was so quiet that Professor David Gates read a couple of paragraphs from a section that described the man who lived at the Sad House.

*From what I could tell, the man ate pastries and sandwiches from the deli at the local grocery store, and drank coffee with a lot of Kahlua. He liked to golf and gamble at the casinos in the area. They had a really nice boat in the garage, along with a CJ Jeep that I saw a picture of his wife proudly standing in front of. He smoked unfiltered Camels out of his bedroom sliding glass door, or on his front porch when the weather was decent. He watched old VHS movies of family holidays, surrounded by photo albums, on his recliner in the living room. The toilet often had a lot of piss on the seat and a floor with drops of blood which weren't easy to remove. His neighbors at the Porn House seemed to look after him, but his son, who lived in the same state, didn't visit much.*

Gates paused, leaned back in his chair, and tossed the papers onto the desk in front of him. "Solid gold, man. That's solid gold." He shook his head a little and let out a chuckle before giving a sort of sly smile, but he had sunglasses on so I wasn't sure if it was aimed at me. I also had no idea what he meant by calling it solid gold and I was too nervous to ask. I could only assume it was good. I didn't think the essay was all that great, but I had never heard Gates read someone's piece out loud or describe another student's essay like that before. I was too mortified to feel complimented, though—I'd just outed myself to my classmates as a single mom who cleaned toilets for money.

Debra finished reading while I burned my mouth on my coffee to the point of making my eyes water. After she put the pages down she looked at me and said my name a couple of times. I smiled and nodded in a hesitant way, not knowing how to respond. "Stephanie," she said again, but deeper. "Stephanie, this is going to be a book. This is going to be a movie! Don't you see how this needs to be a book?"

"A book about cleaning houses?" I wanted to laugh but I couldn't, seeing how serious Debra was.

"This is," she said, and started to read it again.

———

Debra seemed to enjoy it when I brought Emilia to her class. On a week that Emilia had a Thursday and Friday off from school for teacher conferences, I set her up with headphones and some cartoons to watch. My classmates who sat around me smiled at her every time she giggled at something happening on the screen in front of her. This scene felt normal by this point in my time at U of M, but that was only because of my professors and classmates who treated it as such. Maybe they knew that I really needed them to, and I was grateful for that unspoken agreement and that I never felt the need to ask permission.

After class was over that day and everyone left, I sent Emilia up to the front of the room to ask Debra if she would sign my copy of her book *Perma Red*. Debra smiled, leaned over to sign the title page, and I said, "Watch her, Emilia! That's a real author!" Emilia looked at me like she wasn't sure what to do, then she reached up to take the book when Debra handed it to her. They both held the book at the same time for a moment. Debra leaned over to get closer to my daughter and said, "Your mom is a very good writer."

My kid snapped her head around to look at me, like she wondered if Debra meant me, figuring she must have since I was the only other person in the room. I beamed for a second, then blinked back tears. Emilia asked if she could carry the book to the car and I nodded, smiled, and told Debra thank you, wishing I could describe how profound it was for me to witness that exchange. Emilia likely forgot the scene by the time we reached the parking lot, and I wished for it to imbed itself inside of her somewhere. I needed her to know I was good at this thing I fought so hard to become. I needed her to know the vitality of that dream and the requirements to keep it alive, like going to school past her bedtime and reading thick books with a pen in my mouth while I typed things on my laptop without looking at the keys. If she knew, if my kid had faith, then maybe I could believe that someday I would sign my own book for people, too. I could believe it like it would really happen.

This wasn't something I ever said to her directly, and I knew it was deeply sad that I was so desperate for at least *someone* in my family to be proud of me. These moments of wanting this from my six-year-old filled my chest with loneliness and shame. I craved her approval partly because so much of the time we struggled against each other—her little body was filled with rage, planted and tended to by Jamie. I clung to the moments when she felt my love for her and seemed to believe that I did my very best. At the same time, I needed someone who loved me to believe in me, because it was too big a job to do on my own.

---

"Emilia, come on," I said, moving her shoulder around, tempted to tickle her ribs, though that never went over well in the morning. "Emilia. If you don't get up right now we're going to be late and you'll miss the bus."

She looked up at me. "Can you drive me?"

I narrowed my eyes at her and pursed my lips. "Only if you get up *right now*, get dressed, *and* put on your socks and shoes." The last part might have been the most vital. Many outings had not happened because she refused to put on shoes and oh my god were her kicks strong for a tiny person. It took bribing her with a special breakfast of toast with cinnamon and sugar to get her out of bed; then the battle to get her dressed began. Every day required the perfect outfit to go with her mood or something she currently loved. That morning, she had to dress like Michael Jackson, and I couldn't find her glove. She'd worn it all summer. *What the fuck, where could it possibly be?* I tore apart our bedroom before I found it under her pillow.

While she ate, I looked over my notes from class again, and pulled the book we would discuss in class that day out of my backpack.

"Why do you have to read books so much?" Emilia asked, mouth full of sugar, butter, and toasted bread.

"Because I want to be a writer," I said, digging through my bag for a pen. "And if you want to be a writer you have to read and write a lot."

"You must really, really, *really* want to be a writer then," she said, adding a dramatic eye roll.

I chuckled. "It's the only thing I've ever wanted to be. Come on, kiddo, we gotta get going."

I didn't mind driving her to school. We still went in and got breakfast together, only I was sure to remember my coffee now. But it felt awkward when we walked over to where she lined up. Missoula had a dress code for parents my age. In warmer weather the men wore button-up short-sleeve Patagonia shirts with Kühl pants and Chacos. As the weather turned colder, they added a Patagonia fleece or puffy coat and thicker versions of the same brand of pants. The women didn't vary their wardrobes much. Many of them had a patchwork short-billed hat with a button on the side of the brim and the word JAX stitched by it that they most likely purchased at a store called Rockin Rudy's for about forty bucks. Their skirts were made of the same material and patchwork style but I never figured out where they bought those. In the winter they wore tights and knee-high boots and a Patagonia coat or fleece. All of them seemed to have the same stainless-steel travel mugs, but most of the women had tea with the tag hanging out of theirs. I had no idea what any of them did for work, and they didn't seem like they were in any kind of hurry, or stressed in the slightest. I imagined them running their own outdoor clothing companies, or having tech jobs in Seattle that they commuted to by plane.

My wardrobe hadn't varied since my early twenties: wool hat, hooded sweatshirt (likely from a bar, with holes for thumbs cut into the sleeves by the cuffs), worn and unwashed Carhartt pants faded to a nice tint of light brown, and Xtratuf boots. Variations occurred, but slightly. On warmer days, I'd switch out an old T-shirt from a concert or a brewery and flip-flops instead of boots. Occasionally you could catch me in a skirt or some shorts, but only when it was too hot for Carhartt pants.

My wardrobe wasn't the only reason I stood out—it seemed to me that I was the only single mom. Or at least the only one who could watch her kid line up for kindergarten. I wondered what people thought I did for work and hoped none of them knew I cleaned houses for a living. Being asked about my housecleaning rates at my kid's school or in any social setting was unpleasant and set me apart in situations where I wanted to feel like everyone else. I fought to make sure that cleaning houses, a perfectly respectable job that society deemed "unskilled" and therefore one where I felt *less than*, did not define me. I still believed that going to school was my real work.

Besides Sylvie, I knew one other single mom in town, named Becky, who was part of the group that took Emilia camping. Our kids hung out with each other a lot but we hadn't had much in the way of any time together or even a long conversation. My friendships were surface level only. Not because I necessarily wanted it that way. I just didn't have much to give back. There was so much going on in my life between work, kid, and school that I didn't have the bandwidth to sit and listen while someone talked to me about struggles they had. When I confessed this to anyone, they invariably said that friendship was a two-way street, a give-and-take, where one person needs more support and then the other might and so on. "Yeah, but I don't know if I will ever *not* need more support," I would say.

Since Emilia had arrived right on time—on her due date of the summer solstice, almost exactly nine months after she was conceived on the night of my birthday—our lives had been relentless. I knew that some people lauded us as an example of true resilience; it seemed to me that these people viewed living below the poverty line as a kind of strength-training program. Most were likely unaware of how all-encompassing it was for us. They didn't see their participation in how we were trained, but anytime I talked about or posted on Facebook that I was going through a hard time, all the comments were some variation of "You got this!" With every hardship we endured, and in turn every traumatic incident that I had to relay in order to give someone a heads-up that my kid needed trauma-informed care, what I heard most as a response was that I should be proud for getting through it. I was a *survivor*. I was *resilient*. People would tell me "children are resilient" when I worried about Emilia, but I never saw how that could be true. Children didn't have the communication skills or self-awareness to talk to adults about how stressful their lives felt, or that they couldn't in fact handle it. That lack of ability, that silence, seemed to be confused with resilience.

This "resilience" might have been part of what made my writing unique, but it still bothered me that it was a part of my life. Resilience as a virtue is assigned, especially to marginalized groups, when systemic structures have created countless invisible barriers to living what the privileged consider a normal life. Every time I wanted to cry from the crushing hopelessness that life seemed to bring, something inside me hissed, *You must not allow yourself to fall apart.* At first I thought this signified bravery on my part, or that it meant I was a good parent in that I didn't want my kid to worry as much as I did about keeping us fed, clothed, and sheltered. Then I started to realize that I had no choice in the matter: I didn't have the privilege to feel.

If some paperwork got misplaced and I heard the word *declined* after I swiped my EBT card, I wasn't allowed to get mad when the cashier handed me the piece of paper that automatically printed to show my account balance. It had been drilled into me that I should be nothing but grateful for the two hundred bucks a month we received to feed ourselves. I knew that if I dared to get angry at the situation, every word I said would be ignored. This only made matters worse, because I now felt insane as well. Also, angry people were ushered out of places. Only grateful people who followed the rules ran any chance of being heard. My anger had no use or value—it didn't get me anywhere, so I had no choice but compliance.

Immediate acceptance of any shitty situation was what most people seemed to mean by resilience, and they needed poor people like me to be that way. Otherwise, my suffering would be too visible to ignore, and they would have to deal with their feelings about that—whether helplessness or responsibility. If people were made too aware of our suffering—like knowing what Emilia ate for dinner every night or that we shared a bedroom—and if we were deemed innocent or undeserving of that suffering, then those people might feel the need to help out in some way. It was easier for a lot of people to imagine how strong and high-functioning I was, as opposed to how desperate and on the edge of disaster we actually were.

To change our society's worship of the concept of "resilience" would require a whole other way of thinking. But that's unlikely to happen, not when there are whole systems in place to keep low-wage workers so desperate for paychecks that they'll do all the jobs no one else wants to. Not when it would require trusting poor people with money for food without making them prove they worked their asses off for it.

Resilience is a flag we poor people could wave to gain that trust. If we proved ourselves time and time again—if we pulled up those fucking bootstraps so hard they broke and our response was to shrug it off before we found some way to fix them so we could immediately start pulling again—people nodded in approval. They might even have assigned us to the "deserving poor" line when we needed more than what was offered. But if I told people about the debilitating panic attacks that sometimes took hours to recover from? About the times I got off the phone with Jamie after he threatened to take me back to court to force me to move to Portland and I fell to my hands and knees, unable to breathe? Well, that wasn't being resilient!

How did I expect to make it through all of these situations—such as a job with no health insurance or benefits or one fucking paid sick day when my kid's temperature was too high for the day care I could barely afford the copay for? Resilience was the necessary acceptance of that situation. And if I figured it out? If I ducked my head down and barreled through and somehow got to work the thousand other times a similar situation required me to do that? That's not just resilience, that's on your way to success! Look at you, working hard and playing by the rules! That American Dream will be all yours in no time. People thrive on success stories, and I fought like hell to be the one they wanted. Success stories got noticed. They got help because they'd earned enough trust to deserve it.

I sound angry, don't I? I hope I do. I've spent so much of my life pretending not to be angry, and I'm not doing that anymore. And

I don't even have as much to be angry about as a lot of people. I'm deeply aware that while our poverty put Emilia and me squarely in a marginalized group, our whiteness gave us camouflage. Because of our white skin, we weren't immediately *assumed* to be poor and then treated poorly as a result. No one other than the grocery store clerks knew that I needed food stamps to afford staples. No one other than caseworkers offered me the left-handed compliment of noting how "well-spoken" my daughter and I were. I got the occasional break from my poverty, at least in terms of its visibility to others. In terms of how it felt inside, the constant, crushing panic? I never got a break from that.

———

At David Gates's advice, I began to submit essays to publications I'd never heard about before but had noticed were included in a lot of author bios. To start, I stuck with the publications that didn't ask for a reading fee (usually about twenty-five bucks) but didn't pay, either. I knew some publications paid up to a dollar a word, but that seemed unattainable, especially since I thought my only two options for that were the *New Yorker* and the *Paris Review*. No one told me otherwise. I didn't know what freelance writing was, or how to make money as a writer. In college, they taught you that payment came through an impressive bio full of publications in reviews and journals in the company of the almighty "MFA." Getting paid as a writer or having a bestseller from one of the top five publishing houses was considered "commercial" and cheapened the work in a way I couldn't fully grasp. Didn't people *want* to get paid for writing? Wasn't the whole point in going to college, spending thousands of dollars in the process, to learn how to do it?

Over the summer, I had submitted the essay I'd been working on about cleaning houses to a publication called the *Believer*. I had no idea what the publication was, but Gates had suggested it and I trusted that. My only submissions had been to the local magazine called *Mamalode* and I needed to branch out somehow. When I saw the *Believer* had emailed back, I involuntarily scrunched up my face and shut my eyes tight before clicking to open it. Then I peeked.

*Dear Stephanie Land,*

*Thank you for your unwavering patience in receiving a response from The Believer.*

*Unfortunately, we won't be able to take "The Confessions of the Housekeeper" for the magazine, because we don't take personal essays. Having said that, I really liked the narrative voice, which was economical, measured and selective, and adds up to something impressive. I wish you luck in placing it with another publication.*

*Thank you for thinking of us!*

*Best regards,*
*The Believer*

Reading the email wasn't enough. I had to print it out and reread it or else I'd be tempted to hit REPLY and gush a dozen thank-yous to whoever took the time to call my writing "impressive" before asking repeatedly if they really meant that. Sure, it was a rejection, and my first (I assumed) big one. I understood I would receive many, but it seemed like a rarity to get one that came with some feedback. I rifled through the single drawer in my desk until I found a thumbtack to display the rejection on the wall behind it.

# 6

# Sitting in Class

Three girls at the table next to me in the University Center laughed, breaking me out of staring at the blinking cursor on my laptop. I sat back and rubbed my eyes and looked up at the atrium in the center of the building for a second while I debated grabbing more coffee. Tuesday's assignment was to write a short essay with the phrase "evil is the result of boredom" in mind. So far I had fumbled through a few paragraphs about the dark winters I'd lived through in Fairbanks, Alaska, in my early twenties, but it thankfully wasn't due today. Coffee, I decided, was a necessity, since the next forty-five minutes before class would drag along even slower. I packed up my laptop, notebook, and day planner before I stood a little slower than usual after sitting in an uncomfortable metal chair for almost my entire three-hour break. Our favorite table next to the outlet had been free and I didn't want to risk losing it by getting up to use the bathroom after Reed left for his next class. Now that I was on my feet, I realized one was asleep and I had to walk fast downstairs to pee, cursing myself that I hadn't gone before.

Most of the students who poured in and out of the University Center between classes were gone by this time of the day. I assumed they went to their dorms or an afternoon class or maybe even to work, but a few of them hung out here at the tables or in a weirdly dark side room on the second floor with pool tables that always smelled like pizza. After I speed-walked downstairs to the bathroom, I stopped by the snack store. It accepted EBT cards, the debit card used to spend food stamps, but I was too embarrassed to use it. I never saw anyone else using theirs. Usually I brought something from home, like a peanut butter Clif Bar (a staple in my diet for several years by then) or a sandwich that also involved peanut butter. I walked slowly past the back wall of glass, my mouth watering at the sight of the Odwalla smoothie drinks, but couldn't stomach the price to purchase one.

Halfway through filling my coffee cup, the resistance in the lever on top of the airpot dropped and it gave out that dreaded gurgling sound. I looked around for another one and only saw decaf. Two guys at the register in matching polo shirts and knitted beanies were busy talking to a girl with a perfectly disheveled topknot. I debated walking out with my half-filled cup. Instead I let out a sigh, filled the rest with decaf, two creams, and two sugars, and pocketed two more creams and sugars for the cup of coffee I would make that night at home. I walked over to the case with day-old stuff hoping to see a hard-boiled egg, but no such luck, so I grabbed a couple of string cheese sticks to tide me over until six thirty.

"Your coffee things are empty," I said while the boy behind the counter handed me my change for a five. His head swiveled to scan the store, almost like he didn't know where the coffee station was.

My second class of the day and the first of two back-to-back writing workshops was up on the third floor of the building that housed the English Department, which was nice that time of year because it was always unseasonably warm. The Liberal Arts Building was notorious for never holding appropriate temperatures. I shivered through my morning literature class on the second floor. It was in the infamous "Hugo Room," where portraits of visiting writing instructors—including a large one of Richard Hugo holding a glass of whiskey and one of Eileen Myles sitting on a toilet—stared at you unapologetically. Hugo seemed especially disapproving, much like the portrait of Ernest Hemingway I tacked on the wall over my desk at home.

A warm room with a row of windows meant that I could take off my coat and look outside. Since I accidentally discovered during the first week of school that the room was vacant before class, I enjoyed being twenty minutes early to get a few minutes of peace. Sitting for any length of time often blanketed me in a heaviness, though. It felt similar to the sensation of falling asleep after crawling into bed, feeling the weight of your body sink into the cushion below. I had to choke down my lukewarm coffee and hoped that biting a spot inside my cheek would keep my eyes from drooping.

I hated it when I got this tired. Fall semester last year I'd had an American literature class first thing in the morning that I could rarely stay awake for. In my defense, that semester I started my day at five in the morning, drove to the gym to clean it for two and a half hours, came home to get Emilia ready for preschool, drove back to the gym to drop her off, and immediately went to my first class. Halfway through the lecture, the heaviness pulled me into the chair. I could never fight it off entirely. Then came the restless legs and I tried to rub the tops of my shoes together to make it stop, but nothing short of doing jumping jacks would.

Though I no longer had the gym to clean, there still wasn't enough time to carve out for an adequate amount of sleep. Night was my only time to do schoolwork, and I stayed up late to finish it after I had cleaned someone's house, picked up my kid from school, cleaned my own place, and made whatever dinner I could. There was never enough time for anything, let alone sleep.

———

For me, taking Debra's class in the fall wasn't about learning how to write fiction. I honestly had no interest in that. The draw was Debra herself—I wanted to sit in a classroom with her for a little while longer, knowing it would probably be my last chance.

The first hour went by quickly but it was a relief when she suggested we take a ten-minute break, because I'd chugged my coffee to get it down at the beginning of class and I needed to use the bathroom. I reached into the front pocket of my backpack for my phone to check messages. I flipped it open and immediately saw that I had missed three calls and five texts from my new roommate, Seth. I looked at the clock in the front of the room while standing up so fast I bumped my desk, nearly spilling my notebooks and printed-out essays on the floor.

My former roommate, Kelley, fell in love with a traveling banjo player and decided to join him in his lifestyle of train-hopping, busking, and working on farms. After another climbing friend, Michelle, crashed in the room for a couple of weeks, a friend of mine told me about Seth, a freshly graduated law student who needed a place to stay while he studied for the bar exam. I'm not sure how much experience Seth had with kids before moving a few bags of stuff into the empty but partially furnished bedroom one day, but he had worked out well so far. I was particularly impressed when he agreed to hang out with Emilia so I could work after she had puked all over the sidewalk in front of the YMCA. He rarely, if ever, called when Emilia was with him.

"Everything is okay," he said after answering on the first ring.

That wasn't reassuring. I imagined him talking to me from a hospital waiting room. "Okay?"

"Did you maybe forget it's Thursday? Apparently she gets out of school an hour early today?" Seth's voice rose at the end of each sentence, and my head felt like it was full of static. I heard a ringing in my ears.

"Oh my god." I leaned into a wall and slid down to the floor of the hallway. My right hand pressed my phone to my ear while my left thumb massaged the space between my eyebrows, moving up a bit, then back down to start again. While I had mulled over purchasing a bottle of green smoothie, Seth arrived at our place, twenty minutes before Emilia usually got off at the bus stop a block away. On the door, however, someone had left a note with their phone number, saying Emilia was at their house.

"What? What neighbor? I don't know any neighbors!"

"It's a yellow house by the bus stop," he said.

"The bus stop?!" My six-year-old had gotten off the bus that afternoon an hour earlier because it was, indeed, Thursday and school ended at two thirty for teacher preparation or something. Emilia knew Seth was supposed to be there, so she crossed a decent-size street with a good amount of traffic to get home. When she got there and saw the place was empty, my kid, backpack still on, ran back the way she came, across the busy street again, and knocked on the door of the girl close to her age who got off at the same stop. She must have been able to say everything that happened, including going home to discover the babysitter wasn't there. Emilia didn't know my number and I stupidly hadn't written it on her backpack. The little girl's mom wrote a note saying Emilia was at her house, included her phone number, and walked four small children across the street and back to leave it taped to my door.

"Oh my god. Is she okay? Can I talk to her?"

Seth handed the phone to Emilia, who immediately said, "I looked both ways, Mom! I crossed the street by myself and looked both ways so all the cars stopped for me!"

I couldn't believe no one had called the police, but maybe it was normal to see small humans running across the street by themselves at that time of the day. I managed not to say any of this and told her how proud I was of her for remembering to look both ways, then asked her to give the phone back to Seth.

"Thank you," I said. I couldn't catch my breath. "Thank you so much." I walked a bit down the hall to the stairwell. "I feel like I'm having a panic attack."

"Oh, it's totally okay," he said, while I had to force myself not to sit on the stairs and sob.

"I'm so sorry, Seth. I . . . I forgot. I'm so sorry."

We said goodbye and I asked him to take Emilia out for some ice cream and said that I would see them after six thirty. Ten minutes had passed by the time I hung up the phone and my classmates were funneling through the door of our classroom down the hall. I shoved my phone into my front pocket and rushed to the bathroom, peed as fast as I could, avoided looking at my face while I washed my hands, took one deep breath and held it for five seconds, then walked across the hall, took my seat, and sat through Debra's lecture on story arcs while I quietly tried to look as if everything about me was just fine.

I felt so shaken up that I nearly skipped my next workshop to go home. But today's focus in Walter Kirn's class would be a discussion of Joan Didion's *The White Album*, and I knew I wouldn't be called on unless I raised my hand. I could attend and try to get something out of it even while feeling sick to my stomach from panic.

It was only the end of the second week of the semester, so there still wasn't an invisible seating chart. Everyone sat somewhere different, testing out different views from the U-shaped arrangement of desks facing the front of the room, where the podium and whiteboard were. Kirn rarely used either. He sat in a desk like we did, facing us, but usually with sunglasses on, telling us that he hadn't slept because he had been up all night working on edits for his newest book, *Blood Will Out*.

I'd sat in the same seat since the first day of class, when I had pulled out my notebook and pen, and looked up to see Evan walking through the door. We hadn't spoken since the night we hung out over the summer on my back porch. He drank a few beers and spent most of that time gushing about how relieved he was that I got an abortion.

"I mean, what would you be, four months along by now?" he had said before downing the rest of his second beer. "We really dodged a bullet."

I had agreed with him then. I didn't want to tell him how much I'd grieved for what I felt was my last chance to have another child, even if I had no desire to have one with him.

My stomach had flipped and then turned when I saw him walk into *my* writing workshop. The class I had looked forward to since I heard Kirn would be the instructor for it. Evan's right hand was linked, as in fingers laced together, with a girl I had never seen before. He had talked about her when we hung out over the summer but only to explain that she was out of town. She looked nice and was probably shy, and had hair that was a bit longer and darker than mine. Evan and I had made eye contact immediately, since I was one of three people already in the room. While I froze, he smiled at me as big and sincerely as he could without showing any teeth, nodded, and took a seat a few desks to my right, at the back of the arc. The girlfriend sat next to him, in the desk farther away from me. If she knew who I was she didn't show it. I wanted to tell her everything about my short time with Evan, especially how fast we went from sitting next to each other in class to chairs in the waiting room at the only place in town that offered abortions. I wondered if he used protection with her. I wondered if he still remembered the due date had been Christmas Eve.

I still clenched my teeth whenever he walked into class. I didn't look up, but I knew him by the sound of his boots. He had never been openly affectionate with me, so the fact that he always held hands with his girlfriend hurt more than stung. Maybe he had fallen in love for real this time. I breathed out through my nose, and imagined putting his boots on to kick him squarely in the shin before yelling that his poems weren't any good.

My memory of Didion's *The White Album* was faint and I hadn't been able to find my copy to review before class. Thankfully Kirn led the discussion in a different direction, going into how a writer's personality comes across on the page.

"You know, I've been to jail," he said as an example. "Always pay your speeding tickets in St. George, Utah." All of us chuckled. "Whatever makes you an outsider is what makes you a writer." I scribbled that one down.

These little nuggets of brilliance from my writing instructor—a real, actual writer—were the reason I took these classes. They would utter profound things in between explaining plot and syntax, or while mapping different story arcs before asking the class which was the hero's journey. They all counted as electives, since I'd taken more workshops than my degree required, but it was the whole reason I'd fought to attend. Plus, I needed letters of recommendation for my

MFA application, and I really wanted one from Kirn. David Gates, with whom I did an independent study that semester, and Judy Blunt were the only other nonfiction professors. They couldn't write letters for me since they decided who got selected for the nonfiction program—although everyone knew that Gates tended to agree with whatever Blunt said.

Judy and I had met in her office before I officially switched my degree program from sociology to English. She'd been a guest speaker for the Introduction to Creative Writing class I took that summer to talk about the MFA program and the possible trajectory of a writer. Her memoir, *Breaking Clean*, told her story about leaving her marriage with three young children days before starting her freshman year at U of M. She then went on to graduate with an MFA in nonfiction and eventually directed the whole program. Our stories had a lot in common, and I told her so, and that my intention was to earn my MFA. She seemed to smile approvingly and asked how old my daughter was.

"She just turned five," I said, "but she's at her dad's for part of the summer in Oregon."

"That's good," Judy said. "Babies don't belong in graduate school." She went on to tell me how her kids were passed around during writing workshops, since they met in professors' houses back then, and classmates would babysit other times. I didn't ask why that privilege wouldn't apply to anyone else. Judy went on to tell me about working construction, particularly sanding floors, and getting up at four in the morning to work on her book just like she would for any other job.

"I guess I never thought of writing as real work," I told her. "I *want* to be a writer . . ." I paused for a second to feel the weight of those words. I had never said them out loud to anyone in a professional setting. "It just seems frivolous to do that, you know, as a single mom. That's why I wanted to come talk to you."

Judy spoke of assistantships where graduate students received funds for their tuition through teaching introductory composition classes. "Sometimes the committee will offer full scholarships for unsupported writers without the teaching requirement." She reached for a piece of fuzz on her slacks, picking it off and smoothing the fabric before uncrossing and crossing her feet again. "Most of our writers come from Ivy League schools or have families who can pay for their education—even beyond what we offer. But sometimes the committee will take on a student who doesn't have that support and shows a lot of promise." I straightened up in my seat, thinking she meant someone like me, unaware that "the committee" was basically her. "Unfortunately, they just accepted a writer from Alaska who is in that position. I'm not sure they'll want to do it again so soon." She changed the subject to books, motioning for me to look at a rolling metal shelf not far from where we sat, and suggested I pick up some Mary Karr.

"Would you be willing to be my advisor?" I asked.

Judy nodded. "Bring in your forms and we'll take a look at what classes you've taken to see where you're at. Have you done two years of another language?"

"I did four semesters in Fairbanks, Alaska," I said, not mentioning what it was.

"Good," she said, standing and walking to the door. "That one always seems to trip people up."

Judy's demeanor changed from pleased to annoyed when we met again in her classroom, and I couldn't help but wonder if it was because she saw that my four semesters of language were American Sign Language (and not a Latin-based spoken one) *after* she had approved my acceptance to the English degree program. My "solid gold" moment with Gates faded when she led the class in a discussion on my first assigned essay in her Advanced Nonfiction Workshop.

She wrote, "It's pretty relentless," in the notes for a sixteen-page essay I had submitted for peer review, spending twenty-seven dollars on printing copies for everyone. Then, to my humiliation, she also called my essay *relentless* out loud in front of everyone. She clearly didn't mean this in a good way, so much so that after class Evan tried to tell me it wasn't that bad. Judy had praised his essay, so he must have felt generous. It often seemed like some classmates—especially male ones—would only say nice things about my work if the instructor had said something nicer about theirs.

The word *relentless* lived up to its definition as it throbbed in my head for several days after. When our class met the following week, Judy Blunt walked in wearing her usual tennis shoes, slacks, and button-up shirt under a vest and I thought, *I'll show you relentless*.

More workshops with different instructors meant more opinions about the work I handed in. No one else used the word *relentless* to describe my writing, but I let it become part of my motto as a student. *My life may be relentless*, I wrote in a notebook, *but goddammit so am I*. It would have been possible for me to graduate halfway through my senior year, but I couldn't because of a required Shakespeare class that didn't fit into my fall schedule. I didn't mind. Not only was I already taking fifteen credits that semester, but I jumped at the opportunity to do more advanced nonfiction classes with visiting writing instructors. This semester was Kirn, and the next was Sherwin Bitsui; both had refreshingly different styles from Blunt or Gates. Judy taught us never to change even the smallest detail in our writing from how we remembered it—not street names, colors of houses, or wardrobe hues. We all assumed she felt this way because the family she left behind said a scene in her book didn't happen. After Judy had to admit they were correct, she and her publisher offered apologies while deleting the scene from future printings. Kirn taught more on the side of creative nonfiction, and told us that if it works better to have a blue dress instead of a white one, write it as blue. But Judy's cautionary tale stuck, and instilled the fear of family retaliation if I changed details from the way I remembered them. Memory wasn't always dependable by default anyway. However, I immensely enjoyed the supportive environment Kirn created and the lack of public shaming, which seemed to be one of Judy's favorite parts of teaching.

Emilia had no idea any of this was going on, but if she'd known what the word *relentless* meant, she'd have recognized it in me. Time off from school meant attempts to make up for the fall and spring seasons when I would disappear into a shape that barely got up from the kitchen table, hunched over a laptop or varying sizes of books—shutting out the blaring sounds of *SpongeBob SquarePants* while I did it.

For her part, Emilia had to learn how to occupy herself. We had adopted a long-haired Chihuahua puppy a couple of months after we moved to Missoula that I thought might work as a companion. But Emilia's habit of jumping on the mini trampoline while she watched cartoons or squishing the dog into toy strollers made him extra skittish. This tiny thing we named Token (as in "the token dog") would, however, comfort Emilia during the stretch of months when her dad stopped calling her and wouldn't answer his phone whenever Emilia wanted to talk to him. Jamie told me later that he had been depressed, but I couldn't help feeling that it was a product of anger, and that he was punishing both of us. I hoped he wasn't intentionally breaking his kid's heart, but in the end it didn't matter; the effect was the same.

———

A six-year-old-sized shape bounded toward me when I got home later that evening. Before I could put down my backpack, Emilia rushed over and told me about crossing the street and getting ice cream. Seth mumbled something about needing to go get some noodles and brushed past me to walk out the door. I looked for evidence that my kid had eaten dinner and found nothing, then looked in the cupboard for a box of mac and cheese and didn't see one of those, either.

"You wanna go get dinner somewhere?" I asked, reaching in the front pocket of my backpack for my wallet and phone.

"Yay!" Emilia said, reaching down to chase Token, who finally succumbed to being picked up. "Can Token come, too?"

"No, they don't allow dogs inside places. You know that." Besides, Token wasn't exactly housebroken, just litter box trained, so I never fully trusted him. He had a tiny bladder and lifted his leg on anything. Despite his size, he was a good little hiking buddy, and had summited the nine-thousand-foot-high Lolo Peak with us over the summer. He also proved himself as a crag dog, curling up and sleeping on backpacks while everyone's attention was on the huge boulders or rock walls. We just had to keep an eye out for eagles that might try to swoop down and pick him up.

We walked out the back door, then down the alley toward North Higgins, the main street that went through downtown. There wasn't really anywhere close to us downtown where we could both sit and equally enjoy a meal within our budget. Plus my kid would only stop bouncing around long enough to take bites of things like fries or pasta, and forcing us both through that experience would not end well after the day's events. I pulled Emilia into Taco del Sol for a burrito big enough for two meals and that cost only about eight bucks, then walked across the street to Worden's Market for her to pick something.

Emilia had grown up almost completely on a food stamp diet—one that was painstakingly budgeted and had no room to purchase expensive produce for the sake of multiple introductions. I had to keep to things I knew she would largely consume without leaving leftovers, since she wouldn't eat those, either. When we had a bit of extra money, like the beginning of the semester when the loan money came in, even if I took her to a huge grocery store and told her to get anything she wanted for dinner, she would still pick out a box of mac and cheese and a packet of crackers with the bright orange cheese substance in the middle, which is exactly what she chose that night. I picked up a six-pack of hard cider.

We were dangerously close to Emilia's bedtime when we got home so I told her we had to eat dinner quickly. I bent over to take bites of my burrito while I checked Facebook and looked at my planner for the weekend. Two houses to clean the next day, but they were both pretty easy. Sunday evening was Second Wind, a weekly thing where all the MFA students gathered in a bar to watch two of their peers, each partnered with an established writer, read their work. My homework load was light that weekend, except for finishing that "evil is boredom" thing, so I could work on polishing some other essays to submit for publications. In my independent study with David Gates that semester, I planned to work on a second-person piece I thought might be good for *Creative Nonfiction* or the Sustainable Arts grant they offered only to artists who had children to care for.

Emilia ate while I cleaned up the kitchen, then asked if she could sleep with me that night. I nodded but said, "If you brush your teeth super-duper fast!" I read most of a chapter of the first book of the Harry Potter series, then turned off the lamp and gave her my arm to lie on. I sang "Goodnight Sweetheart" a few times and waited for her to fall asleep, only to wake up an hour and a half later when Emilia flung her hand onto my face in her sleep. I whispered "shit" into the darkness before I forced myself out of bed. Everything was still brightly lit in our living area and kitchen, and Seth's door was closed. Since it was almost ten thirty I assumed he was home. I fished my notebook out of my backpack and pulled out the essay Kirn had handed out in class for next week.

"'Shooting an Elephant,'" I muttered, flipping through the xeroxed pages of George Orwell's essay. I grabbed one of the hard ciders out of the fridge and turned off the lamp over the futon before I poked my head into our room to make sure Emilia was fast asleep. Like a teenager, I tiptoed to the drawer to the right of the kitchen sink where I kept a pouch of tobacco, some rolling papers, and a lighter. My thickest, oldest hoodie hung by the door, and I reached to grab it and put it on. Stepping out onto the porch felt like entering a different world, one where I was myself again. If I slept on the futon that night, it would be a whole eight hours before I would be "Mom" again. For now, I sat on the top step of the porch, opened my drink, and placed the assigned reading in the spot with the best light.

Orwell, predictably, couldn't hold my attention that well. I leaned back on the post to close my eyes for a second or two. My phone buzzed in my pocket and I checked to see who it was. A text from Daniel, telling me to go out to the bar, but I closed it and put it back where it was without responding. I didn't feel like saying no. I just wanted ten minutes, maybe thirty, to smoke a cigarette, have an adult beverage, and maybe read a few paragraphs of Orwell, before I had to scrub my face, brush my teeth, and collapse on the futon in my clothes—then wake up and do it all over again.

# 7

It's Buildering, Not Bouldering

"Let's go!" I said, pulling Daniel down the sidewalk. Then I gasped. "We should go buildering!"

Daniel had been staring back at some guys yelling at him to come and play pool, but swung his head to look directly at me. "What? Did you say 'buildering'?" He laughed again. "You're something else, Stephanie Land."

My face broke into a smile while I tried to hide how much I liked it when he called me by my full name. Daniel had someone else he hung out with. All I knew about her was that she was a lot younger than he was, and she was not as interested as he was in getting serious. They called each other "babe" over text while I rolled my eyes and waited for him to finish the conversation. Daniel was a couple of years older than me and would probably live as if he were still in his twenties for as long as he possibly could. We had fun together, but only when Emilia wasn't around. He was for good times only, not someone I had any illusions about. Still, I really liked him. "Come onnnnnnn," I said, pulling him to walk with me. "I don't want to go home yet."

"Why, you don't want to make out with your boyfriend?" Daniel sounded jealous, but I knew he was faking.

"He's not my boyfriend." I added an eye roll to my flat tone.

"He used to be and he's sleeping in your bed right now! How is that not a boyfriend?"

Daniel thought this was amusing. I did not. Part of what he said was true. My ex-boyfriend, Travis, had called out of the blue a few days before to say he had some time off and he was thinking about coming to Montana. It was rare for him to take time off, so rare that I wondered if he'd quit his job. Travis ran his family's farm, where they boarded around a hundred horses and used the back field for growing hay to feed them. Emilia and I had lived there for about six months before I realized the role of Farm Wife did not mesh well with my personality.

"Have you . . . Haven't you only left Washington once?" I had asked him when he called. I had no idea why he wanted to come see me. I could only assume that he wanted to get laid.

Travis told me he would hang out with Emilia the whole time he was there, which meant I'd have a break from school drop-offs and pickups, dinners, and bedtimes. "You can stay with me," I said. "There's a futon in the living room that one of us can sleep on. But I don't think I'll be home all that much, if that's okay. It would be kinda nice to go out while you stay with Emilia."

His voice had a false brightness to it when he said that was fine. "I just want to go somewhere. Go on a road trip."

The evening he arrived, Emilia assumed he was there only to visit her. Travis looked a little disappointed when I said sure, they could walk downtown for ice cream without me.

"Come on." I pulled Daniel again. "I have this place I like."

Daniel seemed amused and possibly turned on by the whole situation and let me lead him by the arm a block away, turning once before ducking into an alley. I scanned for police cars before I walked over to the fire escape, then I took off my flip-flops one at a time and stuffed them into each of my back pockets. I had done this once with Theodore and another time on my own, climbing up in a dress with a plastic cup of whiskey clenched in my teeth after seeing the Wailin' Jennys play. They had ended with "Callin' All Angels," a song I had listened to on repeat after the abortion. Instead of crying at the bar by myself I went to a rooftop where it could be just me and the stars.

"You really climb up that thing?" Daniel said, looking up and craning his neck a bit. "There's a . . . What is that, a metal plate?"

"Yeah," I said. "It doesn't go up that far." The plate covered the bottom four or five rungs of the ladder, and was undoubtedly there to keep people from doing what I was about to, but there were a few pipes attached to the brick wall that made for good footholds. This never seemed like a huge risk, since the actual ladder began about fifteen feet off the ground and there were secure holds on either side.

With full knowledge that I was showing off, I grabbed on to the side of the ladder with my right hand, got a good grip on the second row of pipe with my left, and swung my left foot up to grip the first row of pipes with my toes, simultaneously pushing and pulling up to wedge myself between the fire escape and the wall before I could reach up higher on the ladder and stand on the lowest pipe. Daniel let out a "Jesus be careful" as I turned to face the metal plate, then reached up to grab the closest ladder rung above it with my left hand, turned sideways, then bent my right leg up to grip the next row of pipes with my toes, fully smooshing myself between the plate and the wall of the building, holding all my weight with the hand grasping on to the rung. Then, repeating all of that again, I stood on my right foot to straighten my leg, inching my bent leg higher. When I reached for the next rung on the ladder above me to move up, my right foot pushed off the pipe and slipped. My left arm flexed as I fought to get my foot back on the pipe while my right hand kept hold of a pipe above it. My bent leg sank about an inch before my right foot steadied itself again, the outside of my left leg catching the corner of the metal plate in the process. After that I moved my right foot up to the next pipe, stood on it, and turned around to climb the ladder the rest of the way. Halfway up, I felt liquid trickle down my leg. At the landing by the roof, I lifted the rolled-up leg of my Carhartt pants. In the dark I could see two blackish lines of blood making their way to my foot.

"You good?" Daniel asked from the ladder, already above the plate.

"Ay, ay, a scratch, a scratch," I said, then stretched out my arms. "A scratch!"

"What?" Daniel sounded a bit annoyed.

"Mercutio! Never mind." I walked to the front side of the roof to look over the main stretch of downtown and the sidewalks still full of people. Daniel came up behind me and tugged at the top of my pants and turned me around to bring me toward him, then tilted my face to his with the fingertips of his free hand. I smiled as our lips touched, feeling his tongue toy with mine while his fingers traced the inner waistband of my pants. I gasped a little when he brushed by my hip bones and he chuckled, pleased to have found something to tease me with. My right hand went from where it rested on his hip straight to rub what was under the zipper of his shorts. He took in a huge breath, pretending to be shocked, saying something coy like he wasn't that type of girl. This is what I liked about him: We played. Nothing was direct or serious. There were no feelings involved. When we did have sex it was primal and loud and exactly the fucking I needed, but I didn't want that tonight. I was too distracted. My mind was still focused on the short paper I'd just trudged through (after Emilia went to sleep and while I tried to ignore my ex's loud snores in the next room) to give a "Formalist Analysis" to the film *Citizen Kane*. My leg caused me to wince a bit as I lowered myself to lie on my back and watch the sky. Daniel and I stayed up there for an hour, looking at the stars, and told stories of stupid things we did as kids. Sometimes we made out, then stopped to listen to the sounds of people talking and laughing on the streets below us.

Daniel got up on his knees to look over the side of the building after someone screamed, and I lifted the cuff of my pants. The light from my cell phone screen was just bright enough to see my leg better. He turned to ask me something as I got my pant leg up to my knee and revealed what could only be described as a hole about the size of the pad of my thumb. Blood had smeared all around it with several dark lines trailing to the top of my foot, but it didn't seem to be bleeding now.

"Holy shit!" Daniel said before I could make sense of what I was looking at. "What the fuck! What the fuck did you do to your leg?" He bent forward, then stood up straight again, crossing his arms, put his hands on his hips, then crossed his arms again.

"I don't know, I slipped," I said. "I didn't think it was that bad. I thought it was just a cut." I couldn't tell how bad it was and didn't want to touch it.

Daniel put his hands on his hips again. "You've gotta." He paused. "We." He cleared his throat, then said, "We need to get you to an emergency room," in a formal voice I'd never heard him use before.

I laughed and told him he was cute before I reminded him I didn't have health insurance. Deep down, I also knew Daniel wasn't able to truly invest in caring for someone other than himself. That's what made him "safe"—I had no illusions about him and knew better than to put myself in a position where I needed him. Caring for each other wasn't part of our relationship, and I would inevitably get hurt if we tried to add that element. Another heartache wasn't something I had time to deal with.

"Just walk me home," I said. "I'll be fine." Blood had started to snake down my leg again by the time we reached the fire escape (which was much easier to climb down, thank goodness) and continued as we walked slowly toward my house. Daniel was quiet and gave me a long hug once we got to my door.

"You sure you don't want to come in?" I tilted my head toward the house, purely to tease him. He never came over when Emilia was home.

He looked around me, almost like he expected to see Travis standing at the window. "No," he said. "Not with homeboy in there."

I rolled my eyes. "You better text me when you get home."

Daniel waved me off as he walked in the direction of campus, saying, "Yes, Mother," over his shoulder.

Our entryway was dark and I turned on the light to get a better look at the gash. My eyebrows went up when I saw it had torn a hole through my Carhartt pants, too. But my view was partial and upside down, so I fished my digital camera out of my backpack and took a picture. The photo, framed perfectly from my knees to the floor, revealed the large size. I forced myself to breathe out and in again in a feeble attempt not to faint. I zoomed in on it and tilted my head a little. Its shape was an almost-perfect heart.

With the exception of a serious car accident at sixteen, I'd avoided any sort of injury that required stitches or even extensive wound care. All I knew was that it was best if it bled a lot and got a good scrubbing with hot, soapy water. The door frame to the bathroom steadied me for a minute while I looked at the floor. I pivoted my right foot to lean against the open door so I could stare at myself in the mirror to give myself a pep talk. I now wished Daniel had stayed to help me because I couldn't stand the sight of blood and washing this thing carried with it a good chance that I would pass out or puke. I grabbed the hand soap, rolled up my left pant leg, and sat on the edge of the tub with one leg on either side. I turned on the hot water. Steam surrounded me as I sat there for a minute. My bloody left leg was about an inch away from the hot water as I worked up the nerve to rub a palmful of soap over the wound. I sucked in a breath and held it, turned my head and clenched my eyes shut, slapped the soap on my leg, and started to rub quick and hard.

My fingers grazed the hole and the texture reminded me of hardened salmon roe. *Was that . . . was that fat? Was that the inside of my leg?* Sweat sprang out of every pore in my body and wooziness took hold. Luckily, we had some Neosporin and bandages and they were sitting on the shelf behind the toilet. I dried off my leg with a hand towel before I stood, steadying myself with the help of a towel rack, and inched my left toes back into my flip-flop. My left hand held up my pant leg as I carefully walked into the main room to sit on the edge of the futon. I squeezed some Neosporin onto my trembling finger, took a big breath, held it, and reached to apply it on the wound. The entire tip of my finger sank into my leg.

"Oh god," I mumbled. Surely this would be an occasion for me to pass out. This was bad—maybe ER type of bad, but that wasn't an option. A few minutes passed as I sat and took deep breaths in an attempt to calm myself enough to stand up and walk again. Travis and Emilia were in the next room sound asleep as I inched my way over to reach out and gently shake my ex-boyfriend's shoulder. He looked at me, confused at the sight of a dark silhouette looming above him. He sat up, startled. "Is everything okay?"

"I, uh, need you to help me with something," I whispered, then walked back out to lie on the futon with my left leg propped up on the chair. Travis was a farmer. He got injured all the time. He could handle it. It would be fine.

"Holy shit!" Travis exclaimed at his normal voice level. "What the fuck did you do to your leg?"

"Ssshhhhh!" I said. "Just cover it with a few Band-Aids."

"I think you're going to need something bigger than Band-Aids." He stared at my leg with his hands on his hips, then looked at me. His face showed alarm. That couldn't be good.

"I don't have anything besides that!" I whispered so loud I almost hissed at him.

"Well, what do you have?" he whispered back in what sounded like a hushed yell.

I looked around the kitchen. "Hand me that roll of paper towels and unclip my climbing shoes. There's a roll of athletic tape tied on to my chalk bag." He brought those two things and watched me fold two paper towels into a square. "Wait. Go wash your hands, then help me tape this on. I don't think I can look at it again."

---

Travis took Emilia to the bus stop in the morning while I emailed my first professor of the day, thinking I could still make it to my afternoon classes. *I tore a rather large hole in my leg,* I wrote. *I should also add, this is the first time I've ever done anything so stupid. At almost 35, I figure that's doing pretty well. However, the hole is the shape of a heart. Figures.*

Professor Katie Kane wrote back five minutes later: *Epic and, there-*

*fore, excused. A lesser story would not have done the trick, but this one . . . yep. Be careful out there, Ms. Land. P.S. I most definitely recommend a tetanus shot.*

Travis probably gave himself a gash this bad every year, but I doubted he'd ever gotten a tetanus shot. We used to get in arguments about whether or not Emilia or I needed to see a doctor, because he didn't think it was necessary. I didn't think I could drive, and I didn't want my ex-boyfriend to take me to the clinic on campus that was covered by my student insurance. I decided to call my old roommate Kelley, who was back in town for a visit. I sat in the passenger seat of Kelley's car an hour later, surrounded by cigarette ashes and empty bottles of water, and gave her a sheepish smile while I buckled myself in.

"Tell me again what you did?" Kelley asked, half-laughing. "You climbed a fire escape?"

"Yeah," I said, and leaned my head against the headrest. "Just seemed like a good idea at the time, I guess."

Three nurses gathered around my leg in a room I'd never seen at the Curry Health Center on campus. My arm draped over my eyes while one nurse gave me a tetanus shot and the other irrigated the wound. The third nurse described the hole in my leg to me with agonizing detail.

"Looks to be about a half inch across, three-quarters of an inch in length and—" She tapped my shoulder so I would look at her. She pointed to the other nurse, who held a syringe with a teeny metal straw poking an inch out of the top. "That went almost all the way in."

"It's too big to stitch up," the nurse by my leg said. They all made noises of approval. "You need to keep it covered," she said rather sternly in my direction. "But air it out. Wash out the dead, yellow, or green tissue. Come back as soon as it starts to smell or go straight to the ER."

I put my arm back over my eyes. "I think I'm going to throw up."

They sent me home with some bandages and a pat on the shoulder as if to wish me well on my journey toward healing and learning how to touch the inside of my leg without fainting.

———————

Walking to class was impossible and luckily my other professors understood. Before Travis left to meet Emilia at the bus stop, he paused for a moment and I thought he was about to lecture me. "Does Emilia have a bike?" he asked.

"Not really," I said. "There's that small one out there that someone gave us, but she hasn't ridden it. Jamie had promised to buy her one over the summer and that never happened."

"Do you think she would like it if I got her one?"

"I think you'll have to ask her."

Emilia ran past me to throw her backpack on the floor and yelled something about a bike over her shoulder on the way back out the door. I smiled. Travis and I had been together off and on for just over two years, which was a very significant percentage of Emilia's life, and they really seemed to have a good time together. Still, it felt weird to have him there in a worlds-colliding sort of way. Part of why it felt so strange, I realized in that moment, was that Travis was the *only* person who had come to Montana just to visit us. My father not only hadn't visited, but it had been six months since he had said he'd call back and didn't. Most of my friends and I were no longer close or had never been all that close in the first place. My mom and I hadn't talked to each other in about a year, and I couldn't remember the last time I had any kind of message from my brother. All my other relatives hadn't seen me or Emilia since long before we moved to Missoula. If I needed proof that I made the right decision in moving us here, this was it. "Back home" wasn't a home for us at all anymore.

My leg remained wrapped in gauze until my friend with EMT

training said I should probably stop doing that. "It needs to breathe," he said, staring at the hole in my leg with a flashlight. I had been so nervous about it getting infected that I didn't let it air out long enough to form a scab. "Boy, that's definitely the shape of a heart."

I snorted. "I won't take it too personally that you just told me my heart-shaped wound needs room to breathe."

"How old are you again?" he teased.

"I'm . . ." I paused to think. "Whoa, I'm thirty-five in a week!"

Thirty-five seemed like an important milestone that I couldn't fully comprehend. How could I be thirty-five? My birthday party the year before consisted of a bunch of friends who went out for pizza with me. Emilia spent most of the time under the table, removing all the contents from my bag and all the cards from my wallet, then refused to walk anywhere else—even for ice cream. Her full weight got too heavy for me to carry after a couple hours. By the time we got home I sank to sit on our porch, exhausted and defeated, while my kid happily walked inside, sat on the couch, and turned on the TV. That's how it usually went, though, whenever I tried to carve out a day—or even just a few hours—for myself: life and responsibilities had a way of invading. There was no taking a vacation from them, no one who could sub for me fully. Most of the time I didn't even try to plan anything special for my birthday.

I started to get some hints that this year might be different, though. First, Professor Kane took *The Scarlet Letter* off the syllabus and several of us hooted and whooped while Richard Hugo grimaced in disapproval from where he hung on the wall. Then a few of my friends swooped in over text message like sparkling birthday fairies to ask if they could take Emilia camping for the whole weekend. "The whole weekend?" I kept asking, like it just didn't make sense. That would be Friday after school to Sunday evening. Two days to sleep in. Two nights to go out. One night to have a birthday party.

I gave my friends a hearty *Heck, yes!* and told about a dozen people that if they brought over some whiskey I would feed them well. Someone procured a large jar of pickle juice and I stashed it in the fridge with the hamburger for my dad's special chili recipe and the pile of cheese for my favorite mac and cheese from scratch. Work on Friday would be quick, since a client had switched to Wednesday that week. Homework was light, with only a short reading assignment, and we weren't even discussing Orwell until the following Tuesday. All I had to do was clean up a bit, cook, and have fun.

Daniel came over shortly after Emilia bounced out the door to join two other kids her age in the back of a Volkswagen camper van. He walked in the back door while I concentrated on the roux for the mac and cheese.

"Well, happy birthday, Ms. Land," he said in a deep voice.

"Thank y—" I started to say, then saw he had on a button-up shirt and a vest instead of his regular T-shirt and shorts. "Wow, don't you look nice! Got a hot date?"

He rolled his eyes and feigned a dramatic sigh. "No!" His head bowed a bit and he smoothed the front of his vest. "I wanted to look *man beautiful* for your birthday."

"Aw, Daniel!" I stopped stirring long enough to give him a quick kiss and a hug. "Thank you. You're always man beautiful. Can you stir this for me while I add stuff to it?"

Sylvie came over first, then a couple of other friends from the climbing gym showed up with small bottles of whiskey. "Um," one of them said while nodding in Daniel's direction, "who is that?"

"Yeah, who is that, Stephanie?" Sylvie asked as well, to tease me a little—or maybe a lot.

"That's my friend Daniel." I tried to be nonchalant but I couldn't keep a straight face. "He's my bestie."

"Best fuck buddy," Sylvie added before grabbing a beer from the fridge and ducking outside.

The two girls looked at me with raised eyebrows.

"Okay, yes," I said. "Best fuck buddy, too." They smiled and took sips from their red cups before going over to look at the food. With the exception of Sylvie and Daniel, who were both older than me, most of the people at my house were ten years younger than I was. I guess some of them could have been closer to my age. Dirtbagging tends to keep people on the younger side. Oddly, I had more in common with them than with the parents of kids in Emilia's class. I couldn't afford the other parents' lifestyles, and finding a younger-minded crowd that I fit in with—who still had to rent, instead of owning a rental property—usually made me feel less at a disadvantage in that way. My discomfort with the other parents at school was also a resistance to their state of domestication, my word for "settling down." I had tried cohabitation several times by then and felt suffocated by it, much like a feral cat that suddenly found itself indoors and forced to use a litterbox. But usually cleaning, cooking, and grocery shopping fell on my shoulders, which I hated, and I didn't have the relationship skills at that point (or any good example growing up) to have discussions about gender roles. The thought of doing someone else's laundry without getting paid for it made me grimace. There was nothing domesticated about the group of people I hung out with, and that usually suited me just fine. Even if every once in a while I had the sense of being the old weird dude at the party.

Most of the food was gone by the time it got super dark, and almost everyone had tried a pickleback, which is a shot of whiskey followed by a shot of pickle juice. Daniel gave me a long hug and kiss on the cheek, saying he had to bounce because he was meeting someone downtown. I felt confused and showed it. He knew I had the place to myself that night. Wouldn't he want to spend the night with me? Daniel, who seemed to know what I was thinking, shrugged in a comic sort of way, then walked off. Only a few remained out in the driveway and I stood in the kitchen with Sylvie, gawking at the amount of whiskey I suddenly had.

"Well?" Sylvie said, putting her arm around the waist of her date, who towered over her like almost everyone did.

"I guess we should go out," I said.

Missoula had already changed quite a bit in the two short years I had lived there. The dirty floor and pool tables at one of Emilia's and my favorite places where they had Family Friendly Fridays was one of the first to modernize by way of revamping the whole place to cater to a crowd that had more money than the regulars. Most of the bars downtown had live music on Friday nights, and the others had DJs who played music with a lot of bass, but I tended to avoid those places. The dudes in those crowds would dance by grabbing from behind whomever they pleased and pressing their dick onto them unless they got a solid elbow to the chest.

In Missoula in the spring of 2012, just a few months after we arrived, a local news station reported that another football player on campus had been accused of rape. This brought the number of rape accusations toward the football team to eleven in the previous eighteen months. The website Jezebel deemed Missoula the "rape capital" of America, and hordes of people, including the then president of the university, wrote letters to the editor. (One writer in particular detailed passing out next to a platonic male friend only to wake up to him having sex with her, which helped me realize I'd been raped twice in my twenties.) The U.S. Department of Justice announced in May of that year that they would investigate the Missoula Police Department, the Missoula County Attorney's Office, and the University of Montana for gender bias. Most of us who were local avoided a couple of bars in downtown Missoula on the weekends when the college kids were in town for the "rapey vibe" they had. In any of these places where the majority of the crowd looked barely twenty-one years old, it was known that you didn't go out on the dance floor without expecting to get groped in some way, and you definitely didn't leave your drink unattended while doing it.

Every sidewalk on the main stretch had crowds of mostly college students walking from one place to the next. Food trucks started to come out at midnight and every once in a while a literal party bus— complete with a dance floor, colored lights, and disco ball—came rolling past, blaring music. We locals shook our heads at the college kids who only came here for school; we were annoyed we had to wait for a drink and nostalgic for the short weeks of summer when most of the university students were gone. It seemed like everyone was downtown that night, filling the sidewalks and moving at a crawling pace.

We popped into the Union first, showing our IDs to the old guy on the stool out of courtesy, since he was always there and probably knew us by then. Sylvie scanned the crowd and frowned a little at the band. One of the regulars playing pool yelled at a younger guy to stop crowding the table. I couldn't believe how many people were there. The line for the bar was four people deep and stretched the whole length of it.

"Let's get out of here," I yelled toward Sylvie, who tugged the hand of her date to follow her out. We walked slowly down the side-walk outside, sharing a cigarette, occasionally stopping to watch the crowds. In a vacant lot a few guys had a boom box and a large piece of cardboard laid flat on the pavement to do some kind of break-dance moves on; in another some stood in a circle kicking around a hacky sack. Most of the alleys weren't crowded, so I turned abruptly into one of those. "You wanna go to the Rhino?" I asked. Sylvie and her date nodded. She now had her arms wrapped around his waist, hugging and walking beside him at the same time. Which was good, I noticed, since she wasn't too sturdy on those platform sandals. I started to tell her this, but I almost walked right into Theodore. He had his back to me, talking and smoking with a small group. He said a soft "hey" when he saw me.

"Hey," I said, shoving my hands into the front pockets of my jeans. Sylvie and her date went inside. "I, uh, thought I'd see you earlier."

"Oh yeah," he said. "We had a thing on campus to go to." He motioned to the guys; half of them looked at me with curiosity and the other half looked down to avoid eye contact. I thought I recognized one as an MFA student. "Happy birthday," he said, giving me a half smile that caused my chest to ache.

There was enough whiskey in my system that I had an urge to tell him that he shouldn't have given up on us so easily, or something probably worse. Instead I looked down at my feet, dug the toe of my Chacos into a hole in the pavement for a second, then looked up and said, "Thanks," before walking past him.

Inside the bar, Sylvie and her date were nowhere to be found. I had wondered if I would see Daniel there playing pool, but I only recognized one of the players before I remembered that he'd kissed me once where I'd just seen Theodore. My mind stretched to recall his name, then he looked up and smiled at me. I suddenly remembered meeting him there—he'd stuck out his hand and said, "I'm Max." I smiled back, gave him a little wave, and turned to walk toward the front door.

"It's hopeless here," Sylvie said when I found her. "Even he can't get a drink." Her date looked annoyed, but that could have been his natural expression. I couldn't really tell.

We decided to leave and try the Top Hat. First we had to squeeze out past the bouncer and everyone else who was lined up to go in.

Sylvie was close behind me, but her date was stuck inside, blocked by a group of girls. I turned to go down the sidewalk and ran directly into Daniel, who had changed his clothes back into his usual cargo shorts and a faded T-shirt. "What the hell," I started to say, then noticed his arm stretched out in the direction of the alley, pulled by a bubbly blonde with long hair. She looked young, maybe early twenties.

"Babe, c'mon," she said, turning back to look at him while laughing.

Daniel stood expressionless for a few seconds before his smile returned and he said, "Hey, babe, this is my friend Stephanie." He gave me an apologetic smile. "It's her birthday."

"Nice to meet you," the girl said sweetly. Then she pulled Daniel again to follow three other guys, all as young as her. Daniel gave me a shrug as an explanation, then held up a fist to his ear and mouthed, *I'll call you*.

"Who was *that*?" Sylvie said.

"That, um," I started. "I guess that's Daniel's girlfriend."

"I thought they weren't serious."

"Well, it looks like they're serious enough for him to make plans with her on the night of my birthday."

The Top Hat had a DJ playing dance music and the whole place was half-lit with neon lights. Sylvie immediately brought her date on the floor to dance and rub up against him. I wanted to go home. *Actually*, I thought with a bit of a pout, *I want to get laid*. Or at least kiss someone.

My night was decidedly over. I walked out the back door, past all the people crowding between the three bars that shared the alley space, and headed toward home. I looked up after a few paces and noticed someone familiar walking slowly by himself. Max. Without thinking, I threaded my left arm through his to hook his right elbow and said, "You, sir, are walking me home."

"Oh?" he said, not surprised in the slightest.

"Yes. It is my birthday and someone should walk me home."

Max laughed (I think he was always kind of laughing) and said, "Okay, then lead the way."

I kept our arms linked for a couple more blocks. We didn't talk much. He asked how my birthday was and I said good, telling him about the party and all the whiskey. I offered him some when we got to my place. Max made a *sure, why not* kind of face and followed me inside. We did a shot together and I asked him if he wanted to do a pickleback. He laughed and said he loved picklebacks.

Max smiled without a hint of confusion when I grabbed his hand to lead him into my bedroom. We kissed when we reached my bed, but not in any memorable way. Maybe it was the whiskey or because my heart hurt so badly, but not much of it was something I would remember later. He was on top, but not for very long. Then he rolled off me and let out a chuckle with his hands on his face and swung his legs off the bed to sit on the edge. My shirt was still on, and I fished under the blankets for my underwear and reached for my jeans on the floor. I held my underwear up in front of me to make sure I wasn't putting them on backward before realizing I didn't care. I mumbled that I needed to go to the bathroom and shuffled out with my jeans dragging from my hand to the floor.

Once I had the door shut behind me, I glanced over at my reflection, then closed my eyes and leaned my head back. *Fuck.* I pulled down my underwear to sit on the toilet to pee and put my feet into the legs of my jeans. I paused to check the toilet paper after I wiped and there was nothing on it. *Did he just fake an orgasm?* I sank my face into my hands for a moment or two, pissed at myself for doing something so stupid. *Really, Stephanie?* My phone buzzed in my pocket, and I looked at it and saw Daniel's name. I let out a scoff and mumbled, "Yeah, right," and my phone lit up and buzzed again.

Max stood out in the living room area, staring at the wall that Emilia had decorated herself. He pointed at one of the drawings of Mount Sentinel and Mount Jumbo and looked at me with raised eyebrows. I nodded. "That's cool," he said.

"Yeah," I said, then crossed my arms over my chest. "I should probably get to sleep."

"Oh yeah!" He smiled and gave me an awkward half hug before he walked out the door and closed it softly behind him.

Someone had cleaned up most of the paper plates and cups, neatly stacking the dirty dishes in and around the sink. My phone buzzed again and I reached down to open it so I could turn it off. One of Daniel's texts said, "Where are you???" but I didn't care. The room I shared with Emilia was dark and my blankets were all crumpled at the end of my bed, and I was alone. I tried not to care about that, either.

---

My phone immediately buzzed and lit up when I turned it on the next morning. It was another text from Daniel and it said "IM COMING OVER" so I closed it and put it back on my nightstand. My hands creeped down to feel for my jeans and they were still on, as was my shirt, so I turned on my side to doze for a bit longer.

"You're just gonna sleep away your whole day off?"

I opened my eyes to see Daniel standing in the middle of the room with his arms crossed, but he dropped them almost immediately. His whole body slouched. I'd forgotten about our "Sure, just walk in the back door" agreement and fought my annoyance over it.

"Take off your shoes," I murmured, and opened the covers for him to climb in.

"She left me," he said, throwing up his arms. "I don't understand what happened."

"I thought you guys weren't serious," I said. "Come here." He lay down next to me and I put my arm on his chest. My laptop was open on a chair next to the bed and I propped myself up on my elbow long enough to hit the play button. A twangy guitar sound pinged out of the speakers and I lay back on my side with my arm across his chest again, letting out a sigh.

"What is this music you listen to?" Daniel always asked this.

"The Lumineers," I said without moving my lips that much. He was quiet for a bit and we both listened to the chorus and the next verse before he asked how the rest of my birthday went. "It was fine," I said into his shoulder. "Why were you texting me so much?"

Daniel sighed. "This music is depressing as fuck. How can you listen to this shit?" He got up and walked to the middle of the room. This wasn't normal behavior for him, or at least that I had seen, so I sat up and turned off the song and waited. "She went home with some dude last night."

For a second I thought he meant me. *Were we not sleeping with other people?* I rubbed my forehead with the palm of my hand like it would help with the headache. Then I remembered the blonde. "The girl you were with?"

"Yes, *the girl*," he mimicked. It was weird for him to talk to me like this, and I winced, registering hurt on my face. He came and sat next to me. "I really liked her. I wanted to be with her." Then he lay back down.

"Daniel," I said, crossing my legs in front of me. He was being ridiculous for thinking a twenty-one-year-old would seriously commit to some guy in his mid-thirties who'd been three credits away from a psychology degree for half a decade and worked as a waiter. But I resisted the impulse to tell him this when he turned to look at me. His eyes were bright blue and watery, and he had a pleading expression that I'd never seen. I sighed. "You know, sad music is kind of nice to listen to sometimes. It keeps you company."

"You keep me company," he said.

"Yeah." I guess I was good for that. I got up and walked out of the room. "Come on. Help me clean up and I'll buy you breakfast. We've got a show to go to tonight."

Growing up in Alaska brought countless experiences that made for excellent stories—like the time my mom got kicked in the face by a moose or when my dad and I fished for red salmon until two in the morning when I was only ten. While all of those experiences made for good conversations over a beer, what Alaska sorely lacked was live music from people who weren't local or whose only chance at getting onstage was open-mic night. Bands rarely, if ever, included Anchorage or Fairbanks on their tours. The ones who did came mostly for vacation. When one of my favorite bands, the Presidents of the United States of America, came, the lead singer sat on the edge of the stage after their final set, shooting the shit with us, asking about places they should visit while signing guitar picks and anything else we put in front of him. G. Love did not do this, nor did he bring the Special Sauce.

Bigger bands also skipped over Missoula for the most part, but a lot of smaller groups took a detour there from Denver to Seattle or wherever they planned to go next. I couldn't believe how cheap tickets were and snatched up as many as I could afford. One time the Smashing Pumpkins' tour bus broke down and they decided to do a show that night. Others played long sets to smaller crowds, like when Kelley and I stood right in front of the stage to see the Tallest Man on Earth. A few, like Indigo Girls and Trampled by Turtles, seemed to make it every year. Seeing as much live music as possible became a sort of mission that extended to Emilia, who, at age six, got asked, "Is this your first rock concert?" by the guy selling T-shirts for Dr. Dog. She looked at me, then back at him, and nodded without trying to hide her smile. She fell asleep halfway through the show, but proudly wore her new shirt for days. Most of the time I went to shows by myself, but lately I'd been getting two tickets just in case.

For the Saturday night of my birthday weekend, I had two tickets to see Shawn Mullins.

"Who?" Daniel asked when I reminded him that he had agreed to go with me.

"Shawn Mul— He has this song I like," I said. "I used to listen to it a lot."

"What's it called?" Daniel looked at me like I was making this up.

"'Rockabye.'"

"'Rockabye'?!" He laughed. "What does that even mean? Rock-abye." He crossed his arms and looked at me with more suspicion. "Sing it."

"Sing it? You want me to sing 'Rockabye.'" Daniel nodded and raised his eyebrows. I let out a breath, took in another one, and managed to sing "Ev-er-reething's gonna beee all riiiight. Rockabye," mostly in tune.

We left soon after Shawn Mullins sang it onstage. Daniel said he had to go find the blonde, which was good since I wanted to go home anyway. After last night, staying in with a movie sounded pretty great. The small menagerie of whiskey also helped in keeping me company.

———

Daniel wanted me to join him at the Top Hat on Sunday morning, my last day before Emilia came home, and bribed me by offering to buy me a Bloody Mary. He wanted to watch the football game, but I did not. "Steph," he said over the phone. "They have a Bloody Mary bar. Like salami and cheese and all this fuckin' shit." I could hear the game in the background.

"Pickled asparagus?" I rubbed my eyes.

"Are you kidding me? They have like a whole section of pickled things."

"Okay," I said, looking at the clock next to my bed. Almost eleven. I couldn't remember the last time I slept that much. "I'm up," I lied.

"Liar," Daniel said. "You better get down here."

I snapped my phone shut. It was so quiet. Emilia wasn't due back until that evening, and a Bloody Mary did sound good.

Outside the bar, several men in Green Bay Packers jerseys gathered on the sidewalk to smoke. Their morale did not seem high. Daniel had a high top table to himself, a couple of pint glasses and a mug of coffee in front of him. "You want breakfast?" Daniel got up and walked toward the bar before I could answer and returned with a pint glass half-full of ice and a couple of inches of clear liquid. I looked at it, then at him without taking it. "It's vodka," he said, raising his voice as men cheered around us. They had Styrofoam hats on in the shape and color of cheddar cheese. This was not my idea of a fun time. "All the shit's over there."

I took the glass and walked to a bar in the back of the room, raising my eyebrows at the line of ingredients. "They really do have salami," I said, but decided against taking any. I wasn't what you'd call a fan of that, either.

"Where's the meat and stuff?" Daniel asked when I returned with my drink to sit on the stool next to him.

"I got stuff." I pulled my notebook out of my backpack.

"What the fuck, you're gonna do homework?"

"I have no interest in this game," I said. "I just came here to sit with you and have a drink and write. I have an essay due on Tuesday."

"You should write about me." He checked his phone to see who was calling him but didn't answer.

I started to write the scene around me: *A bar in downtown Missoula, Montana, fills with men and a few women wearing green shirts before noon on a Sunday morning. Jason sits at a high table on a square stool, hungover from the night before. In front of him is the Bloody Mary he'd built himself with enough hot sauce to make him blow his nose into a black linen napkin twice. Breakfast for six bucks.*

"Who's Jason?" Daniel asked, pulling the notebook toward him. I responded with a deadpan expression. His phone buzzed on the table. "Fuck!" He picked up the phone to show me a text from the blonde:

Please tell me what I did!

He got up to go outside.

*The game heats up. A player in yellow tights catches the ball and people cheer, giving each other high fives. Jason returns to his seat with a sour look on his face. He orders a shot of Jameson and chews on his nails, then yells to no one in particular, "Fuck we're gettin' our asses kicked!"*

"I don't chew my nails!" he said. I almost wrote that, too, but looked up from the paper instead and saw that Daniel was reading it again.

"Daniel," I said, then looked down at his phone, which buzzed with another text. I caught the words *insensitive asshole* before he picked it up.

*Jason's looking at his phone when the Packers score their first touchdown. He looks up. People around him are out of their seats, arms straight over their heads. Jason doesn't join them, but goes to the bar for the celebratory shot provided by the establishment for touchdowns.*

"What about when the other team gets a point?" I asked him, pointing at the shot.

"What other team?" Daniel said with a raised voice, eyes fixed on the giant screen in front of the stage where last night a guy with a guitar sang "Rockabye."

*The Bengals fumble. Green Bay gets the ball. Full-grown men jump out of their seats to bump jersey-clad beer bellies together. Jason looks down at his phone. She wants to know where her car is. "Are you fucking kidding me?" he yells at the phone's screen as it goes dark. The Bengals get a penalty for holding. Jason downs the shot, then types, "Ask your friend on the floor."*

At this point it became clear that Daniel's "girlfriend" had a "friend" over again when he went to her house last night after the concert. I couldn't tell if he was more upset about that or that she kept choosing someone else over him. Was her other guy better-looking than Daniel? None of this interested me, and I doubted that Walter Kirn, who'd assigned my essay, would be interested, either.

"My mom used to say something," Daniel said to the guy sitting closest to him at the next table. "If you have want in one hand, and shit in the other, see which one fills first." He threw his napkin on the table and went up to the bar to pay.

"I think I'm gonna go home," I said when he returned, stuffing my notebook into its place in my backpack. "I need to do laundry, and my kid's coming back today."

"No, come to my place," he said and reached to grab my backpack. He put his arms through the straps and strutted out of the bar.

"This is annoying," I said when I caught up to him.

"My roommate's got nachos and bratwurst," he said. "Just come get something to eat and meet everyone."

"Fine," I said. "But give me my backpack."

"What do you have in here?" He hooked one finger in the top handle and passed it to me.

"I dunno, homework and stuff," I said, struggling a bit to get it on. "What the fuck did you do, tighten the straps?"

"You carry your *homework* around?"

We walked in silence and I wondered what he might be thinking about, but not enough to ask.

"Hey, man," Daniel said to a guy on the couch blowing out pot smoke when he walked in.

"Hey," the guy said before he coughed and passed the bong to another guy on the couch to his right.

Daniel reached to half high-five and half shake another guy's hand before he pulled it toward his stomach and they both patted each other's backs.

Instead of introducing me to anyone, Daniel turned to grab my hand and lead me through the living room, dining room, kitchen, and eventually to his bedroom. I'd only been there once when we stopped to feed his roommate's cat, have sex, and water her orchid before we left. He still had the same sleeping bags hanging from hooks and a pile of neatly looped climbing rope in the corner.

I felt his hand tug at the waistband of my pants and toward his bed. "They'll hear us!" I said in a whisper, knowing that wasn't true, but it made it feel a little more exciting. He lay down while he took his shirt off by reaching one hand behind his head and pulling it. "No matter how hard I try, I can never get my shirt off that way," I said, climbing onto his bed and walking toward him on my knees.

"Well, let me help you," he said as his hands expertly gathered my shirt by the bottom and removed it as fast as I could lift my arms. He wrapped his arms around me, his chest meeting mine, then tugged at the back of my bra and took the straps off my shoulders while we kissed. Cheers came from the living room while he undid the button and zipper of my pants. I pulled them down and sat on my butt to take them the rest of the way off, and his shorts came off, too, then I was back on my knees, straddling him, trying to decide if I should play with him a bit or just fuck him. I chose the latter.

Daniel started to climax after a couple of minutes but held back enough to keep going, sitting up to clutch my back with one of his arms while he flipped me onto my back and drove himself even deeper into me. *Yes*, I thought to myself, *fuck yes*. I reached my arms out and grabbed his sheets and engaged all the muscles in my lower core and pelvic floor to make the fit even tighter.

"Fuck yes," Daniel said, quickening his pace and pulling almost all the way out before he pushed himself back in. I fought to stay quiet and pressed my forehead into his shoulder, concentrating only on him fucking me hard enough that I'd probably be sore tomorrow morning. I usually was.

"You want me to come?" I said, and kissed his neck.

"You better fucking come," Daniel said, and reached up with his left hand to forcefully cup my breast.

I let my hand come to my stomach before I inched my fingers closer to my clit. Just placing them over it created enough extra pressure while he moved against me. I cried out before I caught myself and Daniel took the hand on my chest and put it over my mouth. That movement alone set off an orgasm with a delicious burst of tingling warmth deep beneath the surface where his pelvis kept colliding into mine. I pulled up my legs to hook my feet behind him, letting him go even deeper while the climax grew and spread. Daniel breathed harder and sucked on my shoulder while I nearly yelled out a "YES" from behind the hand that he still held to my mouth. Every part of my skin felt as if feathers had brushed it, leaving an electric shock behind. Daniel pushed his hips into mine and I felt the sheets under me grow taut as he moved his feet to press in closer. His whole body tensed as he sucked so hard on my shoulder it felt like he was biting. Then he relaxed, his whole weight on me.

We lay there like that for a few breaths before I unhooked my feet and draped my legs over the back of his. He moved his hand from my mouth to grab the blanket so he could wipe his face. "My fucking god you're good at that," he said, rolling onto his hip while I scooted to the side.

"No, that one was all you," I said, desperate for some water. I sat up and spotted my backpack by the door and went to dig out my Nalgene.

Daniel had his shorts on by the time I turned around, his fingers laced behind his head, washboard abs perfectly flexed, watching me with a smirk. "I *hope* my roommates heard you."

"Fuck you!" I said, tossing my shirt at his face. "Anyway I gotta get home." I needed to make our living space look as if there hadn't been a whole weekend of shenanigans before Emilia got back.

"Okay, well, see ya around." He still hadn't moved, and he seemed to enjoy watching me search for my clothes.

By the time Emilia got home later that evening, all the dishes were cleaned and put away. I had even grabbed a few groceries, showered, changed both of our sheets, and did a load of laundry, which was lucky for a Sunday since the machines were typically in use. Our building had an ancient set from Sears that the company didn't make replacement parts for. My landlord and his father-in-law (who were both extremely well-off, mind you) managed to fix it, but I was so worried about the wiring setting the whole building ablaze that it convinced me to get rental insurance for the first time.

Emilia was dirty and exhausted. I gave her a bath and got her into jammies and we read an extra chapter after I agreed to let her sleep with me. She drifted off halfway through and I lay next to her for a while, thinking about the weekend and the entire last month. It was time for me to buckle down with school and my grad school application. My eyes popped open when I remembered that I also needed to turn in my application for graduation. *Fuck, how much is that going to cost?* I wondered. With the fee to apply for grad school, and that GRE test I had to take, I guessed it would be somewhere around a few hundred bucks. Plus, Seth was about to move out and I needed to find a new roommate again. For a second, I thought about not having anyone move in, but I still needed a babysitter three evenings a week between work and class. I sighed. Someday we'd have our own place. Maybe I'd even get to have my own room.

# 8

## Late

"Come on, Emilia, it's time to get up so you can catch the bus on time."

"I don't want to go," she said, turning on her side to face the wall. This scene had become a regular occurrence.

We were nearly two months into the school year and the newness had begun to wear off. Emilia's teacher and I were already well acquainted, since every week seemed to bring a different reason for her to contact me. Emilia had a friend from preschool in her class, but sometimes they didn't get along, which was an easier situation than when they liked each other enough to join forces. Then there were the boys on the playground who enjoyed chasing my kid all through recess and sometimes pulled on her shirt to reveal her bare chest when she hung upside down on the monkey bars.

Some of this I had anticipated. Emilia had always been a strong, willful kid. She'd barely learned to walk before she could make it across an entire soccer field without looking back. I knew she would have a difficult time with school because of the endless rules, the sitting, the lining up to sit again, and I couldn't imagine her being quiet when told to. The year before, when I had the option to enroll her in public school or keep her at the gymnastics gym for a year of what they called half-time kindergarten, I chose what seemed best for Emilia—public school could wait another year, I thought. Now that I looked back, I had regrets. Emilia started kindergarten at age six, a full year older than her classmates. Her extra year at the gym catered to her learning style, since everything involved movement, and I was eternally grateful she had that experience. But for almost half of that year I was exhausted in the deepest way from cleaning the gym every morning. My work and school schedule didn't allow me to pick her up most of the time, either. Every day she went home with a kid in her class or my roommate at the time, who also worked at the gym. Our life had always required Emilia to shuffle from one babysitter to the next. That year, however, the uncertainties we routinely lived with, combined with not knowing when she'd hear from or see her dad, started to pile on her little shoulders.

I had no way of knowing what happened at her dad's house and what he said and did to her. I could speculate, but at the time I still believed (or possibly hoped) he wouldn't be abusive toward her. She'd flown by herself on a direct flight between Missoula and Portland since age five, which seemed to work well. We each bought a one-way ticket for the short Christmas and spring break visits, and usually drove to meet each other in the summer. For the last year I'd sent her with a prepaid cell phone so she could call or text me whenever she needed to, but her dad took it away after she called to tell me she'd arrived okay. If I called other times it was through his phone, which meant he was sitting right there and she didn't say much. This had always been the hardest part of coparenting with an abuser: even though I got us out and moved us away, I was still court-ordered to send my kid back three times a year. It was difficult to decide which was worse—sending her to stay with him or coping with the damage he inflicted on her when he inevitably disappointed her. No part of it seemed to be good most of the time. I often wondered if life would have been better for us if I had not told Jamie about the pregnancy and had moved on my own to Missoula like I had originally planned. At times, my choice to stay burned as the one, true regret in my life as a mother.

All the kids in her class were sitting in a circle and listening intently when I dropped off Emilia. I whispered a feeble "Sorry" before I ran out, went home, showered, got myself to school, parked, and walked to my first class, immediately regretting that I didn't bring more coffee. That heavy-blanket feeling started to come soon after class began. I struggled to stay focused enough to take notes.

"You must *underline* and *bold your claim*," Professor Katie Kane said even louder than usual, lifting the drowsiness that had taken hold of my eyelids. "In a *footnote* or *appendix*, you must identify its parts."

I wrote those two sentences down in my notebook. "What is she talking about?" I whispered to Reed, who always sat on my left.

"Film studies," Reed whispered back, pointing to the syllabus.

"Right," I said. She'd assigned us a response paper titled "A Kantian Analysis of Bennett Miller's 2005 Film *Capote*," which would be due the following week. Plenty of time.

"A *claim* is a road map," Katie Kane said. "You don't have to prove all of it." She looked right at me, and I broke our eye contact to write down that sentence. It felt like a good one to remember.

Reed waited for me out in the hallway when class was over so we could walk to the University Center together. The LA Building's halls filled to capacity with twenty-year-olds between classes at the top of the hour, reminding me of my advanced age. Reed wasn't much older than any of the other kids who passed us, but we had enough in common that I enjoyed his company, often forgetting that he was almost fifteen years younger than me. He, too, was a bit of a loner in a way I appreciated. Reed was also the only other person I knew who absolutely had to work in order to pay rent and eat, sometimes having to decide between the two.

We walked to our usual spot but the table we liked wasn't empty. I sighed, turned, and motioned toward a different one. Wordlessly, we took our backpacks off, unloaded our laptops, and sat in our chairs. I tried to stifle a large yawn.

"Oh man," I said, rubbing my eyes with the heels of my palms. "I don't know why I'm so tired."

Reed shook his head and made a *tsk* noise a few times. "Gotta stop with those all-night ragers."

"I know," I said. "But my kid loves them. And they take naps in kindergarten, don't they?"

"Wow," Reed said, looking up in a daydreamy sort of way. "I miss nap time."

I chuckled. "Maybe I'm coming down with something."

"You better keep that to yourself," he said, looking at me warily.

"I'm fine. But can you please explain what the assignment was again? All I have written down is 'underline and bold your claim.'"

This wasn't the first time I had an assignment that revolved around the film *Capote* with Philip Seymour Hoffman, or the book *In Cold Blood*. It might have been something like my third, but I didn't mind. Every professor had a new anecdote about Truman Capote, or something particular they liked about him. Mine was when he said, "Sometimes when I think about how good my book can be, I can hardly breathe." I wondered if I could somehow work it into the paper to keep my mind more interested.

This was only a short response paper, but in any lengthy report a professor assigned, from British to medieval literature, I always tried to fit in a reference to *Seinfeld*. I started doing it to break up the monotony of academic paper writing, and add a fun challenge. I told myself that whatever professor or TA who had to read thirty papers on the same subject would appreciate that I referred to the Green Knight as "master of his domain," or explained that "the sea was angry that day, my friends" in the middle of a recounting of a Shakespeare play.

*Maybe I* am *coming down with something*, I thought while I flipped through my notebook looking for a blank page. I stopped and stared at the page in front of me, then looked up at Reed. I must have looked horrified, because his smile disappeared. "Are you okay?"

"Yeah, I think I just forgot about something." I reached into my backpack for my day planner. "What's the date today again?"

"Uh, the fifteenth, I think? It's Tuesday, right?" Reed laughed again but I didn't join him, frantically turning pages. Then I remembered this was a new day planner. I'd just switched from using the Living with Intention brand I had used for five years to a Moleskine weekly planner because it had a page for notes for each week and lasted eighteen months instead of twelve. There weren't any entries before the first day of school.

"No, I'm good." I looked up at him and tried to give him a sincere smile. "Just tired is all. Have you, uh, read the whole book *In Cold Blood*?"

———

When I got to my car after class that night, I had no memory of my walk across campus, let alone anything that had happened after I realized what day it was. Only the sound and sensations of my swift walking pace turning into a light jog brought me back into my body. *The fifteenth of October* had been running through my head the rest of the day. *It's halfway through OCTOBER?* Maybe the first of the month hadn't hit as hard because Kelley had prepaid rent? She had only been back for a couple of weeks—just long enough to tie up some loose ends and move out her bedroom furniture—before leaving again, so I didn't have to ask someone for the three hundred bucks I charged to rent the bedroom.

All my landscaping clients had gone dormant for the winter months. I loved walking the streets down by the university at that time of year, when all the huge maple trees littered everything with red, orange, and yellow leaves. I'd always lived in places with spruce and birch or aspen, and the piles of leaves I raked as a kid were half the size of the ones people raked into the gutters in Missoula. Some were as tall as the hood of my car and half as wide. I'd never seen anything like it, and delighted in the piles almost as much as Emilia.

Signs of the passage of time were all around me—so how did I lose three weeks? Had I been that distracted by the daily arguments over what Emilia would wear to school (picture day had been a nightmare) and work, getting to class, and homework?

I dropped Emilia off at kindergarten the next morning, and all but kicked the door open when I got home, scaring the dog into a rapid string of barks before he recognized me and danced a few circles on his hind legs. Token's pee pad in the litter box needed to be changed, and I paused, realizing how strange it was that I had noticed the faint smell that wafted across the apartment. I reached up to forcefully grab my breast with my right hand, relieved to feel nothing. Emilia had left her shoes scattered on the floor of the entryway and I stepped over them to cross through the kitchen and living room to my desk.

Multiple piles of paper covered the entire surface but I knew better than to look there. I needed what was beside the desk on a bottom shelf below my printer: my old day planner.

My fingers trembled slightly and I took a deep breath. I'd been too tired to do this last night and I still wasn't sure if I wanted to, even as I hooked my finger onto September's tab to open it to the calendar where I recorded how much money I got paid for work and when— *what the fuck*. I turned back to August, where almost every day had numbers with a dollar sign to represent how much money I made, but one, on the thirteenth, had a simple "p-start" for the first day of my period. I flipped back to September. *What the FUCK?!* Did I not have a period in September? I had a period, I had to have. I never skipped a period, certainly not without noticing. *Except for last April when you got pregnant and didn't know it for two weeks.*

"Oh FUCK OFF!" I yelled out loud, already sick of these creeping thoughts, and breathed in and out, listening to the dog's nails skitter on the floor around my feet. I sat on the edge of my bed, and glanced at the clock beside it out of habit, as if I thought it might help me figure out the timeline. Instead, I sighed and went over it again.

My cycle was super short at some point that summer. *That* I remembered. Like twenty-five days or something ridiculous like that. Right? I flipped back to previous months, counting days between "p-start" scribbles. May to June, twenty-six; June to July, twenty-seven; and July to August was twenty-four. August to September should have been about the same, meaning I probably started my period on the fifth or sixth, but there wasn't anything written on those days other than a landscaping client's name with a question mark next to it.

That week's events didn't help my memory. Monday, September second. Labor Day, "Ferris Bueller's Day Off" at the Top Hat.

*Did we end up going to that? I don't remember going. FUCK.* Tuesday, Debra's class met in the library and I had meetings with people about my MFA application. Friday I did Melody's yard and Teri's house. Saturday, Portland Cello Project with Daniel; Second Wind on Sunday. Absolutely none of that rang a bell except the show and Daniel. *DANIEL.*

Physical sensations brought me back into myself, away from the panic and bewildered feeling of having no recollection, but my body seemed to be moving on its own. I'd been pacing the length of my bed, back and forth, the tiny dog thinking this was a wonderful game. I felt the edge of the mattress give as I sat down. A twenty-three-day cycle would mean I ovulated on day twelve. My finger tapped on the days as I counted. That didn't make sense for being late, though, because I would have ovulated around the sixteenth and I didn't have sex before or after that. *When was the last time I had sex?* I thumbed through the planners like I would have recorded that, too. This all felt so ridiculous, but I was too panicked to make real sense of anything.

"Oh my god." I couldn't do this again. The last abortion had left me feeling suicidal. Not because of the abortion itself, but the fact that no one had *wanted* to have a baby with me, and I wondered if anyone ever would before it was too late. I went through the days in August of my old planner. Jamie picked up Emilia on the tenth, climbing in Lost Horse, then at the Alberton Rest Stop on Sunday, and so on. Daniel and I met around that time when Emilia was gone, but we didn't have sex until she started kindergarten and even then it was only a couple of times before . . . I flipped back to September . . . my birthday.

I grabbed my backpack and fished my keys and wallet out and got in my car to drive to Walmart. Fucking *Walmart*. "No, that's just fucking *great*, Stephanie. Real fuckin' great." I took a deep breath and closed my eyes before opening them again to stomp on the clutch, tap the brake, and turn the key.

Emilia's conception had occurred on the night of my birthday almost exactly seven years ago. My birth control method was the ring, but I had just started using it that month after trying several different varieties of the pill. An ER doctor started me on the pill at age seventeen because of severe pain from ovarian cysts, not because I was having sex—though I definitely became sexually active right after I had my trusty Ortho Tri-Cyclen. No one talked about side effects in 1996, especially when it came to mental health. Mine was already unstable. I'd been in a car accident the year before and suffered a head injury as well as post-traumatic stress disorder, which created a spectrum of emotions, but the biggest two were anxiety and depression. It would take almost twenty years for me to fully understand how PTSD operated in the brain and what physical symptoms it caused and how it affected me. Depression in the year after I started the pill just seemed like more of the same.

The person I started having sex with after I went on the pill at age seventeen became my first real boyfriend. To have him hold me was one of the greatest feelings I'd ever had, and not like anything I'd experienced before. My parents weren't neglectful, but even as a child, I didn't receive a lot of tenderness or physical comfort from them. They had both checked out by the time I had a driver's license. Mom was well into her affair with another married man at work and chose to "work late" most days, and Dad had an hour commute to a job he hated. I was starved for affection, and the only way for me to get it was to have sex with my boyfriend. Unfortunately, he became emotionally abusive—running unpredictably hot and cold, belittling me, and yelling in my face.

Birth control was a constant through my twenties, along with panic attacks and uncontrollable outbursts or sobbing if alcohol got involved. Not all my boyfriends were as terrible as my first, but they weren't too great, either. One got so jealous I couldn't go out with girlfriends or have any male friends. The one after that broke into my house to steal my hard drive because he wanted pictures of us that I had saved on my computer. I had just kicked him out and gotten the courage to leave him. His emotional abuse and my exhaustion from working sixty hours a week had put me in a psychiatric ward for wanting to die just six months earlier. When I caught him breaking in, he restrained me from running for help with such force I had bruises all over my ribs. My plan to move back to Washington from Alaska was partially to get away from him.

Jamie and I started dating about a year after I showed up in Port Townsend. I'd been off the pill for several months and didn't make the connection between that and being less depressed. Finally, I felt something close to happiness, but I assumed it was due to not living in a dark, cold place like Fairbanks. Then I started taking hormonal birth control again and noticed a host of physical changes—I immediately gained ten pounds, and my breasts went up a whole cup size. It seemed like I was either ravenous or nauseous, and my moods had the same highs and lows. When I called a nurse practitioner at the health department to discuss the symptoms, she suggested something called the ring for its lower levels of hormones. It was inserted correctly when Emilia was conceived.

My doctor implanted a hormonal IUD a couple of months after Emilia was born, but I couldn't stand it due to the near-constant pain shooting down my legs. After that I tried several forms of hormonal birth control, going through the same extreme changes in moods—like suddenly finding myself sobbing for no reason because of a sad song on the radio—until I gave up.

After Travis and I had been together for about a year, I figured it was safe not to use anything at all. Two of my friends raved about tracking their cycles and pullout methods, so with Travis we either avoided sex around ovulation or I told him to pull out, but it was usually both of those things. I kept doing that or used condoms after we broke up. Anyway, birth control is expensive. Most hormonal methods were about thirty bucks a month. While I could get a prescription for it at little to no cost, there wasn't a sliding scale for the birth control itself. I decided that my cycle and all the symptoms that went with it were predictable and dependable enough. I knew to be cautious between day one and fourteen, or, even safer, not to have sex at all, which usually wasn't an issue because I wasn't in a relationship. So, I just kept track of things.

This worked perfectly for me until it didn't. Getting an abortion with Evan wrecked me. It's not that I now regretted doing it—there was no way I would put myself through having a baby with someone who didn't want one. I dealt with the repercussions of that already. My fear was that, at my "old" age of thirty-four, that I had reached a point of no return in terms of having another child, which I did want. When I watched Emilia entertain herself, playing with her toys alone, I physically ached, projecting my loneliness onto her while wondering if she felt it, too.

Getting pregnant when I hadn't planned to felt like an unintelligent mistake at my age. There had definitely been a carelessness with Evan when I trusted him to pull out. But this . . . I had no idea how late I *was*. I hadn't monitored my menstrual cycle for the last six weeks, but I faintly remembered thinking that I was in the clear by my birthday. I must have had a period that first weekend of September, around the time I hurt my leg. There were no current symptoms except maybe feeling a bit bloated, but I had figured that was due to my more sedentary lifestyle during the school year. My boobs weren't even sore. How could I be almost two weeks late and not have any symptoms except shock and humiliation?

Walmart's pharmacy section had a familiarity that lacked anything close to comfort. These aisles contained ghost versions of myself as

I had to make countless, impossible choices, deciding which cold medicine I could afford or if I could put Tylenol on my credit card to get Emilia's fever down enough for day care so I could work.

A sweet-looking older woman made an approving "oh" sound when I put the pregnancy test on the counter. Her hair was teased into a poof like my grandma had for the entire time I knew her. I found myself staring at her pink cardigan and how the yarn had some kind of sparkly silver thread in it, then watched her hands put my test in a white paper bag. "Good luck," she said, her smile sincere enough that I wanted her to stand outside the bathroom door while I waited for the results.

There was no one to do that when I got home, unless you counted the Token dog. He was my witness—anxiously waiting with one paw up—the only one watching when I discovered that I was indeed pregnant for the third time.

———

"Mama!" Emilia said when she got off the bus and ran up to hug my legs. My eyes stung with tears, and I quickly brushed my cheekbone with my shoulder to hide them. "I thought Seth was picking me up!"

"Nope, you get me today!" I took her hand before we crossed the street. "What should we do?" I gasped for air a bit, not knowing if it was from the fast walking or *the pregnancy* because I didn't want to admit to myself that I'd been on the verge of a panic attack for several hours, floating from one physical sensation to the next without knowing how I got there. Emilia skipped as we walked, telling me about a game they played in gym, before she asked if we could get ice cream. "You always ask for ice cream!"

"No I don't! I promise!"

"Emilia Story," I said. "What's the most babysitters you have ever had in one day?" We stepped onto our porch and I opened the door for her to go inside. She put down her backpack and thought for a second, looking at me with suspicion like she already knew where I was going with my inquiry.

"Free," she said, holding up three fingers, causing me to smile and hope she never stopped pronouncing that number that way.

"And how many ice creams did you have that day?" I crossed my arms like a detective expecting a confession.

"But Mo-om, if they didn't think I should have ice cream they should have said 'No'!"

"Emilia, they didn't *know* you already had ice cream!" I tried to fake exasperation, like a TV mom when her kids make a mess that she'll clean up for them anyway. We'd had this conversation many times, and she had overheard me telling people how my kid outsmarted three grown adults in one day.

"So can we?" she asked, folding her hands together under her chin like they'd taught me to do in church when it was time to pray. "Can we walk to Sweet Peaks?"

"Yeah," I said. "But I think I might actually *need* some ice cream."

"Mom," Emilia said. I assumed she was going to tell me nobody ever really needed ice cream. "You should get ice cream every day."

# 9

## What Support

W henever I was home alone over the next two days, I tended to pace the floor, calling offices without giving them my name to ask hypothetical questions. At the university's Curry Health Center I spoke to a nurse named Dale who gave me the phone number and address to the Crisis Pregnancy Center that operated out of a building that also housed the City Life Community Center, Missoula Youth for Christ, and, oddly, a Taco Sano. Dale warned me that the Crisis Center was faith-based, but they had an ultrasound machine and would see me at no cost.

"And they won't report it?" I asked for probably the third time.

"Miss, I really don't know who they would report it *to*," he said.

"Right," I said, trying not to let out a huge sigh. I could name about three organizations in particular that would be incredibly interested to know that I was pregnant. Namely SNAP, Medicaid, and WIC. I had just filled out a recertification for SNAP, and worried that not disclosing information would penalize me in some way. At the same time, I hadn't yet decided for sure what I wanted to do about the pregnancy. Unintentional mistakes were so easy to make with assistance programs. I worried that not asking for more help could be seen as fraudulent, as ridiculous as that might sound.

If I decided to get an abortion, I knew I would need to make an appointment soon. Blue Mountain Clinic, where I'd gone for my last abortion, confirmed an opening in their schedule. I felt my throat tighten but managed to give them my name.

"Okay, Miss Land, that's October twenty-third at nine thirty in the morning. The total cost will be six hundred and fifty dollars, due when you check in. The appointment is fast but expect to need someone to help you for three to six hours."

"Um, okay," I said. "Is that. Is that necessary?" I'd opted to have a nonmedication abortion because I figured it *wouldn't* require several hours to get through everything.

"Yes, we will require someone to drive you. Please wear comfortable clothes and do not drink any alcohol or take any aspirin for three days before your appointment."

"Thank you," I said, writing down what she told me. I needed to register for spring semester classes that same day. The day on which I had just scheduled an abortion.

Someone would need to know I was pregnant if I wanted a person to give me a ride. But I hit the spacebar on my laptop and clicked on the tab to apply for another credit card instead. Depending on how much credit they gave me, a new card could pay for the abortion, or supplement whatever I needed to use out of my student loan funds to cover the cost. At the very least I could transfer some of the debt on my Amazon Store Card to it and buy some of Emilia's clothes and Christmas presents from there instead of having to shop for the cheapest things at Walmart.

I applied for a Discover Card, selecting the style "retro cassette tape," and decided it was time to make the last call I'd been putting off. Even though I didn't know how this pregnancy began or how it would end, part of me hoped Daniel would be nice about it all, possibly even a good friend through it. This was a very small part of me that hoped, but it was present and vocal enough for me to reach out and tell him what was going on. Although I'd always believed that relying on him was a mistake, for the moment I let myself forget that. Not that long ago he'd offered to give me his old truck when my car broke down. It had begun to feel like we were friends.

"Hello, why are you calling me," Daniel said in a flat tone that I knew was not faked. Calling each other in the middle of a weekday wasn't really our thing.

"Because I'm pregnant," I said.

Daniel laughed before a muffled pause and for a second I thought he told everyone who might be around him what I said. I waited for him to say something, watching my feet step directly in front of the other: heel to toe, heel to toe, heel to toe, and spin. Repeat.

"Hello?"

"That was funny shit," Daniel said. "Don't do that again."

"Okay," I said. "I made an appointment for an abortion, but I'm still not sure about it."

"WHAT?" Muffled sounds again. He must have been at his place since it was too early for him to be at work. "Are you fucking kidding me?"

"No," I sighed. "I'm not kidding."

CLASS

"So, what, you're saying this thing is mine? Because I'm not pay—"

"I don't know!" I had to yell over his frantic talking and suddenly he was quiet.

"You DON'T KNOW don't know or you really don't know?"

"What?" I rubbed the spot between my eyebrows with my thumb. "I mean, I guess it could be yours."

"Jesus, how many people are you fucking?"

"About as many as you."

His voice caught in his throat and I could hear a lighter click, then the sound of him taking a drag of a cigarette. "I'm not taking any fucking responsibility for this." His voice had turned cold. "I didn't know you were fucking other people! How many are we talking here—two, three?"

I couldn't believe what I was hearing. "Daniel, I don't expect you to have any responsibility. I just needed you to be my friend."

"Your *friend*," he said in a tone that now mocked me. "A friend doesn't pin a FUCKING KID on you that you DON'T WANT!"

"Daniel, I said I had an appointment for an abortion."

"Well, at least you know how to be somewhat responsible. When the fuck did you fuck another guy?"

"Uh." I let out a breath. "The, uh, the night of my birthday."

"Jesus Christ." He must've held the phone down against his shirt, because the next thing I heard was a loud, muffled *FUCK!* "You slept with some guy and then you fucked *me*? Who the fuck is this guy? Do I have herpes now?"

"Jesus, Daniel. NO."

"Who the fuck is it? Do I know him?"

"It was, uh." I hesitated. I hadn't told anyone about the one-night stand on my birthday.

"You don't even know his name, do you. What a fuckin' . . . I don't know why I ever fucked you."

"Yes, I know who it was," I said, suddenly feeling defensive. "I just don't know his last name. It was Max. He's always at the R—"

"MAX BENNET?" Muffled sound, another *FUCK!* "You slept with that scum before you came over begging for my dick?"

"Okay, I'm gonna hang up now."

"You better get rid of that thing. Don't tell anyone about this. Things are good between me and Tiff right now and I don't want to fuck it up again, okay? It was bad enough that we ran into you that one night."

"Right. On my birthday," I said.

"On your—fuck, that was *the night*?" Did he really not remember my birthday weekend?

"Yup, and then I was with you two days later." When he'd told me that his . . . whatever she was . . . was sleeping with someone else. The thought crossed my mind to remind Daniel of this, but I decided against it. "I guess I thought you'd maybe come with me to the clinic."

Daniel laughed in a maniacal way.

"This was a mistake," I said, feeling like I was going to cry. I had tried to cash in on some form of relationship currency that did not exist.

"You bet it was a mistake." He took another drag off his cigarette. "I'm glad you're doing the right thing." Then he ended the call.

I don't know how long I sat on the floor with my back up against my bed, or how long it was before the dog came in to sit next to me, but I know those were the only comforts I had in that moment.

———

"Mama, are you crying?" Emilia asked for the second time later that evening.

"A little, sweetheart, but I'm fine." She came over and sat in the kid-size seat my crossed legs made. I put my chin on the top of her head. "I'm fine."

"Is Seth coming over for dinner?"

"I'm not sure," I said. "I will ask him."

A few weeks ago my friends who took Emilia camping had invited me to a comedy show they'd planned to perform in. It was at the Union, the bar just a couple of blocks from my place, so I wouldn't need a sitter for very long if I popped in to see their set. I'd stood in the back, laughing along with the crowd, when they introduced someone with the same name as my ex-roommate. Then Seth walked onto the stage. Not only did Seth have a microphone in his hand and a spotlight on him, but he spoke a lot of words to form a funny story that began with "So I've been doing a lot of babysitting lately. . . ."

Seth oddly grew more and more attractive by the minute. I'd never seen him around his friends, or outside of my house. He showed no surprise at seeing me when I came up to talk to him afterward. He suddenly seemed very at ease around me, and I found myself flirting with him. Our whole relationship dynamic felt like it changed.

Since then, we hadn't made out or anything, but we hugged goodbye sometimes and he often came over to make food or hang out. And he still babysat for me, claiming it was "for material" as an explanation for not wanting me to pay him.

Maybe I could tell Seth. I mean, who doesn't want to hear, "Hey, how's it going, can you drive me to my abortion?" There was always Sylvie, but she was dating a guy I didn't like very much and we'd been avoiding each other. Plus she was in nursing school and busier than I was, with four more kids than I had. We barely made it to the gym anymore to go climbing. Reed could be a good person to talk to. No, we talked banter, not anything with substance. I had an urge to go through the contacts on my phone to look for someone who could help me get through the next two weeks. I couldn't think of anyone. *That's how you wanted it*, I reminded myself. *Remember? No relationships.* "Yeah," I softly said.

"What, Mama?"

"Yeah!" I said, wrapping my arms around her small frame. "Let's go figure out this whole dinner situation."

_____

Whenever I looked at my day planner for details on homework over the weekend, I ended up staring at the directions to the Crisis Pregnancy Center for a long time. Despite what I told Daniel, I wasn't all that sure it happened the weekend of my birthday, but it was what made the most sense since it was the only time it could have. I wasn't *sure* sure, but I was pretty sure.

If I really had conceived on my birthday . . . fuck. What were the chances I would accidentally conceive on the night of my birthday twice, seven years apart? What was I even thinking, anyway? Daniel hated me for, I guess, having a uterus that functioned. I could reach out to Max, but I hadn't even known his last name until Daniel told me. We weren't even Facebook friends. "Oh my god." I put my face in my hands, elbows resting on the table. This wasn't who I was.

At night I searched for stories about this situation happening to other people. Maury Povich practically made paternity tests his whole brand but I only found one essay that someone had written for the *Huffington Post* about getting pregnant without knowing whose sperm caused it. She had just separated from her husband and went to her friend's wedding and oops, got drunk and banged one out with the hot best man. One part that interested me was that she did an in-utero DNA test to determine who the father was (spoiler alert: her husband, who forgave her enough to amicably coparent the child with her). But when I googled that, it seemed expensive and not covered by insurance. Society told me it was important to know who the biological father was, but not knowing who had actually participated in getting me pregnant felt freeing. Everything with Jamie had been so hard. How could parenting alone be any harder than *that*? It was, ultimately, my decision to make. What if I *did* choose to do this on my own? Isn't that what I had wanted? Or what I had wished I had done? Did I . . . want . . . to have another baby, like, right *now*? Because given the circumstances, it sure felt like I did.

Taking in a deep breath and letting it out, I tried to center myself enough to write a two-page paper about Truman Capote. My other homework looked relatively simple: read a book called *Reality Hunger* (the only thing I knew about it was it had a red cover with yellow letters), write an essay for part of the midterm for Montana Writers Live, and write a lot of fiction for Debra. My story focused on a character loosely based on a friend who worked his way through college with a DJ business; it was titled, embarrassingly, "The Wedding DJ."

My computer made a ping noise and a message from my friend Kristi popped up. It was in all caps, saying Kevin, my new roommate and her friend, could move in soon. We had all met up briefly over the weekend and he seemed nice, tolerating Emilia immediately climbing into his arms. I guessed that was a good sign. He said he was good with babysitting as long as his work schedule allowed, which I worried about a little. But with Seth and the whole house of neighbors who lived in that huge old house, I felt more confident with babysitters for my classes. Plus, it seemed like Kevin wanted something long-term, which was a relief. I had grown weary of having a different roommate every month.

Things with Emilia were in a calm phase. She even put her shoes on without argument and held my hand whenever we walked downtown. From past experiences I knew to enjoy this not-so-difficult moment with her and not to ask why. No doubt trouble was coming, and I didn't need to speed its arrival. Emilia's teacher was happy with her learning progress, but I recognized the expression on her face when we talked: my kid had stopped testing my limits for the time being, and was testing her teacher's instead, like horses sometimes do to electric fences. That was not going to end well.

---

Recorded events in my day planner were the only moments that presented themselves as real for the next several weeks. Evenings echoed, when the house was almost dark and Token's barks traveled through the rooms. Standing in the kitchen alone reminded me of the time I told Seth it had been a long day and he immediately offered to run and get me a taco.

"Mom, I'm hungry," Emilia said as she turned on the television to watch something on Netflix.

"Okay," I said, sighing. "What do you want to eat?"

She put up her pointer finger like she was about to announce the greatest idea. "I'd like a little bowl of ketchup with a spoon!"

"Oh my goodness, are you serious?" I couldn't help but laugh. "Why don't you go grab the mail and we'll see what we can do."

Opening the fridge caused me to lose my appetite and forget everything that I could possibly cook. My constant struggle lately was finding ways to consume protein and produce without it taking the shape of a peanut butter and jelly sandwich, which I'd grown weary of long ago. Sometimes I could find whole chickens on clearance and cooked them in the oven in a cast-iron frying pan. I looked in the freezer and decided on a frozen burrito for me, but that didn't do anything for the kid who hated beans or anything mashed or breaded. "Oh!" I said out loud, finding a frozen meal she might like.

"Emilia, how about a lasagna? It should take about an hour to cook in the oven."

"Okay," she said, throwing a large envelope on the table.

Manila envelopes with white labels caused my heart to race. When I looked closer, I saw the words MULTNOMAH COUNTY DISTRICT ATTORNEY and felt on the verge of a panic attack until I saw the words CHILD SUPPORT underneath. The child support modification from Portland! I'd almost forgotten about it! I ripped it open so fast it garnered my kid's curiosity. It was rare to get something exciting in the mail.

*Child Support Program hereby moves to modify your child support order that was effective 01/01/2012 because there has been a substantial change of circumstances.*

My hand immediately went to my mouth. I couldn't believe it.

"What is it, Mom?" Emilia asked, jumping on her mini trampoline.

"Um, just a letter," I said while I attempted to make sense of the paperwork and looked for a dollar amount. The first four pages explained all the reasons for their decision, which was on the fifth page with **Proposed** in big, bold letters on top.

*IT IS HEREBY ORDERED . . . must pay $689.00 cash child support per month for EMILIA.*

I gasped. "Six hundred eighty-nine! That's almost seven hundred!" Emilia watched me, trying to make sense of what I meant by spouting off numbers, only knowing that it made me happy. On the next page, it said they imputed Jamie's income from Employment Department records. "Well, how much . . ." I mumbled, then saw it on the top of the first page of the Child Support Worksheet they'd included. That fucker made thirty-five hundred dollars a month! His monthly earnings were as much as I made from cleaning houses during the entire school year. More than double what they imputed my income as at full-time minimum wage.

I needed to sit down. "Oh my god," I said.

"Mom!" Emilia said. "What is it?"

I turned to her and smiled, then laughed, smiled again, and felt a tear gather in the corner of my eye. "I just got some really good news, sweetie." She came over to hug me and craned her neck to look at the paperwork, but I flipped it over so she wouldn't see her dad's name. "We should order pizza!" Emilia suddenly looked more excited than I did just a minute before, jumping up and down before she dove into the futon to bury her head into the pillows and blankets and scream. "I guess that means yes?"

"YES!" she said. "Can I have a slice of cheese?" I nodded. "And a cookie?" She folded her hands together under her chin, tilted her face down a little, stuck out her lower lip, and added "Pleeeeease?"

"I don't know how I could say no to that," I said, laughing, and gave her a huge hug.

I read all the paperwork four more times while we waited for our pizza. Seven hundred bucks a month would be life-changing for me, on top of an ongoing life-changing decision I needed to officially make. This money, which added up to an extra three hundred and eighty-nine dollars a month, would be enough to cover my share of rent *and* my car insurance *and* phone bills. I could put more toward credit card debt. I could maybe save up a little money. Maybe we could get a little house with a yard, but I didn't want to get ahead of myself. Not yet.

# 10

## The Crisis Center

$M$y eyes had to adjust to the darkness of the room after I walked through the door. Only one other person sat in a waiting room chair across from where I stood, trying to decide whether or not to turn and leave. She looked young, was very pregnant, and a woman old enough to be her mother stood next to her. The receptionist's desk sat behind a Plexiglas window and I wondered briefly if it was for protection or to create the appearance of a medical office.

Two women behind the window smiled and one handed me a clipboard with a single sheet to fill out. "Front and back, please," she said. I wasn't sure if I should say thank you.

"There's no cost, right? This is free?"

"Yes, ma'am, our services are funded through donations." She beamed with pride. I got the sense that she wanted me to show surprise and ask who on Earth would do such a wonderful thing.

The girl's face quickly moved to look down at the floor when I chose the seat across from her. *Yeah*, I thought, *I don't really want to be here, either.* My visit was for one reason, which, I discovered, was not listed on the sheet for me to check off.

"You don't know the first day of your last menstrual period?" the technician asked, leaning over to look at the paper as she washed her hands.

"Um, no," I said, trying not to fidget. "I'm kinda here to figure that out."

With the lights dimmed, the posters of fetuses created an alien aesthetic. Bible verses weren't present, but I knew they made up the foundation of everything this woman was about to say to me.

"Well, your urine test showed that you're absolutely pregnant. Why are you here today, Ms. Land?" Her voice wasn't impatient, but it wasn't without judgment, either. "I see you didn't give a reason for that."

"I'd like to know how far along I am." I looked down to avoid her gaze. She didn't say anything else, and I allowed the moment to expand in its awkwardness.

"Well," she said. "My name is Kim and I will definitely help you with that today. You have another child?"

"Yes, she's six."

"And you're not married?"

"Why should I be married?"

Kim didn't have an answer for that but continued to pry. "Is your child's father at work today?"

For a second I had no idea why she would ask that question. "Oh.

My six-year-old's dad. He lives in Oregon. I guess he could be at work right now. I don't really know."

"Is he not in the picture?"

More furrowed brows. "Why does that matter for the reason I am here?"

Again, Kim did not have a response and appeared to struggle not to lose her patience. "*Miss* Land, I see you checked that your safety was not an issue, but you can tell me. Is someone in your life causing you to feel unsafe?"

I pressed my lips together, my eyes narrowing briefly before I remembered to breathe. "Ma'am, I really just want to know how far along I am."

"Okay, then," Kim said as the caring moment passed. "We will find that out in a minute." She asked me to lie back on the padded table I sat on, the paper crinkling beneath me. "Could you unbutton your pants, please?"

I raised my head to look. Kim held up a clear squeeze bottle full of light blue jelly that glowed from the ultrasound screen behind it. "Oh, um, sure."

"This will be a little cold." The jelly made a few farty noises as it squirted out before I felt her press the probe thingy into my stomach. Immediately, the sound of a quick pulse filled the room. Kim seemed excited about it, and called it "the baby's heartbeat." I didn't correct her by saying that cells that would eventually be part of the heart had a pulsating movement to them, and that it was nowhere near either a "baby" or a "heartbeat." Maybe science was not their strong suit here. She then continued to press on different parts of my lower abdomen, jelly oozing closer to my underwear, and I wondered how much experience she had at this. "Hm, this isn't showing up. Have you ever had a vaginal ultrasound, Miss Land?"

"Yes." I sighed. This was not exactly what I'd hoped for. But I knew from an early ultrasound with Emilia that if the fetus wasn't visible this way, I must be less than ten weeks along. Kim left the room after handing me a thick white sheet, instructing me to remove my pants and underwear. She knocked as I fought to unfold the sheet. I stood there naked from the waist down and hopped up to the table, barely draping the sheet over my lap before she opened the door.

"Okay!" Kim's voice had renewed enthusiasm. "Let's see who's making all that racket!"

I rolled my eyes, but she didn't notice as she squeezed more jelly on the long wand and spread it around with her gloved fingers.

"Why don't we have you scooch down a bit to the end of the table and put your feet in these funny little sock puppets here." Kim inserted the cold, plastic-covered wand what felt like a foot into my body and I took a sharp breath. "Oops! Sorry about that."

The pulsing sound filled the room again. "Well, would you look at that." Kim sounded as if a line of ducklings had just walked into the room, but when I looked up I saw her pointing at a grayish white blob in the lower right of a larger black circle. Kim smiled at me and looked like she might cry. "That's your baby!"

"How? How far along is it?"

She started to take some measurements, clicking, creating a line or two, then printed out a screenshot. I waited with my head back, not looking at the screen, trying to ignore how uncomfortable that thing inside me was. "The heartbeat is excellent!" Kim said suddenly. "One hundred and forty-three beats per minute!" I heard several more clicks. "Looks like the length of the baby is ten point seven millimeters, so a bit less than half an inch." Then the wand was out and Kim became businesslike, asking me to get dressed and meet her in the next room, and left before I could ask her any questions.

Kim sat in a beige chair in the room to the left of the ultrasound room, across from the bathroom where I'd peed into a cup. With the hand that wasn't holding a clipboard she motioned for me to sit in the other beige chair across from her. I sat and looked around. The room's corner had a large pile of boxes of diapers; the rest was full of baby clothes, hung on racks according to size.

"Are these all donations?" I asked, carefully balancing on the edge of the chair, wondering what this conversation would entail. The reason for that younger girl's presence in the waiting room seemed more clear. I thought about the look on her face, and the older woman standing next to her, and wondered if coming here, choosing to go through with her pregnancy, had been her choice, or if she was able to consent to having sex in the first place.

"Yes, we are very lucky here," Kim said, still writing on the papers on her clipboard.

"All of this stuff just sits here?" I thought back to the times public health nurses told me there weren't any organizations who had diapers because the need was so great.

"If you agree to our services and attend our parenting classes you earn points so you can go shopping." Kim's demeanor became bubbly again for a brief moment. Her short, wavy brown bob moved in one piece as she looked around at the room, like she hadn't been in there for a while. She wore slacks and a white cardigan over a blouse instead of scrubs but I didn't ask why. They hadn't taken my vitals, either. "Okay, Miss Land, we need to have a quick conversation if that's all right with you." She looked up at me and I nodded. "What are your plans for this pregnancy?"

"I'm not sure," I said, shrugging slightly.

"This is your third pregnancy. Could you tell me about that?"

"I had an abortion last April," I said, watching her make a note. "I had an appointment for an abortion last week but I canceled it."

"And why is that, are you considering adoption?"

"No," I said. "I really don't know what I'm considering. I just needed more information first."

"But you've decided to keep the baby," she prodded.

"I really don't know," I said, not wanting to give her any information to record on the papers in front of her because I didn't know what happened to it after I left.

"Miss Land," Kim said as she rested her clipboard in her lap. "Would you like to see what we have to offer you here?"

"Sure," I said, seeing I had frustrated her—not that I meant to. My tone was blunt, but I wasn't dishonest or contentious.

Kim's tour of the Crisis Pregnancy Center was more involved than I imagined. They had several rooms of clothes for babies and children, and one full of professional clothes that Kim pointed out would surely fit me. One room had several bouncy chairs and gliding rockers and the sight of them made me ache. Everything seemed to be kept within the church's basement and I got the impression I would have to become a member to receive any of these things.

When Kim handed me a sheet of paper with all the information she'd obtained from the ultrasound, I stared at the "7w1d" scribbled next to heart rate and measurements. Seven weeks and one day ago would be the estimated day I should have started my period. I speed-walked to my car and drove straight home to find my day planner.

———

Every waking moment of knowing I was pregnant had filled me with shame. After Daniel's response, I grew fearful of telling anyone else. He'd sent a text to check in on me about a week after I told him, and I thought for a second that he might have been sincere. As soon as I told him I was still pregnant he grew enraged again, and his texts filled with almost nothing but words like "fucking crazy." I finally blocked his number. Then came the messages from his friends. One sent me a message on Facebook, telling me to "cut the Jerry Springer bullshit out and get an abortion."

I raced to my day planner when I got home and counted back seven weeks and one day.

"September eighth," I whispered. Days twelve to fourteen of my cycle were the nineteenth through twenty-first of September, the days before and after my birthday.

Along with the shame, though, there was a feeling inside me that was sure I wanted this pregnancy. Somewhere inside me was reassurance, not recrimination, and I needed to not only find it, but allow it to reveal its intentions. I needed to know if I could trust that feeling. Not knowing how to meditate, I decided to take a long shower in the middle of the day. Unsure of how I felt about my body now that it had this clump of cells growing in it, I needed a quiet space to go looking for what I really wanted.

I stared at my hand for a few minutes in the shower that afternoon, then smoothed my hands over my stomach, leaving one there and placing the other on my heart. My lungs filled with the steamy air, and a feeling of freedom began to fill my chest. Whatever word I wanted to use for the pregnancy, be it *situation* or *predicament* or *dilemma*, I realized I did have some autonomy. I had no idea who the biological father was, and while that was something I'd never known anyone else to go through, it gave me the freedom to make a decision solely based on what I wanted. There, in that shower, in water so hot it turned my skin red, I wrapped my arms around myself and whispered, "But what if you did this on your own?" Half laugh and half sob created an odd sound as it left my body from somewhere deep in my chest, then something sprouted, even blossomed, and I felt nothing but love for my whole self and whatever being had begun to grow.

That moment in the shower felt optimistic. Without any way to explain it, I knew with certainty that everything would be okay.

Of course, I still didn't know who had fertilized the egg in my fallopian tube. But not knowing the answer to this question no longer brought feelings of shame—instead it presented an opportunity. This would be a decision I made on my own, followed by thousands of other decisions that I alone would be free to make as well. What place or facility I would give birth, what diapers I would use, what name I would give him or her, and countless other things that I wouldn't have to ask for someone's opinion on or approval for. There would be no fighting over custody or courts getting involved. No one yelling at me for "turning them in" by handing in the paperwork I was required to submit.

"I can do this," I said to the dog staring at me. He rose to his hind legs, gingerly placing a paw on my shin in response. I looked down at the photo Kim printed out for me, showing a small blob in an empty black space.

Emilia was almost done with school for the day and it was so cold out I thought it would be nice to pick her up. It had snowed that morning, but the thirty-mile-an-hour wind had blown most of it away and reminded me how cold our house got in that weather. Maybe Emilia and I could go to the coffee shop down the street for some hot chocolate or something special. As much as I wanted to tell her about the pregnancy, I knew it was best to wait a few more weeks. Closer to the end of the first trimester, at least.

I turned the key in the ignition and nothing happened. "No, Pearl, no, you can't keep doing this to me." I pumped the gas a touch more. Pearl's engine tried to turn over a little, but I knew better than to force it. Her carburetor had been rebuilt the week before and the mechanic said she purred like a kitten, but he'd obviously been too confident in himself yet again. I rested my forehead on the steering wheel, trying not to cry. At least all of this was still considered under warranty, and I could borrow a friend's car if I needed to. "Jesus Christ, not just one good day, huh?"

I got out, slammed the door, and went inside the house to call my mechanic. Pearl had been in and out of his shop constantly for the last three months. When her carburetor first started to give out, I could still jump out and push her, getting her started again by hopping into the seat, pressing the clutch, and shifting into second gear. Lately even that hadn't helped. Now almost every part of her fuel system was refurbished or brand-new. I had agreed to paint the whole interior of a house and do a move-out clean to pay for some of it at the end of the summer.

My car not working never felt like anything less than a personal failure. It was a painful reminder that I needed more help than I could afford. It put more limitations on my ability to work and get both me and my kid to school. We were lucky enough to live in a place where we could get to most places by walking. If I chose a longer route, I could walk by a grocery store on the way home from school. Getting to work, though, with all of my school and cleaning supplies within the time frame I had, was not a possibility. The constant uncertainty of when my car would work likely contributed to what I later learned was complex post-traumatic stress disorder. Even when it ran well, any odd smell, any strange-sounding click, any dip in RPMs at a stoplight caused my heart to race.

This is the way it always went. Every moment of hope was like reaching the very top of a roller-coaster ride—before you go crashing down again.

# 11

# I'm Pregnant

There wasn't much reason to tell people I was pregnant, but hiding things has never been in my nature and I'm terrible at it anyway. Given that I lacked an intimate relationship and had never talked about wanting to have another child, I knew my pregnancy would be a surprise to most people. Most of my friends didn't even know about my abortion. I managed my expectations for their responses by setting a low bar. While it would have been nice to hear some support or to have someone join me in my excitement, I'd always been a prepare-for-the-worst-while-hoping-for-the-best type of person. This, unfortunately, was no different. Conversations began with me signaling that I had something monumental and potentially embarrassing to reveal, then

I started with a huge breath I didn't let out fully, puffing my cheeks for a second before I touched my face in some way, usually rubbing my forehead and wincing a bit. Some would respond with immediate shock: *What? Are you serious?* Others were more restrained, registering surprise on their faces while the wheels turned in their heads to come up with something to say that wouldn't be too offensive.

With Reed I was more blunt. "So," I began. "I'm pregnant."

"What?"

We had chosen the spot at the edge of the balcony to keep a close watch on a table below that was covered in pamphlets and Bibles to entice students to become Jehovah's Witnesses. Since it was only a few days before Halloween, many of the people who walked past the two boys dressed in matching button-up shirts and navy vests were dressed up like zombies. Maybe because of that show *The Walking Dead*? Did I miss a memo?

Instead of looking at Reed, who probably wanted to ask me what the fuck I was thinking, I watched a guy with a Frankenstein mask approach the table, pick up a Bible, and pretend to read it.

"Well," Reed said finally. "Congratulations?"

"Thanks," I said.

"When did this all happen?"

"Uh, the weekend of my birthday."

"Who . . . Is it Daniel's?"

I shrugged. "Maybe? Or, um, this guy named Max."

*"Max Bennet?"*

I winced. *Fuck. Was there only one Max in this town?* "I guess you know him, too."

"I mean, I went to high school with his little sister, but yeah. Everyone knows Max Bennet."

I'd forgotten how young Reed was, and that he'd been in high school just a few years ago. Our ages never mattered when we sat across from each other every Tuesday and Thursday afternoon in this odd area with five or six rarely occupied tables. He was a year behind me in college but about thirteen in age, yet we never had a difficult time connecting.

Frankenstein made a growling noise as a couple of zombies joined him at the table, causing the two boys to cross their arms and look at each other nervously. "I'm only seven and a half weeks," I added, not looking away from the unfolding monster drama. "Kinda hope it's a while before I start showing."

"So no drinking?"

"Nope." I lifted my paper coffee cup. "Just decaf."

"Man," he said, leaning back to look at me. "Well, whatever. I hope everything goes well with all of"—he waved his hand at my cup, as if he were shooing a bee—"that."

"Thanks," I said, letting out a chuckle. I felt the same way about decaf coffee. "That might be the best way to say that."

Reed smiled. "So, what are we working on?"

"This short story about a wedding DJ who can predict if a marriage will fail from their song lists. But I'm running out of ideas for songs that would do that."

Reed took a thoughtful bite of his almond croissant. "What about 'Every Breath You Take'?"

"I've got that one. And the Dave Matthews song."

"Oh, the one about him standing below a window? Total stalker song."

"They played that at my senior prom."

"Ew," Reed said, then looked thoughtful again. "What about that Bon Iver song? 'Skinny Love' or something."

"Oooh!" I typed it into a Google search for the lyrics. "Man. I liked this song, too. This is great."

Five minutes of typing distracted me for a bit, but eventually my worries took over again. My food stamp amount would decrease by about twenty bucks a month in a few days. They had sent out letters about this a couple of months ago to inform recipients that the boost they gave us after the recession had expired, or run its course. That sheet of paper Kim gave me after the ultrasound would qualify me for Medicaid, more money for food, and possibly cash assistance. But every time I considered applying for Temporary Assistance for Needy Families, I reminded myself that it was more trouble than it was worth, which was absolutely the intent. The fewer people who signed up meant more block grant money for the state to spend elsewhere.

"Cash assistance" was a stretch, too, since the amount I would receive in "assistance" was less than what I got in child support from Emilia's father. One of the obligations to sign up for TANF was not only to have a child support case open through the state, but that you had to sign a waiver for them to reroute the payments to go to their office. The first time I had gone to a local office to inquire about it, a woman in front of me burst into tears and said that asking for child support would mean revealing her location to her abuser, but the woman behind the counter wouldn't budge and repeated that it was a requirement of the program. I never understood why I had to exchange child support for TANF when the amount of financial help was so small. If I signed up, I would actually be out thirty bucks a month. I wondered if they would require me to open a child support case for this pregnancy. What if I signed up two months before I gave birth? Would they force me to get a paternity test?

Then I remembered that I'd just filled out the twice-yearly re-certification paperwork for SNAP (they always wanted to check on how many hours you worked and if you had money squirreled away somewhere) and I was waiting to hear about what they would decide. I needed Medicaid to see a doctor for the pregnancy, but I hated the thought of telling anyone I was pregnant so I could get more money for food. I didn't want to fuel their prejudices by playing the role of the woman who has a baby solely for the bigger welfare checks, even though there was no such thing as welfare anymore.

Meanwhile, Emilia still needed a costume, which was the part of Halloween that I hated the most. I wasn't creative enough or gifted in the area of sewing to make something, so we always ended up at the Halloween Store, where I begrudgingly spent the last of the money I had for October. We had to shop for her costume at the very last minute, because any costume bought before then would get tossed aside like it was from last year and not last week.

These thoughts must have been playing out on my face because Reed asked me if I was okay. For a second I thought I might start crying, but I managed to make a joke about zombies who used to be Jehovah's Witnesses. There was no way to tell Reed, or anyone else for that matter, about all the thoughts that just went through my head in a way they'd understand. Besides, this was my creative writing time, when I was supposed to get a break from those thoughts.

"What about that Taylor Swift song?" I said, typing her name into the search engine. "It's like a *Romeo and Juliet* song?"

"Can't help ya there," Reed said, puffing up his chest in a show of masculinity that made me burst out laughing. He looked so sad for a second, I thought I might have hurt his feelings, but then he coughed and started to laugh, too.

"Wow, those big blue eyes of yours can be pretty convincing," I said.

"I know," Reed said, adding a hair toss. "It's one of my many talents."

———————

"Stephanie, what are you going to do with a newborn baby in grad school? I'm just not sure you've thought this through."

I shrugged. Kristi had given me a ride home because my car was still with the mechanic, and she used it as an opportunity to demonstrate how unprepared I was to have another child. We were parked outside my apartment in her Volkswagen van, and I had my hand on the door handle, wanting to escape. I had hoped Kristi would be supportive—she always had been before—and I was simultaneously hurt and angry at her judgmental tone. Not for the first time, it struck me that the most unentitled people felt entitled to judge. People who'd never known a day of food insecurity in their lives, who'd been too proud to accept a handout, or who had the perception that their success was self-made, were usually the ones who felt justified in judging my decision-making as a single mother who lived in poverty. Kristi didn't have kids and her husband was a grumpy asshole. I didn't say it to her then, but I thought to myself that she was in no position to judge my parenting abilities, or to tell me what I could or couldn't handle. At least no one in my household yelled at anyone else. I felt whatever bits of friendship we had fade away the more she voiced her opinions on my life.

"I just want the chance to have a kid on my own," I said. If I tried to explain why, or how much I wanted this baby, I doubted she would understand. There wasn't a way that I could explain it, since it was a feeling so deep down in my gut. I *believed* it would all turn out okay, but I had no evidence to support that.

"I'm worried you're not making good decisions here," Kristi said. She stared at me and I refused to look at her. I was older than her by several years and really didn't appreciate condescending tones from someone who was supported by a spouse.

I wanted to make a joke about scratching her off the babysitter list for grad school next year, but even that seemed like too much effort. Did she honestly think I hadn't thought about all the concerns she brought up? Why wasn't it enough for me, a thirty-five-year-old, to say "I want to do this," and why wasn't her response "Okay, then how can I help?"

I was so private about most of the things I struggled with that maybe she really assumed I didn't consider the *how* of having a baby, and had only focused on the *why*. In truth, the *why* mattered more to me in most areas of my life. It would be impossible for me to achieve good marks in the five classes I took that semester while working and single parenting without knowing every single minute of the day *why* I needed to do it. The answer to *why* was Emilia: envisioning her smiling at me from the audience as I walked across that stage to accept my diploma. Only now, I guess I had to change that vision to me carrying a third-trimester fetus under my gown.

"Thanks for the ride," I said. "I guess." Closing the door to her van felt like a metaphor for the end of our friendship, or at least any possibility of a deeper one. I had no tolerance for concern trolling. Every time someone did this, I immediately felt like a child. It wasn't real concern—it never was—it was an opportunity to act as if they knew better than me. If Kristi truly was worried about me, she could have checked in more, or asked me out for tea or some decaf coffee. But the *point* of faking concern with an edge of judgment seemed to be to knock me down a notch. To make the other person appear higher in intelligence, or even class. Kristi could have said, "Well, that's a pretty low-class thing to do," and it would have come out the same way. What she apparently needed in that moment was for me to know she thought my decision was irresponsible and rash. It would have been more honest if she'd said that, but that would have made *her* feel bad. This way, she could drive off and gossip about my decisions with *concern* rather than show me any kind of real empathy or compassion. Empathy takes work, after all. Gossip does not.

When I got inside, Seth said, "Look, Emilia! She's home!" before giving me an exasperated look. Seth still refused my offers of money for babysitting, insisting he considered it a trade for new material.

"I'M CAPTAIN UNDERWEAR!" Emilia said, emphasizing every word with a jump on her trampoline while holding a half-eaten sandwich in her hand. A Nutella sandwich, judging from the dark brown marks on the sides of her mouth.

"I see that!" I said, trying not to laugh. I glanced at Seth, who shrugged and said he had to go since Kristi was his ride. Emilia had the show *MythBusters* on and wore only a pair of underwear and her favorite fuzzy blue blanket, which she called "Nemnie," safety-pinned around her neck like a cape. I wondered what had transpired in the few hours that passed between picking her up from the bus stop until then, but I also kind of didn't want to know.

"Mom!" Jump. "Mom!" Jump. "Mom!"

I set my backpack down on the chair by our small table and rubbed my eyes. "Yes, Emilia, what is it?"

"Can we? Carve pumpkins? Tonight?"

"Um, yeah, I think we could do that." After the conversation with Kristi, I had almost forgotten about my least favorite holiday happening that weekend. "Did you eat anything other than that sandwich?" She pointed at a bowl on the table. "What am I looking for?"

"Cereal!" she said, then patted her stomach, sticking it out as far as she could. "In my belly!"

I laughed. "You know, Emilia Story, you're a pretty cool kid."

"I know," she said, like I'd just told her the sky was blue.

"Let me figure out something to eat and then we'll get to that pumpkin, okay?" I pulled my day planner out of my backpack to lay it open on the kitchen island. My writing assignment for Kirn's class on Tuesday was to make the class cry. I had even underlined "cry" in my notes. *Write a piece on regret. A strong regret.* Despite my current situation, that was a difficult one to come up with. There was always the option to dredge up an event from my childhood. I didn't feel like writing something from my current life that carried enough emotion to make a group of twenty-somethings cry. I wondered what their essays would be about, what *Evan's* essay would be about, and already wanted to miss that class altogether. "Hey, Emilia, what did you want me to carve in your pumpkin this year?"

I had discovered a hidden talent for pumpkin carving over the years, done completely with my trusty old Gerber pocketknife, which I'd gotten in my early twenties. Though I was still particularly proud of the giant Curious George, there had been some other good ones, like Skippy John Jones, and one year it was just "a fart." One year we painted pumpkins, and I had hoped she would want to do that this year, too, since nausea and severe exhaustion had started to rear their ugly heads. But my kid had stopped jumping on her trampoline, the gears visibly turning. Her face lit up and she started jumping again.

"La! La! Loopsy!!"

"Lala what?"

Emilia pointed to her backpack, which had a doll on the front who had tight ringlets and buttons for eyes.

"Sure," I said, rubbing my forehead with my palm. In addition to the fatigue and nausea of pregnancy, I'd been battling sinus pressure and congestion. My favorite pain reliever, ibuprofen, wasn't on the list of things I could safely take while pregnant. Before Emilia could jump up and down and yell *yay,* I was sure to add a sincere "I'll try." Then I remembered: "You're going to a birthday party on Halloween!" A friend who didn't have any children had asked to bring Emilia to a kid's birthday party on Halloween and I'd completely forgotten about it. All I had to do was bring a pumpkin for the carving activity—and get her a costume.

Convincing Seth to go with us on this adventure the next evening wasn't difficult. Seth actually enjoyed Halloween. He was one of the first people I'd told about the pregnancy after I decided I wasn't getting an abortion, and he'd been really sweet and nice since. Sometimes it felt like we were dating, but it was more like we were playing house. Seth was one of Emilia's favorite people, and she was acutely aware that he came over to hang out and have dinners more and that we had begun to hug goodbye. When I told her Seth was joining us to go pick out a costume, she jumped up and down, saying, "We're all going together?" This worried me a little. I loved Seth and wanted him to stick around, but I could never be sure how long people would be in our lives. I had promised myself I wouldn't be the cause of disappointing Emilia again. But then, in the car on the way to the costume store, Emilia reached up to tap Seth on the shoulder and said, "Are you going to be my new dad?" I glanced at Seth, and he looked as if he wanted to jump out of the moving vehicle.

"Emilia," I said, then stopped as I realized I didn't know what else to say beyond that. Seth looked at me in a desperate way and I took the cue and said, "No, Seth is not going to be your dad." This clarified something for me as well: based on Seth's response, I knew he wasn't fantasizing about the three of us forming a happy family forever after. We were close friends who got kinda cuddly sometimes. He loved my kid, and he even seemed to tolerate the dog. This had to be enough for me.

For the rest of our outing, Seth made jokes and fended off my kid's attempts to make him uncomfortable while I fought a desperate urge to rush home, throw up, and crawl into bed. I hated that I felt so disappointed about Seth, that despite all the lectures I'd given myself, I had set myself up for a letdown. I was no more capable of fighting to protect my own feelings than I was of protecting Emilia's.

# 12

# Testing Hunger

The response to my recertification for food stamp benefits dealt me
a blow I had not expected. I knew our benefit amount would decrease
after the recession boost expired, but I was shocked to find out that it
was decided that I shouldn't receive food stamps at all. Emilia would
continue to get them, but since she was now over six years old, I was
considered an able-bodied adult without a dependent. According to
the letter, the rationale was that my kid was now school age, which
allowed me to work full-time, even though she was only in school
for six hours a day. Of course I worked. I worked my ass off. But I
also had fifteen credits that semester, which spanned over five classes
I scrunched together on Tuesdays and Thursdays, plus homework.

On my "free" days, I scheduled work, which included four weekly and biweekly housecleaning clients. All of this had to be done while caring for Emilia alone.

Food stamps are, technically, a supplemental assistance program. For us it was hardly ever that. It was our entire budget for groceries. Most of that went to my kid's food. I was rarely able to afford fresh produce or meat unless it was heavily discounted; instead the benefits went toward boxes of rice, pasta, and staples like milk, cheese, and eggs. If I had some extra work that month, we ate better or could at least get some kind of treat, but Emilia's diet by that point didn't vary all that much. Her pickiness about what she ate may have been a developmental stage—lots of kids exert what little control they have over the food they put in their mouths. But I suspected that Emilia's anxiety around food wasn't just a stage. Food insecurity ruled our lives, and Emilia knew that it was somehow "bad" if she didn't like something I served her. She became afraid to try anything new, looking up at me in defeat, saying, "But what if I don't like it?" I tried not to let my own anxiety spill over onto her, but it was difficult when she refused to finish her food and also refused to eat leftovers. Every ounce of food I purchased was for a specific purpose and supposed to last us a certain amount of time, but I always stretched it beyond that. If Emilia decided to stop eating two bites into a bowl of pasta and sauce or cereal or applesauce, that meant it would go to waste if I didn't choke it down.

Panic had taken over my system when I opened the benefits letter saying that I had been denied food stamps and ten minutes later I still fought to unclench my jaw. Our monthly amount dropped to under two hundred dollars, less than fifty bucks a week. *There must be some kind of mistake.* I called the office and waited for half an hour to learn that because of Emilia's age, I was now required to work twenty hours a week—between five and ten hours more than I could do—to receive food benefits. I didn't ask why, and it never occurred to me to lie. The chance of getting caught was too big of a risk, and there was no asking why. Society's view is that people like me should be grateful for the amount we receive. By this rationale, I was lucky they didn't require me to do more for the benefits, like submit urine samples for drug tests. Or worse, take a bunch of pointless job training classes in the middle of the workday like applicants for the cash assistance program had to do—ostensibly to teach me about the many types of low-wage jobs that existed without offering fair compensation, child care, benefits, or anything useful.

My pregnancy qualified me for the WIC checks, another type of nutrition program. Pregnancy was an automatic acceptance to receive large paper coupons for gallons of milk, a jar of peanut butter, a bag (or cans) of beans, a set number of ounces of cereal, a particular amount, type, and brand of juice (or cans of frozen juice concentrate), a dozen eggs, some cheese, and ten bucks' worth of fresh produce. With our food stamp amount diminished, this became the foundation of our diet.

Fortunately the Discover credit card I'd applied for had been approved, but only for five hundred bucks. I used that to purchase lunch on campus and tried to conserve it as much as I could, but, for example, a grilled chicken sandwich and some fries from the cafeteria ran at least ten bucks. I reserved the card for those times I really needed something hot, either to lift my spirits or fill me up enough to get through the rest of the day.

My creative flexes with meals at home didn't always turn out the greatest. One night I came up with a can of refried beans cooked in a pot with pieces of string cheese and some enchilada sauce, topped with crumbled pieces from the remains of a mysterious bag of Fritos. Shoveling food in without tasting it, hoping it would stay down through the morning sickness, became essential.

Losing money for food felt like a punishment. My value, it seemed, was entirely based on whether or not I worked at a job that could be verified with a real pay stub. I didn't understand how I could be denied what they called a supplemental amount for food. Through TANF, certain types of classes would count toward work hours, but they were ones that taught specific trades, such as car mechanics. My hours spent doing homework and physically being in class not only didn't count, they worked against me. How was I supposed to feel good about getting any kind of degree after I was denied money for food? I veered between two opposing thoughts: On one side, maybe Jamie had been right; maybe getting an English degree while struggling to put food on the table was the height of selfishness. On the other side, I hated that whole argument, and that I tortured myself by returning to it—over and over again. How could I be selfish for getting a four-year degree at a state college? Of all the things in my life that I didn't have access to or felt like I didn't deserve for some reason, an education hadn't crossed my mind as a thing I wasn't supposed to have.

Although the denial of food assistance and my pregnancy were arguably unrelated, the timing felt like another punishment. My awareness of the "bad decisions" I supposedly made was heightened by how much they went against the grain of what I *should* be doing as a food stamp recipient. The government, society as a whole, and even people who knew me had opinions on how I should act, speak, parent, and live. But becoming pregnant and choosing to have the baby was, ultimately, my right. I had the *right* to choose this, just like anyone else did. I had had the same right *not* to be pregnant and have a child six months earlier. I should also have the right to an education and a degree that would help support my family. I should have the right to an adequate amount of food. It all felt like part of the "poor people can't have nice things" mandate. In this case the thing

I wasn't allowed to have was free will. How dare I make decisions for myself?

This denial of access to food was a defining moment in my life. That letter symbolized a kind of death for me—an end to any hope I had of the system working in a way that would help me get out of its web. According to several reputable opinions, I had done everything right. I was in college, about to graduate with a four-year degree. That was supposed to be a major milestone on the imaginary path out of my situation of food and housing insecurity. Great things were to come from this magical slip of paper that marked my passage out of college. Once I had it, the opportunities were supposedly endless. But what society encouraged and what it actually supported were two different things depending on what economic class you found yourself in.

Nothing made me question my life choices more than knowing that my hours spent cleaning other people's toilets to put myself through college weren't enough—and that my hours spent earning a degree didn't matter. By kicking me off food stamps, it seemed like they were telling me that higher education was something I simply could not afford. If I spoke up about this, I imagined people would tell me to be grateful for what little help I did receive. But the one-step-forward-and-two-steps-back dance the government forced me to do felt purposeful, like the whole thing was meant to keep me poor. If I couldn't eat, if I was hungry, then I couldn't afford to aspire to anything better and I would have to keep working shit jobs that would qualify me for a small amount of money to buy food. Maybe my "place" in society, the *real* class I found myself in, amounted to that.

Most days, if all went well, I had accomplished my biggest challenge by seven fifty-eight in the morning: putting a fully dressed six-year-old on a big yellow bus. However, midway through my first trimester, a few of those late mornings were not Emilia's fault. Halfway through November, the school sent a letter home informing me that if my kid was late to kindergarten more than twice in one month, instead of eating lunch in the cafeteria with the rest of the class, she would eat in what they called "the reflection room," which to me sounded a lot like detention.

Tardiness three times in one month didn't seem like a big deal for a new kindergartner and her parent trying to get everyone used to a new routine. It also didn't seem to make any sense for my kid to be singled out and receive a punishment when it was my responsibility to get her to school on time. It felt the same as when her dad would do things to punish her when his ultimate motivation was to hurt me. I worried that she might be treated differently at school because they would assume I was neglectful or inattentive or didn't care about my kid's education. I'd worked at a Montessori school in my early twenties and saw this happen with kids who were dropped off first and picked up last. There wasn't a lot of empathy or understanding directed at the single mom who rushed in five minutes past the time aftercare ended. Emilia was underweight and wore clothes from the clearance racks at Walmart. It was difficult for me to keep up with her need for new clothes and shoes and then gym shoes or a new winter coat. I feared she would be seen as a "bad kid" or "the poor kid" from a broken home, and treated differently because of that.

Emilia seemed unfazed by her detention, and even said it was nice to sit inside and read away from the other kids. It was strange for her to say things like that, though, since normally she ran, jumped, climbed, and talked constantly. I wondered why she would prefer to sit alone.

After Emilia spent lunch in the reflection room, the emails from her teacher had a tone that felt like they were more on the stern side.

I'm sure that wasn't her intent, but every couple of weeks, there was a new incident or difficulty with my kindergartner's behavior. In my return emails, I voiced my concern about being seen as neglectful, and noted that most of the time the tardiness was due to my exhaustion or not feeling well in the mornings. Her teacher offered some reassurance, but I of course didn't trust its sincerity. I struggled through this first trimester in a way I hadn't with Emilia since I was food insecure, but I couldn't admit to her teacher or the principal that we didn't have enough to eat. It's another way that poor people are discouraged from seeking help, or from being honest about their struggles: my biggest fear as a single parent living under the poverty line had always been someone calling child protective services. They would then inform her dad and possibly open up a can of worms with custody while giving him leverage to use against me.

In the days following the letter saying I would no longer be a SNAP recipient, the child support office in Portland notified me that Jamie had filed an appeal on their decision about the modification. Now, on top of everything else, I had the task of gathering evidence of expenses and getting it submitted to an administrative law judge who would hear our case in January and make a decision based on that hearing alone. Thankfully, I could appear via telephone. Jamie had already submitted printed-out bank statements detailing every single expense he had for feeding and caring for Emilia while she was at his house for ten days that summer. His feelings of hatred toward me went beyond resentment, and I wondered how much Emilia heard about those, or what he said to her. He'd told me countless times I had ruined his life. I hoped he would never tell his daughter that, too.

College classes began to pale in comparison to everything else I had listed in my day planner. Between homework assignments and notes about meetings with instructors, Emilia had early-release days that week and no school on Friday. I had to figure out what to do with her while I was at work and meeting with my professor for independent study. Then there were the WIC appointments, and the initial appointment with my midwife, who clucked her tongue and shook her head when I told her I didn't know who the father was.

I also needed to get signed up to take the Graduate Record Examination (GRE) as another step in applying for grad school. The exam fee was a mind-blowing two hundred and fifty bucks. Luckily I could take it on a Monday afternoon when I didn't have any work or other classes scheduled. Most people told me not to worry about it, since I didn't need good math scores anyway, but the size of the book to study for it intimidated the hell out of me. And unlike others, I couldn't afford to take it more than once.

———————

My independent study that semester was entirely to go over the sample essays for my MFA application and to receive advice on where I could possibly get them published. One was a piece called "A Baby with Him" and the other was the "Confessions of the Housekeeper" essay, which I had now expanded to twenty-five pages. It was the longest essay I had ever written. I'd grown weary of looking at both.

David Gates, the professor who had once called my essay "solid gold," had been more than agreeable about offering me time. He'd suggested some books to read during our first meeting and I told him what I hoped to get out of our one-on-one time together that semester before handing him copies of the essays I wanted him to look at. He had them sitting on his desk when I arrived for our next meeting, but once we started going over them, he read the lines he wanted me to revise out loud. After the first few, I noticed that there was a common thread among the excerpts, and I grew so uncomfortable that I squirmed in my seat.

"'Your body begins to change in odd ways,'" he read. "'If anything brushes one of your breasts, which have almost doubled in size, the pain makes you clamp your jaw.'" He paused to look up at me, pen in hand, and said, "Maybe if anything brushes *past* one of your breasts?"

I nodded and resisted the urge to cross my arms over my chest. It felt like I was in a skimpy tank top instead of a large, hooded sweatshirt. Gates gave a slight nod, marking the essay with his pen. "'He tells you you're too fat and too tall and that he's attracted to other women,'" he said, reading another line. "'He only has sex with you in his sleep, grabbing you from behind while you lie on your side, waking up the infant cradled in your arms.'" Gates looked up at me again and said something about changing the wording to make it more visual, but didn't have any specific words in mind.

I grew nauseous by that point. His tiny office shrank and our chairs were suddenly too close together. I would have to move my chair slightly to open the door, which I wanted to do immediately. This man was on the decision committee for my MFA application, and was one of only two nonfiction writing instructors who weren't visiting professors, like Walter Kirn. I couldn't believe he picked those sentences out of all the others and had asked me to expand on them in this voyeuristic, creepy way. I wondered how many more of these meetings I would be required to endure for a "pass" grade.

"Okay, well, thanks, but I need to get going, my kid's out in the hall waiting for me." As I got up, Gates did as well, and in the tight space it was hard to get around him. I kept my head down because I didn't want our faces to be close to each other. Emilia sat on the floor in the hallway, her legs crossed and her chin resting on her closed fists, eyes fixed on my laptop to watch a cartoon. She didn't have school tomorrow and I would probably have to take her to work, but at least it was a regular client who didn't mind if I brought my kid with me. "Hey, sweetie," I said. "Thank you for sitting so patiently. We need to get home, okay?"

With the exception of my meeting with Debra, this had been the only time I had met one-on-one with a professor about where to publish a specific piece of writing. Other than Gates telling me how much he got paid for a piece in the *Paris Review,* there was never any mention of payment for getting published. I probably could have asked more teachers for their time, but I thought "office hours" meant that was the only time I could reach a professor outside of class, and that it was intended only for an urgent question or emergency—sort of like a doctor's office hours. No one explained what office hours meant when we went through the syllabus; if the professors talked about them at all, it was a sort of mumble in passing as they got to the first item we'd go over as a class. I found out later that some of my fellow students took office hours as an opportunity to introduce themselves, build a relationship, and eventually get letters of recommendation or suggestions for scholarships. I already felt like it was asking a huge favor just to take up space in their classes. I didn't want to seem entitled to their time, or burden my professors more than absolutely necessary. My independent study was, I thought, my only opportunity to meet with an instructor regularly. I had also incorrectly assumed my choices were Gates or Blunt, since they were the only ones who specifically taught nonfiction writing.

If I had gone with Judy Blunt, I risked having to answer a bunch of questions about my life that would definitely not be included in my application and were probably illegal, which I knew would affect her decision about my candidacy. (This was a particular risk for me in applying to U of M. They already knew me and the obstacles I needed to overcome to get to class. They knew what I looked like, how I presented myself, and how it was to have me as a student in their classrooms.) Also, I honestly wasn't too excited to take another workshop with Judy. My hope had been that I wouldn't have to rely on her to mentor me. Now, after that meeting with Gates, working closely with him didn't seem like it would be that great, either.

Despite my concerns about U of M's creative writing program, I couldn't move or apply to anywhere else. The terms of my custody arrangement with Jamie required me to ask the court's permission to relocate us, and I knew the mental and financial stress to do that again was too much. I had to see things through at U of M, and my situation didn't afford me questions like *What can this school offer me?* In my mind, the question always was, *What can I somewhat desperately offer this school so they'll accept me?*

Acceptance to an MFA program was what I'd pinned all my hopes on. The biggest opportunity the MFA degree offered me was job security. It would be my ticket into the academic world, I thought, and possibly ongoing employment. A lot of the grad students went on to get PhDs and most of them taught at either U of M or another university. That part of it, perhaps naively, was my main reason for wanting to drag my kid through two more years of watching me stare at computer screens all evening. Well, I guess now it would be two kids, but if I could do it with one I could do it with two, right? Wasn't it only supposed to get *really* chaotic when you went from two to three kids? Ultimately, though, this was what I wanted more than anything. I had chosen this, and my stubbornness would always find a way to make it work. That part I knew.

I had heard about the other opportunities that an MFA program presented, namely the connections you supposedly made with other writers, who would then introduce you to more writers. They were your cohort, a tight-knit group who would hopefully cheer you on and share contacts and offer some good feedback and advice on where to submit pieces. I imagined everything short of sleepovers and braiding each other's hair. With instructors, I had the same expectation, though I wasn't sure why. Perhaps because the visiting authors and other special guests of the program might be friends of theirs and they'd introduce you personally and maybe describe you with words like "up-and-coming" or "fantastic" and we'd have deep conversations about stuff we'd read and what I was working on.

All of this bonding sounded important, vital, and, well, pretty nice. Attending this huge academic conference for writers called AWP sounded great, too, but between child care and travel costs I couldn't afford to go and they didn't offer scholarships or stipends. For similar reasons, things like writing residencies and specific, weeklong intensive workshops also weren't on my radar.

It was only later that I found out I'd gotten it all backward. The connections you made weren't a side benefit of an MFA, they were the primary goal. If someone had sat me down and explained this to me—if they'd told me that the *real* opportunity was not in the extra workshops, feedback on your work in progress, or training in teaching via your own Composition 101 class—I wouldn't have tried. Honestly, none of that "networking," which felt so smarmy, fake, and creepily transactional, really interested me. Especially since most of the time those conversations were with privileged people. I really just wanted to learn how to make it as a writer from writers who supposedly already had "made it" in some way.

When we got home I checked the portable digital thermostats I'd set up to test temperature and humidity. I had been experimenting with them, trying to figure out where the biggest drafts were coming up from the floor. The windows would definitely need some weather stripping, and I had wondered if a rug could also help. A couple of friends had offered their extra ones to give me. On the floor of our bedroom, when it got colder than thirty degrees outside, the thermostat stayed in the high fifties. Another one that I'd placed on the mantel wasn't much higher at sixty-two. I tried to imagine a baby crawling on the freezing floor. Add to that the feral cat who lived under the front porch of the house that Emilia and I were allergic to, the mildew and mold growing in the bathroom, and it was a perfect formula for constant illness. We'd already been through this when we'd spent a winter in a cold, moldy studio apartment in Washington when Emilia was three. Whatever virus she had brought home from day care bloomed in our bodies, already worn down by environmental allergens. We both had hacking coughs and runny noses for a whole year.

My current constant headache and runny nose were getting worse, and while I tried as long as I could to deny that I was sick, that became increasingly impossible. This would be a horrible situation under any circumstances because I could never afford to take sick days, but the timing was even worse now. A huge research paper was due soon and I had to turn in the first four pages and meet to discuss them with my professor, the GRE was fast approaching, and because of the pregnancy I couldn't take much more than Tylenol to control my symptoms. This meant that I had to take workdays off—partly out of caution for my clients, and also because the postnasal drip made my stomach turn to the point where I threw up. Once again I felt like I was on the speeding-downhill part of the roller-coaster ride. Mucus took over my entire head that weekend, making it impossible to concentrate *and* parent a person who asked constant questions. A single-mom friend offered to take Emilia all day on Sunday to hike up the "M Trail" behind campus, which went halfway up Mount Sentinel to a large letter *M* made out of concrete. This would give me the chance to study whatever I could for the GRE. I still wasn't sure I knew what I had to study *for*, but I figured if I looked through the study guidebook enough times, I might figure it out.

My head felt like someone had filled it with pudding when I showed up to take the exam at twelve thirty on Monday afternoon, trudging through a fresh several inches of snow to get there. Emilia had the same cold and had awakened a few times in the night from coughing. She finally drifted to a deeper sleep after I convinced her to drink some cough medicine and rubbed her back, and mumbled an "I love you, Mom" as she did. These were some of the tender moments I lived for, but I lost a lot of sleep because of them.

While the student sitting behind a large desk checked me in and figured out what computer I should use, my eyes drifted to a box of donuts sitting on a table behind him. My mouth watered and my stomach growled but I didn't want to ask if they were for everybody on the off chance they weren't, hoping he might offer one instead. I'd brought an apple to eat and a cleaned-out Adams peanut butter jar full of tea to drink, albeit slowly. We weren't allowed to get up to use the bathroom unless we'd made accommodations with them at registration, and it hadn't occurred to me to do that.

Most of the exam was a blur. I hadn't taken a math class in years and skipped a lot of the questions. Someone told me a skipped answer was better than a wrong one and I hoped that was true. The verbal sections were pretty easy, since they focused on reading comprehension, and the ones requiring a typed response were annoying but fortunately I had a lot of experience writing out a long answer to a boring question when I was hungry, tired, and ill. I didn't want to be there a moment longer than I had to; I was anxious to get home and finish two essays and a reading assignment for tomorrow before Emilia was done with school.

When I got home I saw that I had an email from my professor, Robert Stubblefield, who taught Montana Writers Live. A short piece I'd written about a visiting photographer had been published on the local radio's website that day, and the university had it featured on

their home page. Emilia came with me to his class the following evening, and he had the home page projected on the screen. Stubblefield
gave us a huge grin when we walked in, saying, "Look at that, Emilia!
Your mom's photo is on the home page for the whole school!"

Her eyes got big when she saw it, turning to beam at me for a
quick second before asking if she could have her Happy Meal now.
I nodded and told her to find a seat toward the back, but she already
knew the drill. Stubblefield smiled at me again and gave my daughter
a little wave. I thanked him, hoping to convey how grateful I was for
that moment. Without his kindness in allowing my kid to join us—
while watching cartoons with her headphones on and loudly sucking
the last bit of chocolate milk through her straw—I wouldn't be there.

# 13

# Christmastime with the Big Sister

Only a few weeks away from the end of the semester, and I had already begun to advertise on Facebook that I was available for work over the six-week winter break. Usually I took a class during the break, but I had only two required classes left. A former client had reached out to ask if I was available and one of the grad students got me connected with a third-year nonfiction MFA student who needed, of all things, a nanny for his infant daughter. I tried not to dwell on the irony. He seemed about the same age as me, and his wife worked full-time. He had a composition class to teach over the break, so the job was temporary and only a couple of hours a day while the baby napped. My job was to arrive, see him off to school, and wait for his wife to get home from work. I marveled at how a six-month-old could be so reliable for that long of an afternoon nap, but they assured me she would be asleep the whole time. One small hitch was Emilia getting home from school, which we also easily solved because she could take a different bus home and I would run out to meet her with the baby monitor.

It had been a while since I'd had a job with this many hours all at once, and I relished the small amount of relief that it brought. Loan money for spring wouldn't hit my bank account until the end of January, and some extra expenses for car repairs, the GRE, fewer food stamps, and Christmas were depleting my bank account faster than normal. A lot of the five-hundred-dollar balance on my Discover Card had gone to food over the last two months, and I had to use the rest on Emilia's plane ticket home from her dad's, and on her big Christmas present. She'd asked very specifically for us to see the local production of *The Nutcracker* and I'd been shocked at how much tickets were. I hoped seeing the afternoon performance and getting some treats after would be okay.

———

Emilia spent the entire morning before the Sunday matinee of *The Nutcracker* with her arms outstretched, spinning around in her nicest dress and tights. We'd never been to something like a ballet performance. We'd hardly been to the movies. I wondered how well Emilia would be able to sit through it, and how much they'd charge for refreshments during the intermission.

My tools to primp were limited to things from my teenage years, plus an old tube of lipstick and some eye shadow, but Emilia seemed thrilled at the opportunity to look fancy. As I bent over to apply some purple powder to her eyelids, I heard a forceful knock on our back door. This door had two long, side-by-side windows in the top half and was next to where we stood in the bathroom, but with the door closed I couldn't see who was knocking. No one ever knocked on that door. "Um, Emilia, just give me a second," I said, handing her a mirror. She puckered her lips and batted her eyes, turning her head to the right and left. When I opened the door to sneak out of the bathroom, I still couldn't see who'd been knocking—or they were no longer standing close to it. Daniel's face suddenly appeared, and in the same amount of time it took him to look up and see me standing there, I instinctively shot my hand toward the dead bolt to turn it to lock. Daniel watched me do this, then looked up at me with wide eyes before narrowing his eyelids to slits.

"What the fuck have you done?" he yelled, his voice muffled but the look of rage on his face absolutely clear.

"Go home, Daniel," I said, not knowing what else to do. I wasn't sure where my phone was, or who I'd even call. "Emilia can hear you."

"Let her hear me! She should know what a whore you are!"

At this, I got nervous. Since I'd blocked him from my phone, Daniel had taken to emailing me. His last email ended with "I hope you get hit by a bus," and I wasn't sure if he would be physically violent toward me.

"Daniel, please," I started to say.

"My fucking girlfriend hates me because of you!"

My face crinkled in confusion before I remembered a conversation with my upstairs neighbor last week when she interviewed Emilia and me for a video project she did. She was a friend of Daniel's younger girlfriend, and when she heard that I was pregnant she must have felt the need to tell Tiff about the situation.

Token barked from inside the bathroom and I scanned our kitchen area. My purse hung from a chair just a few feet away. Daniel went for the doorknob with his right hand, turning it forcefully, while he slapped the glass repeatedly with his left. "I'm not leaving until you get out here and talk to me!"

"Daniel, you need to leave," I said, dashing for my purse to grab my phone. Emilia cracked open the bathroom door, almost letting Token escape. "Just wait for a minute, sweetie! I'll be in there in a minute to finish your makeup!" She closed the door and Daniel slapped the glass again. Was it even glass? It seemed more like Plexiglas, now that I looked at it. Maybe it was really old glass.

"You're not going to get away with this, you fucking bitch!" Daniel continued. "You can't get away with ruining people's lives!"

I involuntarily barked out a laugh. "Ruin your life, Daniel?" I dug in my purse for my phone. "What life? What life do you have to ruin?" I didn't look at him for a response. "Daniel, please, Emilia is right here."

"Another kid you ruined! Did you ruin her dad's life, too?"

"Okay, Daniel, I need you to leave."

"You're fucking insane, Stephanie!" He slapped the glass again for emphasis.

I pulled my phone out of my purse and showed it to him. "Okay, Daniel, I need you to leave or I'm calling the police."

"Mama?" Emilia had opened the door enough to show her small frame draped in a dark purple velvet dress I'd found at Goodwill. Token came running out, nails scraping across the floor. I closed my eyes at the sound of his rapid barks. "Mama, can I come out now?"

"Just a second, honey, okay?" I opened my flip phone and looked at Daniel through the glass before raising my voice to say, "I just need to make a phone call."

Daniel nodded slightly before slamming his palm against the door again. Emilia and I jumped as Token completely lost his mind. I wished my tiny dog could have been at least forty pounds bigger.

Emilia looked up at me and a feeling of helplessness washed over me like someone had dumped a bucket of cold water on my head.

"I'm calling, Daniel," I said, looking at him directly through the glass.

Daniel took a step back and paused, staring at me the whole time. I wondered if he thought the look on his face was intimidating, but he seemed scared more than anything else. I wondered if I looked that way, too. For a moment I wished I had someone to be terrified with me, someone who was simultaneously confident things would work out, and would reassure me of that. Daniel turned, dropped the two steps down from my porch, and threw open the fence's gate so hard it let out a loud creak before it slammed back into its place again. I took a deep breath. One hand clenched my phone while the other shook at my side. I looked down at Emilia, who had an expression that mirrored my feelings of relief and confusion.

"Well," I said, turning my arm to look at my watch. "We need to get going soon. How about some lipstick?"

Emilia sat perfectly still at the ballet, mesmerized while she watched people twirl and dance onstage. In Washington, close to Travis's place, a dance studio had offered scholarships and I had enrolled her for the spring season when Emilia was three. Rehearsals where the instructors let the parents watch were always my favorite, because I was right there in the room, witnessing her raise her arms with all the other little girls. After we moved out of Travis's place and to a neighboring town, the drive back and forth wore us down, and Emilia barely wanted to perform in the final show. I couldn't find a closer studio that offered scholarships, so she stopped, and I always felt bad about that. I knew that watching this would renew her dreams of being in *The Nutcracker*, and maybe that was part of the gift for me. I wanted her to dream, and have something to feel passionate about. I just hoped I could find a way to afford supporting that passion.

During the intermission she sipped a cup of juice and picked up a nutcracker ornament with such gentleness I asked the woman on the other side of the table if we could purchase it.

"Really, Mama?" Emilia said. "We can have our own?" She cradled the small painted wooden figure like Clara had in the ballet earlier.

I smiled at her, rocking an ornament in the crook of her elbow, putting my hand on her shoulder to pull her in for a side hug. My whole body ached to give her more. She deserved cookies shaped like ornaments and going out to dinner after this or a dress that wasn't a size too small. She deserved ballet lessons if she wanted them and for someone to show her that it was okay to dream. I hoped I was showing her that. Maybe she'd know by the time she went to college that she could do anything she wanted simply because I'd done the same.

———

Holidays are the hardest on the poor. Especially poor parents. As I looked down the barrel of Christmas that year, I had even more to worry about than usual.

My caseworker at the Montana Department of Health and Human Services said they hadn't processed my paperwork to get back on food stamps due to the pregnancy, but she had no idea why. I couldn't get emergency help unless I went to the food bank, and because of the recent cold weather most of the organizations in town were out of grant money for the year. Because of the morning sickness I needed to eat something all the time, and it wasn't always easy to find food I could stomach. I feared what would happen if I ran out of credit, cash, and food stamps at the same time during the holidays, and that was very likely, especially if clients canceled unexpectedly or roads were bad or any other unexpected emergency occurred. That was the thing about relying on this kind of work that was usually a "bonus" instead of a necessity—clients could easily cancel because of the slightest excuse without knowing it meant that I possibly wouldn't be able to pay for food or rent.

In one regard, this was business as usual for Emilia and me—we were always on that roller coaster. But as Christmas approached, it was difficult to balance the basic needs with things that were still important but not as urgent. Sure, my kid would be fine in the long run if we didn't purchase a small toy at the grocery store that was five bucks, or a Happy Meal, but among the dozens of times I told my kid no, it was important for her to hear a yes once in a while. I wanted her to know that childhood could be magical, even if it meant me being hungry for a few hours.

As it got difficult to hide my stomach, which seemed to grow at twice the rate of my first pregnancy, I decided it was time to tell Emilia about her pending big-sister status. I thought we could go to the place in the mall with the huge freezer full of about twenty different flavors of gelato. We didn't go to the mall often, but Emilia would always beg for samples and a little cup. Maybe we could have a whole night together.

When she ran to me after she got off the bus, I couldn't contain my excitement.

"Hey there, Emilia, how was school today?"

"Fine," she said, and grabbed my hand before she started skipping. "Did my teacher call you?"

"No," I said, trying to not sound alarmed. "Is she supposed to?"

"Yeah." She stopped to look both ways before crossing the street. "And maybe the principal, too."

I took in a deep breath and tried to be nonchalant. "Well," I breathed in and out again, "I'm sure they were just busy today." We were almost to the alley behind our place and I couldn't wait until we got home. "So I was thinking we could do something kind of special tonight."

Emilia stopped skipping and looked up at me. "Are we getting ice cream?"

"Not just any ice cream, the fancy ice cream in the mall."

She gasped.

"And . . ." I continued, trying to act all sneaky or like it wasn't a big deal.

"What? What?"

"I thought me and you could have a girls' night and get haircuts, too."

"Really?"

"Yes, really." I paused to open the door and let her in. "*And* I thought we could maybe have a sleepover in the living room and watch a movie!"

Emilia gasped again, threw down her backpack, and said, "Come on, Mom, let's go!" while pulling my hand to get us out the door again.

"Okay, okay," I said. "Just let me grab the keys." Evenings like this were few and far between. As much as I loved to see my kid excited about a special few hours at the mall with her mom, it made me a little sad, too. Especially when it wasn't unusual to see videos of parents surprising their kids with trips to Hawaii or Disneyland on social media. I ached to be able to do that for her, but for now this would be our best night ever.

We skipped Great Clips this time, deciding the usual twenty-minute wait for Regis Salon was worth it. Although Great Clips was the cheapest, the last few times we'd paid for it in other ways by getting haircuts neither of us asked for, or ones we would need to pay someone else to fix.

"We're having a special night!" Emilia told the receptionist when we checked in.

"You are?" the woman said, winking at me.

"Yes!" Emilia did two quick little jumps. "We're having a girls' night!"

"Well, then." The receptionist looked around and checked the schedule in front of her again. "Let me see what I can do about that."

Our wait didn't end up being that long, and the receptionist smiled broadly at us when two hairstylists came to greet us at once.

"We heard this is a special night!" one said.

"So we thought you two might want to sit next to each other!" said the other.

Emilia nodded and smiled at me in a way that briefly made me want to pick her up and nuzzle my face in her neck. "Come on, Mom!" she said after grabbing my hand.

This was not an unnecessary haircut for me. Although I'd finally grown out the last not-wonderful one enough to have someone hopefully fix it, my hair and scalp had changed a lot through the first trimester. I needed less hair or a professional's opinion. Or both.

"Is that your mom?" Emilia's hairstylist asked.

Emilia nodded, breaking her contemplative gaze into the large mirror in front of her. "She's the best mom."

"Aw," my hairstylist said. "How old is your daughter?"

"She's six," I said, following the stylist to the line of sinks.

"Such a fun age," she said while I leaned back to rest my neck on the divot.

"Mhm." Personally, I missed age five. I missed last summer. I missed the times we weren't both in school and working all day.

When we got back to my seat, Emilia was already sprayed down and getting her bangs trimmed. I tried to explain what was happening with my hair without using words like *pregnancy* or *hormones*, but the lady seemed to understand. Both stylists began cutting and chatting away, sometimes turning to laugh with the receptionist. They turned us both around several times and used blow dryers and straighteners and whenever I looked over at my daughter she was excited as ever but also trying as hard as she could to act like she'd been getting fancy haircuts her whole life.

"She's really cute," my hairstylist said.

"She is definitely that!" I said with a chuckle.

Both our stylists said "Ready?" at the same time, then turned us to face the mirrors. Emilia's mouth formed the shape of an O and then she turned to smile at me. We'd both gotten, without discussing it first, almost the same sleek, chin-length bob. Hers with long bangs that framed her face and mine with none.

"They're perfect," I said. "Thank you so much."

Both of the hairstylists nodded and smiled. I wished so much that I could have left them a huge tip. I wanted to tell them that, but maybe they already knew. They stood at the front desk with the receptionist and smiled at us and waved to Emilia when she said goodbye and thank you. She waved back like she would see them next week before she grabbed my hand and pulled me to the gelato case.

I always found it difficult to tell her no when she pressed her nose up against the glass, getting her fingerprints all over it in the process. They weren't that close to closing, though, and I knew other kids would be along to do the same before they had to wipe it down that night. The college kid behind the counter sensed Emilia's excitement and seemed genuinely happy to offer her tastes of four different flavors before she chose her usual chocolate.

"Anything for you?" she asked when we got to the register.

"Um . . ." I wanted, possibly needed, a double twelve-ounce Americano with room for cream. "Maybe just a hot chamomile tea?"

Emilia had long since sat at a table, carefully digging through her cup of frozen chocolate. By the time I sat down it was half-gone. I asked her if she liked it and she nodded without looking up. I cupped my hands around my tea, even though I was already a little too warm in my winter boots and long-john shirt under my sweatshirt. "So, I uh, I wanted to tell you something," I began. She barely glanced up. There was a charming, thin line of chocolate around her lips that I chose not to wipe away. "It's kind of a surprise that I've been waiting to tell you about. And it's one you've been asking about for a while." Now I had her attention.

"What is it?"

"Remember that time I asked you what you wanted for lunch and you asked for a sister?"

"No." She cocked her head a bit in thought. "Did I really order a sister for lunch?"

"You did," I said, and we shared a laugh together for a moment. "And I didn't get you a sister that day, and you still don't really have one now, but you will be a big sister really, *really* close to your birthday next year."

"Really?"

I nodded, and tried not to visibly wince. I knew what was coming. This kid knew how babies were made.

"So is Seth the dad?"

"What? No!" I said, possibly too loud.

"Well," she said, frowning a bit. "Who is the dad?"

"There's no dad, or he's not around, anyway." I let out a breath I'd been holding in. "This baby is just ours."

The smile that kid gave me. Man. I melted into my chair. Then she got up and walked around the side of the table to hug me and sit in my lap, almost knocking over my tea and causing the two older women sitting a few tables away to turn and smile at us. We sat like that for a few minutes, her asking soft questions and me whispering answers. For the first time since I'd found out I was pregnant, I felt some kind of peace. Maybe it was more of a knowing. I would call it reassurance but I knew that I shouldn't need a six-year-old to offer me that. In that moment, though, it was a nice feeling to have.

I don't know what movie we watched that night. I know we got home and took selfies of our new haircuts with the camera on my laptop, Emilia standing in front of me in her Monster High pajamas with her arms outstretched. I know she fell asleep in the crook of my arm right after looking up at me and saying, "Thank you for everything you do for me, Mom." I know I slept, too. I know I slept well for the first time in a while.

———

Every winter weather advisory for that first week of December seemed to be in a competition to outdo the last. A storm that began with thirty-two-mile-per-hour wind gusts and negative temperatures in the low thirties ended with winds blowing through at almost forty-five miles per hour, some snow, and temps as low as negative thirty-five. Emilia wore her winter coat over her footed pajamas or wrapped herself in a blanket while she watched television on the futon. Even with the added electric heaters (that my landlord did not approve of) going full blast, all the thermometers stayed in the low fifties. When I started to think the inside of our house was too cold, I'd take off my coat and go stand on the porch for a minute or two so when I came back in it felt a lot warmer than it had before. The plastic I had taped around the windows moved so much with the wind gusts that I thought it might come loose.

On the first Saturday of December, several downtown Missoula businesses joined together in a daylong celebration of the Christmas tree lighting, complete with a parade ending with Santa Claus joining a choir singing carols, where they had fires burning in barrels and hot chocolate and cider passed around with candy canes. That year, despite the negative temperatures, Emilia and I joined our friend Britt and her son to hit as many free activities as we could. Britt had also moved to Missoula from Alaska with her son, Canyon, and worked as a local musician. We'd connected after an old friend of mine from Fairbanks mentioned us to one another and I'd gone to one of her shows to introduce myself. We thought bundling up to spend the day outside at negative thirty-five degrees would be a fitting activity for a couple of former Alaskans.

We waited in line for almost an hour in the main lobby of the Florence Hotel for the kids to get the chance to sit on Santa's lap. Emilia wouldn't tell me what she was going to ask him for, but I was happy to snap a photo of her sitting on his lap in her bright pink snow bibs and the tennis shoes her dad bought her.

"I know he's not real, Mom," she said to me afterward. "It's just a nice thing to do for Christmas." She skipped ahead of me, her coat, which was also from her dad, unzipped despite the bitter cold.

We hit almost everything on the list of shops giving out free food or opportunities to do a craft project. Bernice's Bakery had a long table set up for kids to decorate their own sugar cookies. The carousel down at Caras Park had fires outside to roast marshmallows for s'mores in addition to free rides. One of the fancy restaurants, Scotty's Table, offered free fries. I'd never been there before and felt like an imposter, especially with two rowdy kids jumping up and down from the sugar rush.

We all went back home to warm up and met again for the parade. This was our second Christmas parade in Missoula, and even though we'd stood on the same street to watch countless marching bands and decorated cars with people throwing candy go by, it was especially shocking to see so many people braving the below-freezing temperatures. We all stuffed our chins in our scarves, waving hands covered in huge mittens to welcome Santa, sing carols, and watch a bunch of tiny white lights draped around a large tree turn on after we counted down from ten to one. Everyone seemed so happy to stand around barrels with fires blazing inside, drinking free hot chocolate and cider offered by a coffee shop close by.

Downtown Missoula came alive with the community who filled it during these times. I'd never experienced anything like it. The time felt precious, even then, before we knew how much gentrification would change it all. Somehow I knew I was lucky to get there just in time to witness and feel Missoula's community in its purest form. Maybe we all sensed we were lucky to get these last few years together after the recession and before inflation raked us through the coals. For now we could afford to work and live there, and that was all that mattered. We were home in what felt like the purest sense, huddled together to warm our hands while a choir sang the second verse of "Jingle Bells."

There wasn't a feeling of a class divide that day. I never felt like my kid was the one on food stamps showing up to take advantage of charity. For a whole day, we were able to enjoy all the activities with everyone else, and no one knew we wouldn't have been able to afford it if they'd charged money.

———

For those two weeks between my school semester ending and Emilia beginning Christmas break, almost every one of my clients gave me a cash tip for the holidays, totaling nearly one hundred dollars. I decided to use some of it to buy myself a pair of maternity jeans, since none of my pants fit anymore. I didn't know where to go except the maternity clothes place in the mall. With Emilia's pregnancy, several of my friends had been pregnant around the same time or just had babies, so there were piles of maternity clothes that got passed around from one person to the next. Here the only place I knew about was that Christian organization—where I'd have to earn points to get clothes—and I was too tired and weary to ask for help from anyone else. Although I was increasingly at peace with my decision, I didn't have the energy to answer questions about my plans or why having another child was even a possibility for me, or how I thought it would all work out. All I knew was that I had a feeling it would. Judging by Kristi's reaction, it seemed like my impoverished status shouldn't allow me that kind of confidence, and had robbed me from sharing my joy with others.

Now that Emilia knew (and seemed to be excited) about her pending big-sister status, for the moment she was the only one I felt like I could share my giddy feelings about the pregnancy with. In the maternity store, she oohed and aahed with me at the dresses and lacy shirts. When I tried on the jeans, pulling the large elastic piece of fabric over my belly, sticking it out as far as I could, Emilia exclaimed, "Wow, Mom, your belly is gigantic!" I heard the women who were helping me chuckle. They had a clearance rack of maternity jeans, so I decided to get two pairs for thirty bucks. Emilia needed new shoes again and having someone measure her feet and help her try on different pairs made us feel fancy.

Afterward, I suggested we go out to eat at Red Robin. Eating at this restaurant was usually saved for occasions like birthdays and the last day of school, but I figured we needed the boost in morale. She got the mac and cheese with a cup of mandarin oranges and I got the teriyaki chicken burger with fries. For a few minutes it felt like we were normal: Like this was something we did when cooking at home was too daunting of a task. Like we went to the mall once or twice a month as opposed to hardly ever. Emilia could feel the crossed dimension, too. I know she could. Or maybe she just felt so fancy, sitting there, having someone ask her if she would like another Sprite with a maraschino cherry.

# 14

# I Want to Be a Writer

Professor Katie Kane's office was an entirely different experience than the space I'd occupied with David Gates. For one, Katie loved my research project idea on attempting to pinpoint the beginning of the desensitization of rape culture through media meant for children, giving me glowing feedback on the first four pages I'd handed in. We also had a shared experience of coming from different backgrounds. Katie had the same hard look of determination in her eyes that I did and knew the life of grasping tightly to your dreams, and holding on to them wherever they took you. Also, she was just really cool and I had been in awe of her since our first day of class.

"I've kind of gone way beyond the requirements for this assignment," I said, handing her my list of works cited.

Katie's eyes got a little wide and she chuckled. "I wouldn't expect anything else from you, Ms. Land."

"Well, I plan to use it for my expository essay to apply for my MFA candidacy."

She made an approving face. "Aren't the applications due relatively soon?"

"January third or something? Maybe it's as late as the tenth." I took a deep breath. "I took the GRE earlier this week. I'm pretty sure I did okay, but I've been having all those lovely illnesses from elementary school run through me lately."

"Say no more," she said, turning her head to one side and holding up two hands. "I remember those years." Katie, too, had raised kids on her own, and I suppose she still was, even though hers were older.

"I'm nervous about the application," I said, looking down at my hands, wanting to muster the courage to tell her I was worried about Judy Blunt finding out I was pregnant. I could still hide my belly under my biggest, baggiest sweatshirt, but those days were coming to a fast end. I hoped to avoid Judy just long enough that she wouldn't find out before my application was decided upon. I also wondered if they might possibly let me delay my start date by a semester. I had no idea what was reasonable to expect or ask for. Ideally, the decision committee, the gatekeepers, understanding a broader spectrum of my history and work, should have been in my favor, but it felt distinctly the opposite. They didn't only know my work, they knew me—including the fact that I was a poor single mom. I saw no reason why I would want to share with them that I was now pregnant by an unknown and assumed absent biological father, but they'd eventually know that, too. "I'm nervous about Judy saying kids don't belong in grad school."

"Judy said that?"

"Yeah, a couple years ago when I first met with her about my intent to change my major and apply to the program."

"Interesting." She held eye contact for a moment or two, possibly considering what to say. "Ms. Land, you are the type of person this program needs the most."

"Me?"

"Absolutely." She held up my research paper for emphasis. "Yes. We need more of this kind of work ethic from people who don't have an Ivy League background, you know what I mean?"

"You mean working class?" I wanted to believe her. Instead I glanced down at my fingers to keep them from fidgeting. "Yeah. Judy said something about that, that the committee will only occasionally accept a, um, scholarship case from a needs-based background, but they'd already done that recently." I was uncomfortable admitting these things, even though I was in the safest place to say them out loud.

"Oh did she." She sat back in her chair, but didn't say anything else.

"I wanted to ask if you might write a letter of recommendation for me."

"I would love to," she said with conviction. "When are they due?"

"Ten days after I submit it, so mid-January sometime."

She turned to her desk to write something down on the large desk calendar that took up most of the surface. "Could you email me to remind me? I write a lot of reference letters."

"Sure, I can do that. Thank you." I gave her a half grin, trying not to let tears well in my eyes. I wanted to tell her how monumental she'd been that semester, yet at the time it was more of a vague feeling and one I couldn't put into words. Generosity usually felt that way to me, like a scratch that satisfied an itch I didn't know the source of. I wouldn't be able to fully comprehend how much that meeting in her office affected me for several years. Our twenty minutes were almost up so I started to get my stuff together to go.

"Best of luck to you, Ms. Land," she said before adding, "Come and talk to me anytime."

Almost halfway through my senior year of college, and that was the only time any of my instructors and professors—through three different colleges—had said that to me.

———————

Emilia's time at her dad's was never simple or easy, for about a dozen reasons. First, it forced me to communicate with my abuser, who still relished opportunities to call me a selfish piece of shit, and to tell me that no one would ever love me. Then we had to organize when our daughter would fly on a plane, alone, from one house to the other, and when. When she was gone that holiday week, I moped. I watched movies and entire Ken Burns documentaries about a war, not moving far from the couch except to pee or eat, both of which had become increasingly necessary as I entered the second trimester of my pregnancy.

Whenever she returned from a trip to her dad's, my kid wasn't the same as the one who'd left me just a week or so before. Maybe that was a huge part of my moping: anticipating the return. At six years old, she couldn't articulate the rage she felt. Emilia has never been the type to tell me everything that happened in one sitting. I got snippets, like puzzle pieces, that I'd have to parse in order to figure out the bigger picture. This time, though, her rage was apparent. She yelled.

The anger she showed one morning before school didn't resemble our past four months of mornings in the slightest way. It came as a surprise; she'd clung to me all weekend and cried, asking to sit with me and watch movies. Since her return on the plane, I'd heard that Jamie told her about the child support modification in his own, manipulative ways. When Emilia had picked out a necklace at a store for her Christmas present, Jamie told her he couldn't buy it because he had to pay me so much money, then added that I would just throw it in the garbage anyway. His mom, who'd flown in from North Carolina to take care of Emilia while Jamie was at work, cried with my six-year-old over the tragedy of me supposedly putting a piece of jewelry in the trash.

Jamie packed a lot into those ten days. He made it clear that he might not be able to see Emilia again because I had gone to court to ask for more money. It alarmed me to hear my daughter say this. This was, frankly, none of her fucking business, but protecting his daughter from worry didn't seem like it was that important to Jamie. Emilia returned from her dad's house absolutely hating me. This was always his way, but this time it was worse, and more than I could handle. About five minutes after I had to leave to drive Emilia to school, she sat on the entryway floor, pulling on her rubber boots. We hadn't made it to catch the bus and she would be a little late, but that was fine, comparatively speaking. My sweet kid's heart was broken for the hundredth time. Five minutes late did not matter in the grand scheme of things. Her school wouldn't understand, but that didn't matter, either.

I watched her, sitting in her pink snow pants and purple coat with the hood nearly covering her face, struggling to pull on her boot. I knew I couldn't help her; I probably wasn't supposed to be watching her. She'd get mad if she caught me. Nighttime had been a different story. Every bedtime routine since she'd gotten back from her dad's had been full of guttural sobs. She begged me to tell her when she would see her dad again, and my chest hollowed with helplessness. Inwardly, I hissed and seethed. How could any human being do this to a child? With absolute certainty, I knew he wanted this scene to happen.

I turned away from her to the kitchen, where I'd left my precious one cup of half-decaf coffee, and Emilia let out a primal growl. I swung my head around just in time to see her scream and kick off her boots.

"What are you doing?" I blurted. "Emilia, we're late!"

She stuck out her chin and crossed her arms. "I'm not wearing socks today!" To emphasize, she pulled off both her socks and threw them at me. It had snowed a foot over the weekend. She absolutely had to wear socks. I stomped to her dresser and pulled out a different pair of socks, came back to hand them to her, and she slapped my hand to bat it away. I tried to grab her feet to put the socks on myself and she kicked with such strength I thought she might catch my jaw. So I did what any exasperated parent would do: I picked up my fifty-plus-pound child and carried her like a large sack of potatoes to the car, kicking and screaming all the way.

I'm sure the neighbors heard, but I didn't care. My breath came out in huffs by the time I sat in the driver's seat. I put my hand on my stomach, attempting to calm a Braxton-Hicks contraction that had spiked from the sudden movement while Emilia screamed at me from the backseat. I don't remember what she said, or what I said in response, and I'm grateful for that. We both probably are.

When we got to her school, I parked by the curb nearest to the front door, since there weren't any buses or other people around. Emilia opened the door and took off running before I stomped the parking brake into place. She'd never done something like that, and a wash of terror swept over me. She ran for the entrance to the school and stood watching me with her hand on the lever to open it. When I was ten feet away, she pushed it to enter, letting the door close behind her. I took a deep breath and walked inside, catching a glimpse of Emilia at the top of the stairwell to go down to her class. I signed her in, smiling at the woman who worked at the front desk, and walked toward my daughter to escort her downstairs. Emilia took two steps down, one step up, three steps down, two steps up, and I finally told her to hurry up because she was late. She repeated the sequence, only gaining one step down in about twenty seconds. I firmly said, again, that she needed to get to class. Her hair parted away from her chin to reveal her smiling mouth. I'd had it. I walked back to the front office, trying my hardest not to burst into tears, and asked the woman sitting behind the glass if she would please escort my kid to where she needed to go. "I can't," I said, a single tear streaking down my cheek.

Back in the driver's seat of my car, I gasped to stifle sobs. I had a lot to do that day. My MFA application was due, I had my first day at my new (temporary) nannying job, and I had to gather evidence to make the case that I deserved more child support. I'd spent the last of my money on rent and had three weeks until I'd get my student loan check and didn't feel like I could ask to be paid on my first day after we agreed they'd pay me on Fridays. There wasn't any food for me to eat. All I had was what I could purchase with my WIC checks and whatever food I'd bought for Emilia.

At home, I walked into the kitchen without looking in the fridge or the one cupboard we had. Every cent in my bank account was spoken for. My credit cards were maxed out. I didn't need to scan the shelves to know what there was to consume: grape juice and peanut butter. They'd been my staples for the last week, and they didn't sound appetizing in the slightest. I sat in the chair at my kitchen table, defeated, and glanced over at the digital clock on the back of the electric stove. Nine o'clock. The food bank would open soon, but just for a few hours.

Missoula's food bank at that time was a small, one-story building nestled between Flipper's, my favorite bar, and Bernice's, my favorite bakery. During the hours it was open, parking in that area was impossible, and I'd heard people complain about that. The street the food bank's front door faced got a lot of local traffic, and people crowded outside waiting to be let in. It was all very *visible*. In my present state—pregnant and about to enter a legal battle for more child support and a potential candidate for a local MFA program—the last thing I wanted was for anyone to know I needed free food.

But I was also hungry.

I was almost six months pregnant and hungry.

Without housecleaning, decluttering, or organizing to do (because I'd done all that in December), I sat in my chair, tucked under our small table, and watched the minutes tick by. I knew what the food bank's limited hours were because the lady on the other end of the line when I had dialed 211 told me.

I just couldn't bring myself to get up and go do it. To me, my hunger was my fault. I'd chosen to go to college instead of work full-time. I'd chosen to keep a pregnancy. I'd chosen to, what, live in a town with almost nonexistent affordable housing? How many more failings could I list in that moment? A lot. I seemed to come up with a new one every fucking minute. My resounding conclusion was that I'd brought this on myself. My last fifty bucks was on hold for the fee to officially apply for a Master of Fine Arts in nonfiction creative writing. I'd been working on the essays I would submit for writing samples for two years. But it was fifty fucking bucks that I could have spent on food. How ridiculous was that? I'd made decisions that got me to where I was, sitting at that table, wiping tears and snot from my face, watching time tick by, attempting to garner motivation to go to a food bank.

Ultimately, I decided that I didn't deserve to go.

My phone vibrated in my pocket, and I frowned at the number before I flipped it open. I knew the number was Emilia's school and wondered if it was the call from the principal that she'd mentioned last month. Had they compounded events? I almost didn't want to know what they were about to tell me.

"Hello, Ms. Land? I have Emilia here with me and she's feeling really sad. She wanted me to call and ask if you could bring Blueberry to school?"

"Blueberry?" I stood and walked to her bed. The small blue stuffed mouse was next to her pillow like he usually was. It had been a gift from a friend when she was born and a constant companion since she turned and smiled at him when she was only six days old. Blueberry was too precious to bring to her dad's for fear she'd lose him or forget to bring him home, so Emilia would ask about him whenever we got to talk on the phone. She seemed to like that he kept me company while she was away, and I would tell her about his adventures to the grocery store.

"Yes, Emilia says that she would really like to have him with her today."

"Um, okay, I'll go there right now."

Later that day, when I was already at my nanny job, I got another call from the school, but from the principal. Apparently two older boys thought it was great fun to chase my kid around on the playground and tackle her.

"I guess they held her down and told her they were going to have sex with her," the principal told me. He sounded merely exasperated, not horrified.

"They did *what*?"

He repeated what he said and not much else. I asked if the boys got in trouble and he said they had to sit on the wall for the rest of recess. My kindergartner got a detention for being tardy three times in one month but when kids held her down and threatened to rape her they got a time-out. No wonder she'd needed Blueberry. I felt simultaneously furious and heartbroken. Emilia was due to get off the bus in ten minutes. His timing had been impeccable. I offered a flat thanks for letting me know before ending the call.

Emilia didn't run to me when she got off the bus. Our horrible morning had faded from both our memories—or been replaced with other sources of anguish—and I wished we could go home and curl up in bed and eat some french fries from McDonald's. Instead we walked to the house where I'd been quietly sitting for the last hour and a half while an infant slept upstairs, reviewing the two sample essays I planned to submit with my grad school application. Emilia walked at a pace that was half her normal speed, looking down at her feet dragging on the ground.

"Did Blueberry keep you company today?" I got a nod in response. Blueberry was nestled in the crook of her arm, and she hugged him a little tighter. "He's a good friend, huh."

I wanted to be able to tell her we could go get some ice cream or a Happy Meal, but all I had were a few crackers and a juice box. Most of all, I wanted to find out who the boys were that tackled her so I could see their faces in my fantasy where I yelled at them and kicked their asses and they begged me for mercy. It unnerved me to know that my daughter wasn't protected from things like that in kindergarten. The principal promised it would never happen again, but I cared that it had happened in the first place. I also wondered what the *other* call was supposed to be about. What else had happened to Emilia? Had the principal decided not to tell me?

"Can we go home, Mama?" I opened the car door to put her backpack in the seat next to her booster.

"Not yet, sweetheart," I said with a sigh. "We still have an hour."

That night, after she was asleep, I paid the application fee and clicked SUBMIT. I was officially an MFA applicant. Three of my professors had agreed to write letters of recommendation, and I'd be able to see those when they had submitted them. I wouldn't know if I was accepted for several weeks but I couldn't imagine not getting in. I wasn't sure what I would do if I didn't. The MFA program wasn't important simply for the degree; it would offer job security and a possible career as a teacher. Also, as a funded student, I hopefully wouldn't have to take out more student loans since I would get paid a stipend to teach a composition class and tuition would be covered. My GRE score had been surprisingly good and I made the dean's list again, so I wasn't worried about that. Competition wasn't as great as it once was, either. All in all, with the exception of Judy's belief that babies didn't belong in grad school, I was an excellent prospective candidate.

With a sigh, I reached up to close my laptop, revealing the pile of papers behind it. My hearing with the administrative law judge was a few days away and preparation began to feel futile. Jamie had submitted bank statements highlighting every cent he'd spent on food and Christmas presents for Emilia as proof that he shouldn't have to pay more in child support—despite the fact that he made three thousand dollars a month more than I did. Jamie had told me many times that the only reason he paid child support was that he could use it to his advantage if I ever brought him to court for anything. He'd also made it clear that he expected me to save all the money he gave me, put it in a savings account, and give it to Emilia when she turned eighteen. He wanted her to know it was from him. When we were still together, when I was saving every penny to get my own place, he had waved dollar bills in front of my face to make fun of me for not being able to afford to go out to eat. His need to financially control me stretched the whole five hundred fifty-one miles to Missoula, Montana.

I wondered if I should prepare for the hearing by highlighting every hateful, threatening comment he'd made in emails to me. But I knew none of that would matter to the judge. Jamie would be seen in a favorable light because he'd always paid child support. For most judges, that seemed to be like a breath of fresh air. It also wouldn't matter that Emilia had stayed home from school for a day because she couldn't stop crying, since from the outside it was a natural reaction to missing a parent. If I even tried to bring it up and the reasons why, I would be seen as manipulative and vengeful. It wouldn't matter that there was a police report that documented domestic violence, or the fact that I only had ten bucks in my bank account. Instead, I risked those two things reflecting badly on me. Our judge probably wouldn't care that Jamie had paid so little in child support prior to this, because it was the only way I could get him to sign off on us moving to Montana. Or that he'd given up his six weeks of summer visitation twice. I wondered if my daughter and I factored into any of the judge's calculations at all.

The hearing itself would take place over the phone and I would have to call in from the YWCA, since it had to be from a landline. I wasn't sure if Jamie would be there in person, but I hoped he had to call in, too; otherwise he might charm the judge. He was good at that. When the hearing began, I put the phone on speaker and sat on my hands to keep them from shaking. In front of me, on an empty desk in a spare office, were my talking points but now none of them made sense. Jamie had called in, too, but I knew the odds were in his favor just for showing up.

I thought I'd be able to make some kind of statement, but the judge only wanted to know how much money I made and why I was underemployed.

"I'm a full-time student," I said.

"Why aren't you taking classes that meet online or that allow you to work full-time?" Her voice was simultaneously stern and condescending. I wondered what she looked like, but all I could picture was Judge Judy.

"I'm getting a bachelor's degree," I said. "I graduate in May."

"And what are your plans after that?"

"I applied for grad school to get my Master of Fine Arts in creative writing," I said, doubting that answer would go over well.

"So you are voluntarily underemployed," she said. I imagined her taking notes.

"I work full-time in the summer," I said. "I have a part-time job as a nanny currently."

"And what company is that for?"

"It's not for a company, I'm self-employed."

"Ms. Land," she began, her voice growing increasingly annoyed, "when was the last time you worked for an employer?"

"When I first moved to Missoula," I said, trying to remember what the name of the company was. "I cleaned an office building at night."

"How much were you paid for this work?"

"Fifteen dollars an hour."

"Oh!" Her voice changed, but I couldn't figure out if it was due to excitement that I'd revealed something or not. "And you worked there full-time?"

"No, it was part-time," I said, trying to remember how many hours a week I worked there. "It was about four hours a night, between ten and two in the morning, and six hours on Sunday." She didn't respond and I wondered if she was writing that down. "Those aren't normal wages for Missoula, though. I don't get paid that much for other jobs I do. I think I got extra because the hours weren't regular work hours."

"So at fifteen dollars an hour, if you had worked full-time, your monthly salary would be twenty-four hundred?"

"I guess so?"

"Why didn't you include this in your modification paperwork?"

"I only had that job for a month. It wasn't sustainable because I got so little sleep. And it was two years ago."

"So you voluntarily left that position?"

"No, I was actually fired." I hung my head. The job was cleaning a huge building full of realtors' offices. There must have been a hundred. I had to empty trash cans at all their desks along with cleaning several bathrooms and common areas. If I forgot anything or did an unsatisfying job, a realtor emailed my boss to complain. My boss would then compile all the complaints into an email and send them to me. After reading one particularly lengthy list, I replied in a crass way, saying something along the lines of their complaints were bullshit. The next day, my boss emailed to set up a meeting to tell me they were letting me go because I lied on my application. They had finally run my credit report and found a bankruptcy. As if that had any bearing on my ability to empty garbage cans. The job was so awful that I didn't fight it; I shook my head and said okay. I didn't want Jamie to know any of this.

"You were fired," she repeated.

"Yes," I replied, not giving an explanation. I wasn't sure if I could be fired for the reason my boss gave, but I knew it wouldn't benefit me to say any more about that.

"Why didn't you get another job?"

"Your Honor, I have a job. I'm self-employed."

"Right," she said.

I felt flushed with humiliation, and I wondered if that was the whole point. This was a child support hearing, not a criminal case, but I felt like I'd been charged with negligence or worse, and I needed to defend myself for going to college. I didn't have a chance to advocate for myself, or say any of my talking points.

Her questions for Jamie were in a completely different, approving tone. At one point they shared a laugh. He had the full-time job; he worked swing shifts and got overtime. She even seemed empathetic toward Jamie when he mournfully said his summer visits were limited because he had to work.

The implication was that while Jamie was hardworking, I was a slacker, career college student. But the only way my life worked financially or otherwise was to have a job that I could fit between classes and child care. My schedule for spring semester was grueling, and I had to be in class every weekday, not just Tuesday and Thursday like I usually did to maintain my clients. My required Shakespeare class met for one hour on Monday, Wednesday, and Friday, from eleven to noon. There wasn't enough time for me to schedule a house before or after that, since they were all three- to four-hour cleans; either I'd be getting there before everyone left for the day or staying after Emilia got out of school, or I would have to cut their time in half. My roommate couldn't help with child care most days because of his job, and I could no longer afford for him to barter child care for rent anyway.

My hands hadn't completely stopped shaking by the time I got to the house to start the nanny job that afternoon. I'd been so stressed that I hadn't been able to eat before I left home, but suddenly I was ravenous. All I had were Emilia's after-school snacks to last the next four hours, which would be a problem. I figured they wouldn't mind if I ate something at their house but I didn't want to make that assumption and have it turn out to be wrong. I'd always been careful not to sneak a bite of a cleaning client's food they had sitting out on the counters, and at one point learned I'd been literally baited while a hidden camera recorded me. All that paranoia of being watched never left me, no matter how decent the folks seemed to be.

Distraught, I wondered just how much worse I had made things for Emilia by asking for more child support. Instead of helping me, all it did was upset Jamie even more while giving him fuel for whatever he chose to throw back at us. Like me, Emilia hated surprises. Surprise meant instability (a car that didn't start, a father who doesn't show up for his video chat), and we both liked to know what was going to happen. She packed her suitcase to go to her dad's a month in advance. If the dentist or doctor were vague about what was going to happen, Emilia would do anything she could to get away, out of the room, and once hid in the bathroom and refused to come out because she knew they were lying about her getting a shot. Jamie had always used uncertainty as a way to manipulate and emotionally control me, and it was deeply painful to see him now doing the same things with Emilia. When we lived together or nearby, he tended to make me the outlet for his anger. But when I refused to engage, Emilia was his target—and he used her to get at me.

Including pregnancy, most of my time as a mother had been spent weighing the pros and cons between a horrible and not-so-great situation. There hardly ever was a good choice. If a good choice presented itself, there was usually a catch, a barrier, or a hurdle I'd have to jump over and, in trying, I would heartbreakingly discover it was too difficult to make it to the other side. There was not a lot of hope in my life. I had preparation, constant guessing, and bracing myself for the worst. It made for an insecure existence that drained me with its relentless mental acrobatics.

———

Emilia's face brightened when she stepped off the bus, then her head drooped in the five or so steps it took to reach where I stood, waiting with the other parents on the street corner. I longed to be able to talk to her. I had debated finding a therapist for her and maybe it was time to do that. I had signed up Emilia for Medicaid (a program called Healthy Montana Kids) to supplement what her dad's insurance wouldn't cover. But most therapists in town didn't accept Medicaid, or only took on two or three clients who had it. Medicaid paid about half of what therapists billed for their services and a lot of them didn't appreciate that. With the help of the Healthy Montana Kids program, there should be no copays, and a therapist would come at no cost. I just had to find one who would accept it.

"How was school today?" I asked as she reached up for my hand. My other held the baby monitor that, in almost two weeks on the job, had yet to alert me to a crying baby.

Emilia shrugged, looking down as she walked.

"Did you make any art that you liked?"

"We took pictures with what we wanted to be when we grew up written on a chalkboard," she said, perking up a little.

"Oh yeah? What did you say you wanted to be?"

"A writer," she said. "Just like you, Mom."

"You wanna be a writer like me?" I chuckled. "What do you think a writer does?"

Emilia let go of my hand and mimed furious typing while making a stern face at an imaginary computer screen.

"What's that face? Is that a writer's face?" I laughed. "Aw, do I ever look like I'm having fun?"

"Yeah, you and your friends have fun when you're talking about writing and reading to each other."

"You're right, we do have fun when we do that." I missed those nights, staying up with my roommate Kelley, drinking wine and reading poems to each other.

As much as I was flattered that she wanted to be a writer, I knew it wasn't necessarily a profession I wished for my daughter. College was supposed to teach me how to write, and it did, in the sense of forcing me to sit down and produce words that flowed together well and created a story arc. I had learned a *lot* about story arcs. But I hadn't learned a thing about how to make a living by writing them. Most writers I knew didn't make a living at writing. I didn't know how or where I would learn to write an actual book, let alone get one published.

"Did you bring snacks?" Emilia asked.

"Yup, I brought you some of those cheese crackers you like so much."

"The ones with the elf?"

"Those are the ones!" I despised these crackers. They tasted like sweet rubber with cheese-flavored paste holding them together. Emilia pulled on my hand. We were at the back door of the house by then, and Emilia, knowing that a sleeping baby was inside, slowly opened the door and let herself in. By the time I got to the kitchen, she'd already found a seat at the table, unpacked the small tote bag where I kept her snacks, and had the crackers in her hand. I watched her expertly open them and arrange them on the table, then unpack the juice box and carefully insert the straw where it belonged. My stomach growled. Emilia looked up at me and smiled, swinging her feet. Sounds of a baby's babbles crackled over the monitor. We both looked at it and sighed.

"I'll go get that," I said, and turned to walk upstairs.

# 15

# Lil' Sister

At thirty-five, my "geriatric" pregnancy required a menagerie of tests, screenings, and ultrasounds. My midwife's office had an older, portable ultrasound they used to listen to the heartbeat and show an image of a grainy blob that could be baby-shaped if you used your imagination. Emilia and I both were anxious to find out if it would be a little sister or brother. I'd had one official ultrasound already at about thirteen weeks to test for brain or spinal abnormalities, but the one at twenty weeks would be a thorough test for birth defects. They'd also be able to announce the sex with certainty.

Morale had been low in our house lately. My nanny job had provided some much-needed income for January while I waited for student loan money and for me to be on food stamps again. While I braced for the administrative law judge's decision, the "yes" or "no" on grad school, and the boost in food money, I decided we both needed to attend the appointment where we'd get to see this small human who was growing in my body. Emilia already liked to try to feel the butterfly kicks with her hand at bedtime.

My appointment was first thing in the morning the day before my final semester of my senior year of college began, which made it easy to drop off Emilia at kindergarten before lunchtime and then run around to do some final preparations for my classes. I still needed a notebook, computer paper, ink cartridges, and several different types of snacks. Tuesday's and Thursday's schedules were three classes back-to-back with only ten-minute breaks and I honestly wasn't sure how I'd be able to do that, given the first class was all the way across campus, in a building mainly housing instruction for math and science. Until I had my syllabi for the semester, I wouldn't know if I could continue to work or not. With three literature classes, I assumed I wouldn't, since they'd require heavy loads of reading and response papers to write in addition to whatever would be required from my writing workshop. Luckily, all my classes were within the hours that Emilia was at school, but if I was able to squeeze in a house to clean after my Shakespeare class, homework would mostly be done while she wasn't.

After we parked at the building where they had the ultrasound machine, Emilia jumped out of the car and shut the door herself before she stood to wait for me on the sidewalk.

"Mo-om, you're so slow!" I hoped she was trying to be funny.

"Well, I guess we'll get to see who's the reason for that in a minute!" I said, reaching for her hand. Emilia jumped and skipped while we walked to the door but quieted down when we got to the lobby. Every doctor's office was like a tranquilizer for this kid.

In the waiting room, I told Emilia to sit in a chair while I checked in. The receptionist was nice, but peered around me to eye the kid in the bright pink coat swinging her feet while she contemplated the posters of families on the walls. I wasn't sure if they got a lot of kids in there, and I didn't want to explain why mine was with me.

We must have been the first appointment of the day because a woman with a clipboard came out and called my name as soon as I sat down.

"Come on, Emilia," I said, reaching for her hand. She seemed shy all of a sudden so I reassured her about what was going to happen. "They're just going to put the gel on my belly and use the thing that lets them see inside, remember?" Her finger went to her mouth, something she'd done since she was a toddler when she felt unsure.

The woman with the clipboard chimed in. "And you'll get to see your baby sister or brother on the big screen!" I turned my head quickly to give her a grateful look and she added a wink to her smile. Emilia's head popped up to look at the lady for the first time, then she glanced at me. I gave her my biggest smile while nodding, doing my best to hide my nervousness. The technician, of course, wouldn't give me any diagnosis or even a clue there was one, but it was still nerve-racking to walk into that office with a six-year-old who might not fully understand what a birth defect meant after seeing an active baby on a big screen.

My pregnancy with Emilia had been incredibly hands-off. Aside from two ultrasounds to help diagnose something that was going on with me, there were no blood tests or sugary drinks or mentions of possible birth defects. There was one midwife within the city limits who only did home births and used a stethoscope to listen to the heartbeat and a tape measure to judge how the pregnancy was progressing. At twenty-eight, I hadn't been so much younger than I was now at thirty-five, but suddenly it seemed like everything that possibly could go wrong was mentioned more than once. I usually joked with people that I was perpetually twenty-three, stuck at that age both in looks and maturity, but every time I went to my current midwife's office it was like they had to wipe the dust off me before they could take a look at things.

The technician had me recline on a long, padded chair, and I automatically lifted up both my hoodie and T-shirt, then pulled the elastic band down on my maternity jeans. She tucked a piece of paper into them and commented that they were cute.

"I helped pick them out!" Emilia said, her chin almost resting on my shoulder.

"Well, you have very good taste!" said the technician. I wondered how often the person getting the ultrasound was accompanied by a child instead of a partner but blinked a couple of times in an effort to get the thought out of my head. Sometimes I had to force myself to focus on the joy so the sadness wouldn't creep in. Even though I had chosen to do this alone, this wasn't the social norm, illustrated plainly in all the posters and magazines in the waiting area. I'd heard the "children need two parents" messaging through the years so many times it caused my stomach to turn just thinking about it. It screamed *You're not enough!* in a way that could only be silenced by internalizing it. If mothers were generally devalued compared to fathers in our culture, it was even worse for single mothers—it often felt to me as if we shouldn't exist at all.

The room lit up with the grainy blue image that came onto the screen. Emilia and I both gasped when we saw the profile with the forehead, nose, and mouth with a hand not too far away. For a second it looked like the thumb might go into the mouth but the whole image moved as I felt a light kick in my side.

"That's an active one!" the technician said.

"Yeah, I've heard that a few times," I said with a chuckle. "Especially with this one here." I looked over at Emilia and she made a fake grumpy face before her eyes went back to the screen.

Everything was quiet for several minutes while the technician moved the wand around my belly and made lines on the screen and clicked and printed photos. Emilia and I watched the baby move and stretch and look as if it was trying to get away from the thing invading its privacy. Finally, we heard, "Would you like to know if it's a boy or girl?"

I nodded and Emilia said, "That's why I'm here!"

The technician laughed and moved the wand to my lower right side. "Let's see if we can get some cooperation here."

Two leglike shapes showed up on the screen and I whispered to Emilia that we were looking at its butt. She giggled but shushed me. "Is that the cord?" I asked, squinting a little to make out what looked like a smaller, third leg. We got nothing but silence for an answer as the technician pressed the wand harder into my side. Finally, the legs kicked and the third smaller leg thing moved, revealing a crevice.

"Looks like we have a girl!" the technician announced.

Emilia jumped up and down and tugged on the hood of my sweatshirt a few times.

"Are you happy about that?" the technician asked her.

Emilia nodded, and I thought she might actually be speechless.

"Emilia's been wanting a little sister for a really long time," I said.

"Can I see her face again?" Emilia asked.

The technician said, "How about if we use the three-D version?" The screen turned a shade of yellowish orange, filling the room with a warm glow. A human face appeared on the screen, with a flat-looking nose and closed eyelids.

"She looks funny," Emilia said. I laughed while the technician printed out a few more photos for us.

"She's really little," I said. "Like the size of a big potato."

"Smaller than this?" Emilia held up her baby doll who'd seen better years.

"Much smaller than that," I said.

Emilia frowned. "But she'll get bigger, right?" I swung my legs to sit up and pulled my shirt down, struggling to get my hooded sweatshirt back over my stomach. "Will she play with me? I want to play with her." She stood in front of me, unmoving, waiting for an answer.

I didn't want to make any promises like that until I knew the results. "Hey," I said, reaching to put my hand on her upper arm. "Let's get home, okay? Maybe I can make some pancakes and I'll drop you off at school after lunch."

"Can I just stay with you?" She had tears in her eyes.

"Aw, sweetie," I said, putting my other hand on her shoulder. "Do you want a hug?" She took a step forward to stand between my legs so I could wrap my arms around her and rub her back.

"Take your time," the technician said as she left the room.

"Let's get home, okay?" I said again, rubbing her back a bit more. Her six-year-old frame relaxed a bit. "This must be kinda hard, huh? I was really little when I became a big sister, so I don't remember it." I scooted my butt to the edge of the seat so I could stand.

"Did you like being a big sister?"

"Um, yeah," I said, reaching for her coat and holding it up for her to put her arms through the sleeves. "I had a little brother, though, and he could be pretty gross and annoying. You'll be a lot older than your little sister so you'll get to teach her things." We walked out of the dark room and into the fluorescent-lit office, where two other pregnant women sat in chairs. I gave them a half smile as I reached for my daughter's hand on the way to the door.

At home, I asked if Emilia would write "LIL SISTER" on my stomach and pose next to it as a way to announce on Facebook that it was a girl. She made a face at first, then realized it meant drawing on my skin with a marker. In the photo, she's still in her pink coat, smiling, thumb pointed toward my belly. She looked happy, but I had seen the anxiety in her eyes that morning when she realized there was an actual human growing inside me. I'd felt it, too, but in a different way. I still hoped there weren't any heart or lung or brain defects and everything would be okay. I hoped my pregnancy would stay healthy enough for me to finish the semester, where I'd graduate only a month before my daughter was due. I hoped to make it there mostly unscathed.

———

Emilia got a new notebook and pen when we went shopping for my school supplies. I told her she could start drawing pictures for her sister or write some things down about how she felt. I thought it could be a good transition into bringing her to her first appointment with the new art-based children's therapist. Emilia had never been to a therapist before, and part of the reason I felt it was so important now was to document what I suspected was emotional abuse that my daughter experienced. Though difficult, I knew the therapy sessions would be necessary if I wanted to modify our parenting plan. Jamie always fought to have the sections stating the presence of domestic violence removed, and a few times he had refused to sign the modification to allow us to move to Missoula unless I took those paragraphs out. Emotional abuse was almost impossible to prove, and wasn't considered domestic violence in most courts. If I came to court claiming my six-year-old had been emotionally abused, not only would I be laughed at, but they'd probably rule in favor of the father on the assumption I had malicious intent. A statement from a professional would be necessary if I wanted to attempt to shorten his visitation time. There was one thing that troubled me about this: I couldn't be sure if my motivation was to help my kid's current strife or my future self in court proceedings. Given how awful he was to both of us, I ultimately didn't think there was much of a difference.

The midwife called to tell me I had a perfectly healthy baby on the same day the notification about my food stamps arrived in the mail. Not only did it increase by about a hundred and fifty a month, they awarded me back pay to October, so I suddenly had about five hundred dollars for groceries. My absolute need for meat had shocked me with this pregnancy. It wasn't an item I cooked regularly, if ever. With the extra food money I was able to pan-fry the steaks I found on clearance with some regularity. I'd eat them with mashed potatoes or an entire head of cauliflower that I steamed with salt and pepper. Finally I wasn't hungry on a regular basis, and I began to gain weight.

Pearl broke down on the same day my student loan money came in. There was no sound—not even her usual clicking noise—when I turned the key. Knowing I was having a girl caused the reality of my situation to sink in. I now had a vivid mental image of me driving around with two kids, and I had a fucking shitty car that needed to be replaced. I'd grown weary of navigating this tiny car through streets filled with a foot of unplowed snow. The Land girls needed a four-wheel-drive vehicle. We needed something beefy. On Craigslist, the perfect one appeared: a 1987 Toyota 4Runner. This was my dream truck, and the ad included important details like a 22RE engine, lift kit, new tires, and, most important, second owner. It also said it was in northern Idaho, about five hours away. I emailed the guy anyway. After four years with Pearl, our beloved 1983 Honda Civic Wagon that broke down twice a month, I needed a tank to get us through the winter. And, well, life in general. At thirty-five hundred dollars, the 4Runner was half my student loan money for that semester, but we couldn't survive without a car.

Sylvie offered to drive me to Idaho, and the owner of the 4Runner said he could meet us in Coeur d'Alene. The truck purred like a domesticated tiger and it all seemed too good to be true. I told the guy that.

"You know," he said, "I do have a lot of interest in this thing. I bought it from an old guy and cleaned out the engine and made it look nice." He rubbed the back of his broad neck with his giant hand. "It's a good truck," he said, and I believed him. "I knew I'd sell it to you. I threw some better tires on it and there's a stereo in there if you want it. I guess I have a soft spot for single moms."

I wanted to hug him, but my hand still shook as I wrote the check. On the way home, Emilia and I pondered what we'd name the truck and settled on Penny, short for Miss Moneypenny. Sure, it only had two doors, but she ran better than any car I'd had in over five years and tripled my confidence in driving through snow. Penny would get us anywhere, of that I was sure. She also had good resale value, since 4Runners were in high demand in Missoula. If shit hit the fan, I could always sell her, and I'd get at the very least what I paid for her.

In the following week, my mechanic's brother got Pearl running again and I took a few pictures of her engine and posted her for sale on Craigslist. An owner of a used car lot in town called almost immediately and offered to pay me five hundred cash, sight unseen. When he handed me five one-hundred-dollar bills, I didn't question the fact that he didn't test-drive the car. I just wanted it to run well enough to get this guy where he needed it to go before he could change his mind.

When Emilia got home from school, I told her that I'd sold Pearl, and she ran to her bed and wailed, "You didn't let me say goodbye!" Token followed her, lifting his front paw in uncertainty before sniffing out the situation.

"I didn't know you'd want to say goodbye," I said in a gentle but firm voice.

"You never know I want to say goodbye!" she said, and sobs ensued.

I tried my hardest not to read into that. "I'm sorry, sweetie. I didn't know you would want to say goodbye to Pearl." I took a deep breath. "If you had the chance, what would you want to say to her?"

Emilia sniffed a few times. I waited patiently before she lifted her head off the pillow. "I . . ." she started. "I would tell her she is a good car."

"She is a very good car," I echoed.

"And she's the best car we've ever had," Emilia declared.

I wanted to argue. Our Suba-Ruby—who'd met an untimely death on the side of Highway 20 when a car slammed into the back of her with Emilia strapped in the backseat—had definitely been our best car. But it was hard to disagree with the fact that Pearl had gotten us to Missoula. My own eyes started to water at that. "You're absolutely right," I said, voice raised. "Pearl was the best car."

"The best!" Emilia said, rising to her knees on the bed.

A few days later, I saw that the used car lot had Pearl for sale for almost three thousand bucks, proclaiming she could take anyone on a road trip across the country. This was advertising at its most malicious level of dishonesty, since I'd listed all her issues in my ad, and I doubted they'd been able to fix them in a few days' time. I did see Pearl puttering around our neighborhood a couple of times over the next few months, but she didn't appear after that.

Winter continued to pummel us with blowing snow and negative temperatures. Each week brought warnings about the weather, from record-breaking amounts of snow falling or winds that sent temperatures down to thirty below zero. At home we wore layers and had three electric heaters going at all times. I stopped caring if my landlords would find out. Without the heaters, it wouldn't get above fifty—cold enough to lose one of my favorite plants, an African violet I had purchased as a centerpiece for Emilia's first birthday party. I was able to save one of the leaves and put it in some dirt in the hope it would propagate.

Miss Moneypenny the Supertruck was a badass, though, and I felt like a weight of worry had been magically lifted from my shoulders. In addition to the unpredictable mechanical failures, I'd had no idea how much of my anxiety had been caused by Pearl's inability to handle a slight dusting of snow. Our street was considered low priority for the snowplows, and if it weren't for the 4Runner, I'd be walking to campus five days a week, past all the stranded Subarus. One morning in late February, Emilia opened our back door to reveal a two-foot wall of snow. School had been canceled—something I had begun to believe never happened in Montana—and she wanted to go outside to play.

One vehicle after the next got stuck on our street. One of the breweries in town offered a free pint to anyone who arrived on skis. When Emilia stepped off the porch outside, she sank into snow up to her shoulders. The feral cat that lived under the house got stuck somewhere and, despite our efforts to dig him out, meowed for hours. News stations reported skiers missing and the snow falling outside created complete whiteout conditions. Then people on Facebook started posting about an avalanche nearby in the Lower Rattlesnake. Some kid hiked up Mount Jumbo to snowboard down but got carried off by a wall of snow that ripped one house off its foundation and buried another. Dozens of people ran with their shovels and gear to dig out an eight-year-old boy and the older couple who lived in the house.

Emilia and I watched *The Princess Bride* and *The Goonies* under blankets while she snacked on Nutella sandwiches and apple slices. Each time I went to the bedroom to look out at the street, another car was stuck. Our house, at a hundred and fifty years old, had likely stood through countless snowstorms, and I hoped the roof wouldn't cave in this time.

---

"C'mon, Emilia, we need to go," I said for the third time that morning. Her school had a teacher workday so she needed to come to class with me, and I couldn't miss Shakespeare. Our planned discussion was the second half of *Macbeth*. "You have your headphones, right?"

Walking through the LA Building at almost nine months pregnant with a six-year-old in tow was enough to part the sea of students in front of us, clearing a path for us to walk. Some of them smiled down at my kid while others gave us weird looks of confusion and annoyance.

My professor greeted Emilia warmly. I'd emailed him that morning to let him know I had to bring her with me that day. As always, he said it would be wonderful to have her join the class. *Hopefully not the discussion . . .* I'd said as a response.

It was common practice for my professor to assign roles to students for us to read particular scenes. Fortunately, I did not have that responsibility today because my laptop kept dropping the Wi-Fi signal and consequently Emilia's cartoons. She drew in my notebook to pass the time, listening to part of the play.

One student, assigned the role of Macduff, read, "Tell thee, Macduff was from his mother's womb / Untimely ripp'd," and several students glanced in my direction. My face blazed with heat as I tried to sink down into my chair.

After class, Emilia skipped along beside me while we walked back to the car. I'd promised her a Happy Meal if she behaved, which definitely influenced the skipping.

"Mom," she said, lowering the height of a skip down to a little hop. "I like going to school with you."

"You do? I wondered about that. I thought it was super boring."

"It is," she said. "Except today!"

"Why's that?"

"I like when they read plays. It's fun. But why was everyone talking about sex and blood so much?"

Just then, a classmate crossed our path and stopped when he saw us. He had an expression on his face that led me to believe he had heard what Emilia just said. We chatted about the final for our short story literature class, but Emilia yanked on my arm, pulling me away.

"Sorry!" I said. "She just heard a very graphic discussion on *Macbeth* and now we're going out for Happy Meals." After we sat down at our usual table, I brought up something I had been thinking about. "Hey, so, I think I decided on a name. You wanna hear it?"

Emilia nodded enthusiastically. This had been an ongoing conversation, and so far she had absolutely hated every name I came up with. With a last name of Land, names could be comical. I'd gone through phases of wanting to name her Alaska, Homer, Sawyer, and Ellis Irene (Ellis I. Land). The friend we'd just run into had once suggested Novella (a new, little thing) and I was leaning toward the middle name Cairn, but the first name was still undecided. Part of that was purposeful—baby names were my favorite distraction from schoolwork and life stress.

"What do you think of Hadley?" I said. "It's the name of my favorite writer's first wife. Hadley Cairn Land?"

"Hadley," Emilia growled. "I *hate* that name. There's a girl at school named Hadley and she's mean!"

"Are you serious? You really don't like that name?"

"I *hate* it!" She crossed her arms and stuck out her bottom lip for emphasis.

"Fine!" I threw up my hands and shook my head before sighing in exasperation. Emilia didn't waver in her stubbornness. "What do you want to name her?"

"Coraline," she said, pointing her chin toward the ceiling.

"Coraline? Like the movie?" I had only watched parts of it, but I'd listened to it several times. Emilia had been obsessed with the stop-motion movie lately and almost always chose it when I told her she could watch something so I could get some homework done.

"Yeah," she said. "It would be a perfect name."

"Hm," I said. "Coraline Cairn Land. That's not too bad."

"See?" Emilia said.

I knew it was originally a book by Neil Gaiman but that was about it. "Why don't we read the book first," I said, "before we make any final decisions."

"Okay! Can we read it now?"

"I have to order a copy, but we'll start reading it as soon as it comes in the mail, okay?"

Our paperback version of the book, a ten-year anniversary edition, arrived just a few days later. Before Emilia got home from school, I flipped through the introduction, written by Neil himself, who said the story was for his daughters to teach them about being brave, which he said was to be scared and do the right thing anyway. The epigraph, a quote by G. K. Chesterton, caught my eye: "Fairy tales are more than true: not because they tell us that dragons exist, but because they tell us dragons can be beaten."

As far as I was concerned, just those two things confirmed my question of whether or not I should use Coraline, a name created by a typo, for the first name of this human who forced me to be brave every day. For the next ten nights, Emilia didn't put up an argument when I told her it was bedtime. In fact, one night she told *me* it was time to read to Coraline and we both got ready for bed. We squeezed into our tiny bathroom together to brush our teeth, and lay down on my bed, cleared of stuffed animals to make room for both of us, to read another chapter of the story. Emilia's hand stayed on my swollen belly "just in case she kicks" as a sign to see if her little sister approved of the name Coraline. She did.

# 16

## MFAs and Other
## Mother Fucking Assholes

Of course, when things finally started to feel like they might be going well, the administrative law judge's ruling arrived in the mail. I had expected it to be bad; possibly even horrible. My assumption that she was not impressed by my self-employment was absolutely correct. She'd used the job I'd had for a short stint as my imputed, full-time income, meaning I hypothetically made twenty-six hundred a month. This was my potential income, even though I had explained that fifteen dollars an hour at full time in Missoula was nearly impossible. Jamie's overtime pay was not included, and she subtracted his union dues. So I suddenly was a full-time worker, yet she did not impute child care costs. In fact, she stated, "While Ms. Land testified that she incurs some child care costs for Emilia while she is attending class, Ms. Land failed to demonstrate that these expenses are related to her employment or education necessary to obtain a job." Not only was I not in any "real" need of child care, she didn't consider an English degree necessary for my future employment.

Her statement went on about how many nights Emilia spent with her dad and that we do not follow the parenting plan. She calculated that Jamie should only have to pay me four hundred and thirty-two dollars a month, just a hundred and thirty-two dollars more a month than he already did. If she had imputed my income at minimum wage, like the child support office had and traditionally does, his support obligation would be six hundred and eighty-nine. She did not order him to pay any part of Emilia's extra medical expenses beyond health insurance, even though the insurance he had for her through his job didn't cost him anything. He would have to pay back support from October, not the day I had filed for modification. For all intents and purposes, this order ruled in his favor.

A petition to appeal would have to be filed through the circuit court within sixty days. After an hour of calling various offices, I found the correct circuit court clerk who'd be able to send me the paperwork in order to do that. I wasn't sure what else to do. There was no way I could accept that she used that income for me. The fact that she didn't consider my education to be useful also felt like an unnecessary, personal blow.

Jamie uncharacteristically reached out to talk to Emilia the day after I got the paperwork. I assumed he'd also seen the ruling, because immediately after the text about a video chat was another to rub the judgment in my face. *I'm going to appeal*, I replied, after he commented that the judge seemed fair.

*Don't get greedy*, he wrote back.

Appealing the administrative law judge's decision proved to be no simple task. When I could get a clerk of court to talk to me, every single word they uttered was more discouraging than the last. One thing was certain: if I wanted to appeal, I'd have to appear in front of a judge in person.

"There's no way I can do that," I said.

"Well, then find someone who can appear on your behalf," the woman on the other end of the line said, her voice growing increasingly annoyed.

Most lawyers in Portland, Oregon, would not agree to pro bono work or even a sliding scale. When I had reached the point of giving up, a friend gave me the name of one who would. After I explained my case and emailed her scanned copies of documents, she asked for a nine-hundred-dollar retainer. She seemed confident that I had a good case and I tried to trust her on that. With the back child support Jamie would owe, that amount alone would replace the money I put into the retainer. Then I'd possibly get more than twice as much in support money as I received now. It made sense if I did the math and added everything up, but I struggled to comprehend spending nearly a thousand dollars two months before graduation and three months before my baby was due. Without any other money coming in, I knew with certainty that my bank account would empty two weeks after my second daughter was born.

Emilia normally went to her dad's for spring break, but that year we had planned for him to take her the week before, since that was the only (paid) vacation time he could get. He wanted to drive down to San Francisco with her to visit his family. I hated sending her to stay with him, especially knowing he planned for them to sleep in his truck or camp to save money on plane tickets. This wouldn't be the type of camping that Emilia enjoyed. There would be no "setting up" a campsite or enjoying a fire-cooked meal. This was driving all day, pulling over to pitch a tent or sleep in the back of his truck with his dog if it was raining, and doing the same the next day. But if he wanted to use his visitation time, there wasn't much I could do but brace myself for what she was like when she returned. For our spring break, I had received a scholarship to get her into a week of day camp at the gymnastics gym where she'd gone to preschool, and we were both excited about that.

Jamie, unsurprisingly, was not pleased that I had hired a lawyer and did not opt to get his own. This forced my lawyer to communicate with him through dozens of emails, phone calls, and an in-person meeting—all of which came out of the retainer. Since Jamie clearly didn't want to risk going back to court, our goal shifted to getting him to settle on an increased amount. My lawyer thought she could get six hundred fifty, but he wouldn't agree to that. At this point, she informed me that I had used up my retainer and so she would begin to bill me fifty bucks an hour.

I sat, stunned, too anxious to go to class. It was Shakespeare that day, and I'd missed that one a lot. Pop quizzes could not be made up, and I needed to be there for discussions due to the density of the reading assignments. All the productions of plays I found on YouTube weren't enough. My midterm had been a train wreck. Without papers and essay questions I definitely wouldn't have a passing grade. But I couldn't risk missing an email or call from my lawyer, who had a call scheduled with Jamie that day. Hopefully my professor would understand. He usually did, or seemed to. Still, it was a risk—if I didn't pass his class I wouldn't graduate. Sitting at home in front of my laptop, staring out the window, wasn't helping but I couldn't seem to do anything else.

My lawyer's email arrived not long before I had to meet Emilia at the bus stop. The lawyer wanted to know if I would agree to six hundred and allow him to claim Emilia as a dependent on his taxes for the next five years, telling me to look into it and think it over. At a local H&R Block, the woman who answered the phone was kind enough to talk me through what that meant.

"It's a tax deduction, not a refund," she said.

"I can't afford to lose the Child Tax Credit," I said, not sure what either of these things meant. I'd always done my taxes for free online, without any real explanations as to how I got a refund.

"This deductible reduces taxable income over twenty-five thousand dollars," she said. "It's not a credit and will not affect your eligibility for the Earned Income Tax Credit."

"Then why would it be a bargaining tool?"

"If the amount you owe taxes on goes down, then you pay less taxes." She paused. "But it sounds like it's not something you need if you're not making enough."

"Okay," I said. "Thank you for your time."

Five years was a long time. I wouldn't be able to claim Emilia as a dependent until the year 2020. I doubted I would ever need it, and if I did, I'd always be able to claim one child. Jamie had to go to my lawyer's office to sign the paperwork. She insisted upon adding a clause that our agreement could not be modified even if I became successful as a writer. At the time I considered this a cute gesture, nothing more.

I felt no relief until all of it was filed, but I still had to wait for payments to be direct-deposited into my account. At six hundred dollars a month, his payments would be about a hundred thirty-eight dollars a week. For the back support, he'd have a little extra taken out of his paycheck for the next several months instead of a one-time payment.

Sometime around two in the morning, I woke up to shuffling in the entryway of the house, where most of the renters entered. We never used that door because it was mostly glass and hung about two inches above the floor, so I kept some old towels and sheets covering it. The main, outer entrance door rarely stayed locked because it was a pain in the ass to jiggle the key just the right way to unlock it. This shuffling noise didn't sound like it was someone who knew where they needed to go. They sounded lost, then like they'd taken a seat on the stairs.

Our back door was off a main alleyway from downtown that went directly from a bar a lot of older locals went to for its cheap drinks, to a spot with a freeway overpass and a railway bridge that went over a creek. More than once in the years we'd been there, I'd found beer cans around our porch from someone sitting there to drink them after we'd gone to bed. My roommate's bike was stolen while we were all home. One night I'd woken up to the static of a police radio and flashlight beams shining through my windows because someone ran from the cops and threw something toward the bushes out front. My upstairs neighbor came home from his bakery shift once to find a college student, his face still painted for the Homecoming game, fast asleep in his bed.

Thankful for the hundredth time that Emilia was a solid, heavy sleeper, I lay there, my heart racing, listening to whoever it was grow more and more frustrated. He got up a few times and mumbled, shuffling his feet in the entryway, trying the door of the office. Then he jiggled our doorknob. I grabbed for my phone but didn't want him to hear me call the police, or to get out of bed and leave Emilia there alone to go into the next room to call. Right when I opened my flip phone, the person left the entryway, went outside, and then went to our back door, where I heard him knocking and rattling the doorknob.

"No, man, you don't live here," my roommate Kevin, whose bedroom door was directly across from the back one, said in a calm voice. He must have been up watching Netflix.

I crept out to the kitchen area, where I could have a partial view of the door. We used to have a baseball bat there but I forgot what happened to it. It looked like the guy was in a purple suit. He tried the door-knob again. Kevin repeated that it wasn't his house, and calmly reached up to pull the shade on the door down. I quickly went over to the other windows and closed the curtains—bright, brick-red ones I'd bought the year before in an effort to keep it warmer in the winter. I glanced down at the window seat below, where Emilia's watercolor paintings from earlier that evening were still drying. My hand instinctively went to my stomach to soothe another Braxton-Hicks contraction caused by jumping out of bed so quickly. I tried my best to take a deep breath while I walked back over to the corner of the kitchen counter.

"I think he's gone," Kevin said. "You okay?"

"Yeah," I said. "Someone thinking they lived in our apartment is a first."

"My friend said this used to happen at his place down the road all the time."

"Well, in a house this old, I'm sure a lot of people have lived here through the years."

We shared a chuckle then, and I said I should try to sleep a bit more. Emilia moved a bit when I got back into bed. Maybe the land-lord would finally install that new lock for the front door now.

———————

Emilia's therapist, who told us to call her Pam, had a cramped office full of clear plastic bins of toys and art supplies. She sat in the chair by a desk completely covered in papers, and we sat on a small love seat that had seen better days. Emilia spent the time coloring while Pam and I chatted about what had been going on.

"She took something from her teacher one time," I said, eyeing Emilia's movements to see if she paused or signaled that she was lis-tening. "Her teacher held the waistband of her jeans while she rooted through her pockets."

"Is that true, Emilia?" Pam asked.

"She put my face on the desk and her arm on my back," Emilia said. She hadn't told me that part. The principal made it sound like her teacher had grabbed her from behind with one arm while she went through Emilia's pockets with her hand.

"What was she looking for?" Pam asked.

Emilia shrugged for an answer and Pam looked at me.

"It was a small animal figure? I think it was part of a counting game." I sighed. "This was the second time Emilia was caught with something." Though I couldn't say it out loud with Emilia within earshot, it really started to feel like my child had been getting in an unusual amount of trouble at school. Since the principal had called about the boys attacking her, we'd spoken several more times about new incidents. Pam's expression remained neutral. She focused on Emilia's drawing of a house, choosing to ask her questions about that instead.

We'd been late to school a lot lately. They had stopped sending Emilia to lunch detention after I begged them not to single her out since it was often my fault. I couldn't seem to get going in the morning anymore. Sometimes I fell asleep with Emilia at bedtime and didn't wake up until my alarm went off. Every morning was a struggle to get clothes and shoes on. At times, Emilia outright refused, or screamed, and I couldn't do anything but carry her to the truck. I didn't understand what was happening to my child, who months before said, "I'm so glad you're my mom" when I kissed her good night.

When it came time to order my cap and gown, I wondered if I should send announcements to my family. Dad and I had exchanged a few brief text messages at Christmas when he sent a present to Emilia and wanted to make sure I knew so it wasn't stolen off my porch. Mom and I hadn't talked in a long time and the rest of my family I hadn't seen or heard from in three years. When I asked my brother, whom I still chatted with every few months or so, about the announcements, he told me not to bother. *Nobody will care*, he wrote back through Messenger. *Yeah*, I wrote back, *you're probably right.*

Going to an attendance-required class for fifty minutes three times a week sucked the energy out of my entire day. Finally, I made the decision to let my last client go. I'd held on to them because they'd shortened their clean to two hours and I cleaned their office building on Wednesday evenings, too. They had me on the payroll for that, making it easier to apply for government assistance—for all my other work, they had me get written statements from my clients to prove I worked when I said I did.

After one particularly difficult week, Emilia spent the night at a friend's house so I could go to a grad student party. It had been a while since I'd hung out with all the MFA students, and I missed seeing them. Now that I was an official hopeful candidate, I felt more out of place, not less. What if they had rejected me and I just didn't know it yet? If I were rejected, would they even consider me a friend anymore? Their party was centered on a competition to judge the best homemade mac and cheese. Fortunately, I had long perfected the recipe I'd found in an old edition of *Backwoods Home* magazine. Kevin had the night off and I encouraged him to come with me.

"Don't you want to see them?" I asked. He had graduated with an MFA in poetry.

"I get overwhelmed when it gets loud," he said.

"Well, if that happens, just find a way to wave me down and we'll go." It'd been a while since I had socialized with more than just Sylvie or Kristi and Becky to take the kids to Lolo Hot Springs. A lot of the people at this party hadn't seen me in person since I'd started to show, and I was self-conscious about my increasingly large stomach. We parked the truck by a house I'd coincidentally worked at in warmer weather, pulling weeds out of several large flower beds. About twenty people were there, spread out through the living room and kitchen, where a dozen different types of mac and cheese sat on the counters. Each had a card with the name of the dish and the main ingredients it contained. I put mine on the end of the line, deciding to call it "Backwoods Mac," and wrote that it had ham and tomatoes under the crusty cheese top.

"Mmmm, ham," one of the fiction students said from over my shoulder. I turned to him and smiled.

Everyone seemed happy to see me, or at least they were nice about me showing up. I wasn't sure what I'd been nervous about until a bit later when I turned to see Judy Blunt standing in the en-tryway. My roommate was in a cove in the dining room, talking to another poet. In my hand was the small glass of wine I'd been sipping the entire time I had been there, and I felt an incredible urge to hide. Judy didn't know about my pregnancy, or I didn't think she knew, anyway. When she finally made it into the kitchen, our eyes met for a moment before she looked down at my stomach. She immediately dropped her gaze to the floor, and shook her head a few times.

While I would like to believe that moment didn't cost me my MFA candidacy, I know with certainty it did. I'd find out years later that whenever someone brought up my name, Judy would declare, "Babies don't belong in grad school." She also supposedly didn't like the way I dressed, and she thought I had too many tattoos. She told people I wasn't professional-looking because of that. She was especially preoccupied with my personal life, in particular that there wasn't a father involved with my second child. Of course none of this had been in my application or sample essays—she supplied the supplemental information to weigh her decision all on her own.

In recent conversations with a few of my favorite writing instruc-tors, one insightfully told me that the program would have squelched my spirit, saying I wouldn't be the writer I am today if I had gone. "They would have crushed you in workshops," another one said. I believe all of that to be true.

When I told Emilia I wouldn't go to school the next year, her eyes got big.

"No more homework?" she said.

"Nope," I said.

Emilia threw up her arms and yelled, "Yay!"

I thought of the face she'd made to mimic what I looked like when I sat at my laptop to concentrate on a paper due the next day. I thought of how many times I had told her to play alone because I had to finish reading a chapter. How often we couldn't do anything over the weekend due to the amount of studying I had to do. The countless number of classes she'd attended, and the babysitters who'd watched her so I could go alone. She'd trudged through my college education right along with me. Though it made our future uncertain, and I'd have to figure out a repayment plan on my loans before the year was over, if she was happy that I was done with school, then I was, too.

# 17

# Student of the Month

Thirteen days before my last day of college. A month and a half before my due date. In my backpack I carried sixty-five pages of papers and essays and reports with an included works cited. My final for Shakespeare was a week away, focusing on *Troilus and Cressida*, *Macbeth*, *Othello*, and *A Winter's Tale*, and would include half short-answer questions and half a choice of questions that had to be answered with the classic five-paragraph-style essay, complete with a thesis statement.

None of that was at the forefront of my mind that afternoon as I parked my truck a block away from Emilia's elementary school. I checked my purse for the fourth time to make sure I had my camera and a couple of hankies. She had an important event that day and I didn't want to miss a single minute.

Every month, her teacher chose two students as a "Student of the Month" to be awarded a certificate in front of the entire school during a Friday afternoon assembly. For the last couple of months, along with the help of her therapist, Emilia had worked really hard not to make a ruckus at school. This broke my heart, because her willful nature was a beautiful part of who she was as a human. At the same time I had always known this would be something she'd have trouble with. But this was her resilience training. Public school required conforming to a process my kid would not understand or mesh with well. She did not sit still, or not talk out of turn, or wait patiently. From her first breaths, this kid's spirit was one of determination and strong will, and I'd known it would be difficult for her to sit in a circle willingly, never mind follow about a hundred new rules. I wished I could afford even reduced tuition to an alternative school in town, the one that was more focused on the individual student's needs, but I guess I wished I could afford a lot of things.

The woman who sat behind the front desk at school, after witnessing countless mornings when I had to forcefully take my child's hand and physically pull her to her classroom, gave me a knowing smile as I signed in and picked up a visitor pass. A glance in her direction made my eyes sting with tears. I grabbed for one of my hankies as I walked to the gymnasium, where the bleachers had already filled with parents and students. Emilia's class was down in front, on the floor. She looked behind her to scan the bleachers a couple of times to see if I was there yet and I hated that she didn't know I was.

Before calling my daughter's name, Emilia's teacher introduced her with a lot of sentences containing the words "worked hard" in it. My kid stood, holding her certificate, eyes once again scanning the bleachers. I waved at her frantically from where I stood beside them, because climbing the stairs would have been too painful and embar-rassing. Emilia saw me and smiled with her whole body, down to her toes that flexed hard enough to make her lean back on her heels. She wore a brand-new shirt she'd picked out at Walmart for the occasion, a striped one with a kitten on front, and the same boots she'd worn on her first day of kindergarten, now scuffed and too small.

She ran to me when the assembly ended, reaching her arms above her head, the certificate in her hands. I tried so hard not to cry, even when she asked me to take her picture holding the piece of paper under her chin. When we got to the car, she asked me to text a photo to her dad. I hesitated, knowing he wouldn't respond, but did it anyway.

"Should we go get some ice cream?" I asked.

"Can we go get Blueberry first?" Emilia said as she climbed into the truck.

"Blueberry?"

"He helped me," she said with conviction.

"Of course we can get Blueberry!" I checked to make sure she was buckled in. "Why don't we pick him up and then walk to Sweet Peaks?"

When we got home from getting ice cream, I ran into Ashley, our upstairs neighbor who worked as a photographer. She looked like she was just returning home from a shoot. She said hello, shuffling a few heavy camera bags around her shoulders, and I asked her if she could maybe take a picture of us.

"Uh, sure," she said, and immediately dug for one of her cameras.

"Oh, I meant with my camera," I said, fumbling a bit through the words and request.

"No, it's fine!" Ashley said. "Why don't you sit in that rocking chair?"

"Isn't that your chair, Mom?" Emilia said, walking up the steps to the large front porch.

"Yeah, it is," I said. "My dad bought it for my mom when she was about as pregnant as I am!" I stuck out my belly a bit and rubbed it for emphasis. Ashley and Emilia laughed, and I sat in the chair, squeezing my daughter onto the small space available for her to sit on my lap. She held her certificate under her chin, holding Blueberry up behind it. Ashley took several photos of us, even asking if she could take a few with us sitting on the grass. I blushed a bit, beaming and chuckling at my kid telling Ashley all about being Student of the Month.

To celebrate, that weekend I took Emilia to a local theater's children's play and out for a slice of pizza and some ice cream. As we left the restaurant, the hostess told us to have a good night.

"We're not just having a good night!" Emilia jumped up and down. "We're having a *great* night! This is the best night ever, Mom!"

I smiled at her and nodded my head, noticing a few others turn and smile at her, too.

When I read to her at bedtime, the baby started kicking. I moved Emilia's hand to where I felt the last one. Emilia's face lit up when she felt it. "It's like she's giving me a high five with her foot!" she whispered.

I had a desperate urge to sob, but I didn't know if I would be able to stop. All my money had gone to paying a lawyer. In a few weeks I would graduate from college with almost fifty thousand dollars of debt, which I would begin making payments toward after a six-month grace period. Everything I did felt wrong or bad. Nothing felt like a good choice, or even a reasonable one. It's not that I wanted things to be easy, but a little less hard would be nice.

There might have been some senioritis happening by then. Classes were something I had to physically show up for and not much else, and showing up became an increasingly difficult task. In the final weeks of winter snow and ice storms, I had slipped (but caught myself) on the ice a few times and strained my pelvic muscles even more, causing me to waddle instead of walk. I got in and out of chairs at the same pace as a ninety-year-old. The baby also enjoyed the head-down position, which was the birthing position, but she leaned her butt out somehow, and it was enough to cause a hernia at the top of where my abdominal muscles had separated. My midwife referred me to a physical therapist, who gave me a large Velcro belly band to wear to keep the muscle tear from getting worse. Braxton-Hicks contractions happened with such regularity I had begun to time them in my Irish Literature class on Tuesday and Thursday mornings after trudging across campus from the parking lot.

Sleep was impossible. In addition to the stress and anxiety, no position was comfortable for very long and moving from one side to the other caused pain to shoot through my pelvis, jolting me fully awake. One night, I told Emilia about struggling to find a comfortable position and how I missed sleeping on my stomach. She disappeared into our room for a while. At bedtime, I found my bed covered with a thick layer of stuffed animals with a hole carved into the center.

"What's this?" I said.

"It's a hole for your belly," she said. "So you can sleep on your stomach."

"Oh my goodness, Emilia," I said. She reached her arms as far around my waist as she could to hug me. "Thank you, sweetie. That's a very thoughtful thing for you to do."

---

I had reached the end of my college career, and I obviously needed to find a job. I had one maternity dress, saved from my pregnancy with Emilia. When I sat down with a potential employer for an interview, it all seemed so comical. I knew they weren't going to hire me because I was pregnant, and they knew they weren't going to hire me because I was pregnant, but no one would say so for fear of a lawsuit. It felt as if someone might jump out from behind a plant to announce there were hidden cameras.

College hadn't taught me how to use my degree, or how to be a paid writer. All I had to guide me was a twenty-minute commencement address that someone posted on Facebook, coincidentally given by Neil Gaiman, that became daily, required viewing for its incredibly smart yet specific advice on how to become a freelance writer. An editor at *Mamalode*, who had published several of my essays, started assigning me pieces, mostly book reviews, for fifty bucks apiece. My essays in *Mamalode* had always been paid by the click and brought in anywhere from thirty to fifty bucks. Neil's speech became my business plan. I envisioned a mountain with a book I wrote on the top. Every job I took would be one that brought me closer to that.

My one writing workshop that semester focused a lot on lyrical styles of prose. The essay I'd been working on for it had turned into a thirty-four-page monster titled "Relentless," which, in my mind, would one day be that published book at the top of my envisioned mountain. In the time I had between class, homework, and taking care of Emilia, I started to shape it into a manuscript in the form of compiled essays. Without an MFA in my author's bio, I knew I would need to have as many publications and as big a social media platform as possible, but most of the literary journals and contests had submission fees. My website that I'd hidden for two years needed updating. I'd abandoned it after Judy Blunt said during her visit to my first creative writing class that blogging was cheap writing. I opted to pay for a domain name, calling it stepville.com (a play on stephanieland), to showcase what I'd published so far. Facebook had been my only network and whenever I posted a link to something I'd written and published, a core group of friends shared it, but I knew it needed to be bigger. Aside from magazine articles and being a journalist, I had no idea how to turn writing into a career. What made sense, or maybe the only thing that made sense, was to seek out any job that included writing or editing words.

———

My mom graduated from college when I was in the eighth grade, so my memories of the ceremony were vivid, even if I didn't understand the importance of it. She'd worked hard, that much I knew, and graduation was a very big deal for everyone in our family because she'd been the first one to accomplish that. Emilia was too little to understand the impact of my college graduation on us. She probably wouldn't remember anything about it. I didn't know if there'd be anyone to sit with her. Six years of work to get this degree, and I wasn't sure if it'd be worth it (or possible) to attend my own graduation, due to lack of child care.

I honestly still didn't know if I *wanted* to go to my graduation ceremony because it'd be difficult to see everyone with their parents and not have as much as a card to congratulate me from mine. But it was also a bit far from my immediate focus. Each morning, I woke up, got Emilia ready for school, then sent texts to five friends, part of a rotating dozen, who had agreed to be on call. My midwife's birth center was about fifteen minutes away, and I didn't think I'd be able to drive myself safely when I was in labor. Missoula didn't have the greatest taxicab situation, and Emilia needed someone to be with her. Sylvie often had the first spot on the list, and Emilia's former preschool teacher, Jess, agreed to be my kid's person through the birth. According to most of the "Signs Labor Is Near" lists online, it seemed like it could happen any day.

"You should start carrying a jar of pickles to class!" my friend Karl said before our next-to-final class began.

"For snacks?" I asked.

Reed turned around to look at Karl for the answer. He'd sat in front of me all semester, but without that long break between classes, we rarely hung out anymore.

"So if your water breaks you can drop the jar!"

"That's not funny," I said, faking a pouty tone. "I'm really scared of my water breaking in a weird or gross way."

"Just make sure you go into labor right before our final begins," Karl said, making Reed snort out a chuckle before he turned to face forward again.

Most of my social life for the last few months had taken place through Facebook posts, comments, and messages. Sylvie had convinced me to post a wish list for baby items, and boxes of diapers began to appear on my front porch. For the baby shower (which we held at the brewery next to the climbing gym of all places) I asked people to bring diapers and "Soon-to-Be Big Sister" presents for Emilia, saying it would just be good to see everyone. I was never comfortable asking people for things, and now it was near impossible with a resounding *You made your bed, now lie in it!* voice in my head.

*Mamalode* magazine held an event at one of the local hotels for Mother's Day, and it looked like it could be fun. Each room had a different local company showcased, from spa treatments to samples of chocolate, with a raffle you entered by walking in the door. They had free child care at the other gymnastics place in town, and some pretty good door prizes. (I wasn't sure what I would do with a wine fridge other than sell it, though.) I had dragged another single-mom friend of mine with me, feeling like a bad date because my main activity was finding a place to sit down.

"Let's just stay through the door prize thing," I said. "Then we can go."

They had quite a few door prizes to get through, including bottles of wine and a dinner for two. It was fun to see women get excited, and I longed to join them in holding a glass of wine.

"The next one," Elke, the editor in chief, who'd given me several assignments lately, said, "is a two-hundred-and-fifty-dollar gift certificate to the Orange Street Food Farm!"

My chest tightened a bit as I held my breath for a moment or two. That would be a huge, unimaginable thing to win. I glanced around at the crowd of women, who'd made an "ooh" noise but immediately quieted down.

Elke stood by the rail of the upper floor in the main lobby, holding a microphone, her hand deep in a bowl of pieces of paper. When she pulled one out and opened it, her head shot up to look directly at me. With some effort, she pointed the microphone at her mouth and said, "Stephanie Land."

By the time I was able to successfully stand to wave, I let out a laugh that was more like a sob. I'd never won anything like this before. Not even close.

"Boy, you're gonna need that!" a lady next to me said. Everyone around me clapped and smiled as I failed to hide that I was crying. When I looked up at Elke, I saw her wipe her eyes. She knew how much I needed it.

When I picked up Emilia, I asked her about the gym and if she had fun.

"It was okay," she said. "I miss Roots," the place she had gone for preschool.

"Well, maybe you can go there for a week of day camp this summer," I said. "But hey, guess what?"

"What?" she said, disinterested.

"I won something tonight," I said. "Something that you can use, too!"

"What is it?"

"I won . . . TWO HUNDRED AND FIFTY DOLLARS to use at the Food Farm!"

"Really?" Emilia didn't appreciate having to join me at the grocery store, but she loved going to the quirky place off Orange Street.

"What do you want to buy first?" I asked, envisioning their constant, changing display of seasonal toys they always had at the front of the store.

"I want to get raspberries, Mom," she said. "I want to get all the raspberries I can eat!"

I sucked in air for a second, biting my bottom lip. "Well," I managed to choke, "you can get as many berries as you want."

———————

We wore matching pink with white polka-dot dresses to the English Department's graduation ceremony, except I wore my Chaco sandals and she wore her black shiny shoes with one sock that was purple and the other light blue.

"How do I look?" I asked after I put on my black cap to go with my gown.

"Can't you wear your own hat?" She looked like she'd just smelled something bad.

"Nope," I said. "This is all they send you! I really like the tassel."

Sylvie picked us up with her youngest, and we met my old climbing partner Logan and his girlfriend, Mikaila, there. I didn't go to the main graduation ceremony at the football field that morning, opting to attend this one with about fifty other graduates. Half were grad students, and I knew many of them were going on to PhD programs throughout the country. With a month before my due date, I wasn't sure how much more pregnant I could really look under my black gown. I had decided, though, that this was important to me. Whether or not she would remember it, I wanted Emilia to see me walk across the stage. I wanted lots of pictures, or at least one really good one, that I could hang on the wall of our living room to look at every day. Most importantly, I wanted her to know that I'd done this so she knew that she could, too.

Missoula's weather was sunny and warm that day, which was wonderful for the morning outdoor ceremony. By the time we arrived at the University Center, taking a couple of escalators to get up to an auditorium on the third floor, the temperature had climbed to the mid-seventies. Earlier that week the highs were in the low fifties, so the air-conditioning hadn't been turned on yet. They lined us up to walk into the room, and sweat began to trickle down my back immediately after I sat in my seat.

After the valedictorian spoke, along with a couple of other people I didn't recognize, the guy who started the company Submittable stood at the podium, wearing the same cap and gown as my professors, who sat on the other side of the stage. In the last year, I'd gotten to know the Submittable platform. One could say I obsessed over it, since it was the method almost every literary journal used for essay submissions. I'd submitted my MFA application through it (which now coldly said "Declined" in the progress column), all my pieces for *Mamalode*, and countless other pieces that went on to receive rejections. I knew from local folklore in the English Department that the company was based in Missoula, but it didn't strike me as meaningful until I saw the founder at the podium in front of me, joking about how useless a degree in English seemed. At that point, I'd overheated too much to care. Sweat gathered on my forehead and upper lip, creating a film on my skin, and dripped from behind my kneecaps. Emilia's constant movements did not leave my peripheral vision, and I worried she wouldn't last much longer than me.

When they finally got to the undergraduates, each row stood one at a time before they lined up, still in alphabetical order, to walk across the stage and collect an empty holder for the diplomas we would later get in the mail. Different professors called out names of students, and as I walked onstage, Katie Kane was at the mic. She called out the name of my classmate who stood in front of me, then switched with Professor Ashby Kinch, one of my favorite literature instructors. Our class met first thing in the morning for medieval literature, one of the hardest classes I'd taken at U of M. Sometimes Led Zeppelin would already be playing when we walked in. "It's always a good morning when you start it with a little Zeppelin," he would say before doing things like reciting a sonnet from memory.

"Stephanie Land," Professor Kinch said a little too close into the microphone, and a few of the professors gave little "woo!" sounds.

"Woohoo!" I heard from the direction of Sylvie and Logan, and I wondered if Emilia was paying attention.

Then Professor Kinch turned to look at me, and I barely glanced at the dean, where he stood to my right. Kinch stepped away from the podium to hand me my folder as the dean stepped aside. Ashby and I both had tears in our eyes as we involuntarily reached out to embrace. I forgot about being sweaty, and honestly, about being pregnant, and soaked in all the joy he felt for me in that moment.

Down the stairs on the other side of the stage, I took a deep breath. Several of my professors were lined up to congratulate me. Each one had a handshake or embrace waiting for me along with words of congratulations, and I hugged them all, even the professor who taught my Shakespeare class. For about thirty seconds, I felt like Rose in that final scene at the base of the staircase in the movie *Titanic*. It really was that wonderful.

After all the names had been called, after we had each walked across the stage, and we moved our tassels from one side of our caps to the other, we stood and walked in a single line out to the foyer. In a sea of black gowns, a little kid in a bright pink and white polka-dot dress broke through to find me.

"Mom!" she said, jumping toward my outstretched arms. I wished so much I could pick her up and hold her. "Mom! I saw you onstage! Can I wear your hat? Can I, Mom?"

I laughed and took off my cap for her to wear. "Just don't lose the tassel!" When I looked up, my Shakespeare professor stood in front of me, beaming.

"Congratulations, Ms. Land," he said, holding out his hand for me to shake again, which I formally obliged.

"I, uh," I said, giving him a quizzical look. "I didn't think I passed your class."

He chuckled. "You did fine."

# 18

## Coraline

My day planner for the next few weeks filled up with phone numbers. I started to lean on the "211 First Call for Help" line more than ever. Every time I dialed the number, a woman answered who might as well have been an angel, informing me of what local organizations had funding, or gas cards, or a secret closet full of birthday presents, complete with wrapping paper, that I could choose from for Emilia's birthday. I had found two jobs: one, entering events in community calendars and switching out fliers that advertised them in bathroom stalls; and two, a paid internship through the local YWCA. Between the two, I had the possible income of about a thousand a month, and I could do both with a newborn in my lap or strapped to my chest. My new boss at the calendar editing job, who coincidentally was a former housecleaning client, offered me a week of summer camp at Roots as a bonus, since it had been bartered to them as part of a payment for ads. Coraline's due date was June 15, which, ironically, was Father's Day that year, and I chose that week for Emilia to go to camp.

Ten people said they had varying degrees of availability to help us get to the birth center. Five days before my due date, Sylvie told me she couldn't be on the list.

"What?!" I texted back on Messenger. "What do you mean you can't be here? My due date is in five days!"

"Then call an ambulance if you go into labor!"

I stared at her message, not knowing how to respond. I probably said something like she wasn't being a good friend. Sylvie took that as the end of our friendship, and I felt like that was accurate. As someone who'd been abandoned by her family, I had no tolerance for friends I heavily relied on and trusted who let me down when I needed them most. In fact, it just further convinced me I shouldn't trust anyone but myself.

But then my cousin Jen showed up two days before my due date, bringing jam and coffee and much-needed relief. We went for walks around the block, eating ice cream out of dishes, Emilia always running ahead. The Braxton-Hicks contractions were constant. In a moment of desperation, I asked my friend Jess to come with me to the birth center so I could check how dilated I was.

"You're about four centimeters," my midwife, Julie, said.

"Four?" I pushed my head back into the pillow. "Okay, look. I really only have support this weekend. I've been having mild contractions for the last few days. Is there nothing you can do to help?"

"I can strip your membranes," she said rather plainly and added a small shrug like it wasn't a big deal.

"Okay, sure, let's do that." I had no idea I was agreeing to allow this woman to put her fingers *inside* my cervix. Without a warning, telling me what she was about to do, or even instructions to let out a deep breath, her gloved fingers traced the top of my baby's head, just inside the small opening my cervix had expanded to. As I writhed in pain and grasped onto anything I could while she did it, I focused on getting this baby out at a time that fit with other people's schedules.

"I'll leave you here to rest a bit," Julie said, then left the room without another word, closing the door behind her.

Jess came over and sat on the bed.

"Wow, that sucked," I said, the pain so bad that my chest was still heaving. I put my hand near the bottom of my swollen belly in an effort to calm the cramping.

"Yeah, that looked pretty unpleasant," Jess said. "I know you don't believe in this kind of stuff, but would you want me to read her energy? It could help you calm down, too."

"How would you do that, like put your hands on my stomach and get a feel for her?"

"Something like that," Jess said. I nodded and said sure, and she got up to stand beside me. Jess put one hand on either side of my gigantic stomach and tilted her head a few times. Then she smiled. "Aw," she said. "I picture a bright, fair-skinned girl.

"She seems calm and kind of warm and snuggly," Jess continued after another pause. "I see a lot of light, like sunshine. She's just a bright, happy soul." She removed her hands from my stomach and smiled at me.

"So, basically nothing like me and Emilia," I said, struggling a bit to sit up. I still had an absorbent pad streaked with lubricant and blood underneath me, and I wondered if I had any on the insides of my thighs. But, most important was that I needed to place the pad Julie had left for me and get my underwear back on.

Jess attempted to help me, then decided it would probably be best to allow me to do it myself and save my dignity. Because of the pain, we had to walk at a slow pace to leave the birth center. I could barely get myself into my truck.

"We're gonna need some kind of step stool," I said.

In addition to the plans I'd made for getting to the birthing center and for looking after Emilia, there was another reason I was so desperate to give birth on my due date or very soon after. I had never felt like my usual midwife, Julie, liked me very much or approved of my situation. She also just, I don't know, seemed cold. There was another midwife named Autumn, who was young and not long out of school, whom I'd seen a few times and who had never shown any sign of judgment. She was calming, and really nice to me, which I appreciated. Fortunately, Julie was scheduled for a few days off, beginning at 10 p.m. on the night of my due date. In thinking about giving birth with Autumn attending instead of Julie, I felt so much tension leave my body. I decided to call Autumn to ask for some advice.

"I'm not sure what to do," I said. "I'm dilated to four centimeters. I've been having these Braxton-Hicks contractions constantly for three days. I even had the membrane sweep and nothing."

"You need to stop the contractions so they'll restart," she said. "Can you take a bath?"

"Not really," I said. "I mean, we have a small bathtub, but it's not that comfortable. I don't think it would do much to sit in it."

"Do you have any Unisom?"

"I do, actually. Would that help?"

"Yeah," she said. "A Unisom will help you relax and sleep deeply enough to temporarily stop the contractions. People go into labor at night a lot because that's when oxytocin levels are highest. You want your contractions to restart so they'll be stronger. Does that make sense?"

"Not really," I said, "but I'll do whatever I can."

At eleven that night, with Emilia asleep in her bed and my cousin out on the futon, I took two Unisom and rested my head on my pillow. A few hours later, I woke up to abdominal pain, like bad menstrual cramps, that got me out of bed after the third wave. I flipped open my phone to call Autumn.

*I think it's time*, I texted to my friends who'd agreed to be on call that night. My cousin watched from the futon while I bounced on the yoga ball in front of the bookshelf, keeping an eye on the same digital clock I'd stared at six months earlier as I fought the urge to go to the food bank.

Michelle, who'd been my roommate almost a year before and was now a nursing student, showed up first. Jess, Emilia's support person, showed up next. By then it was about four thirty in the morning. I called Autumn for the second time.

"One contraction is big, and the other is small," I said. When she asked if I'd been timing them, I said not really. "I think the bigger ones are every four minutes? With a smaller one in between."

"Just get down to the birth center," she said. "I'm already on my way."

"Okay." I snapped my phone shut. My contractions had paused, and I relished in those moments enough to take a couple of deep breaths. The room suddenly grew so still and calm. I didn't want to say anything until I absolutely had to. I wanted to live in these two minutes between the labor pains. Part of me would have happily traded another month of pregnancy instead of continuing the process of giving birth. Instead, I sighed and said, "I guess it's time to go in."

"I'll drive you," Michelle said. As my doula, that was her predetermined role, but I appreciated her enthusiasm. Jess would follow in my truck once she got Emilia awake and dressed. My cousin Jen would arrive after everything had settled at the birth center. There would already be five people watching me give birth and I didn't need another. Luckily my cousin understood.

I waddled out to Michelle's truck in the predawn light. I had to grab onto the handle above the doorway as I got in and struggled to sit down. As soon as my butt hit the seat, my water broke, filling my clothes and the entire cushion below me with fluid.

"Oh my god," I said. "I'm so sorry! This is . . . this is so gross!"

"I'll, uh," Michelle started. "I'll get a towel."

She came back out with a folded towel that I gladly sat on while we took off for the birth center. I tried to apologize more than once, but every contraction came with pain I couldn't talk through. Michelle drove stoically while we got caught at every red light on our way. By the time we were on the main stretch of road that was the straightaway to where we needed to go, the contractions were so bad I gripped the handle above the door to lift my entire body off the seat like a rigid two-by-four.

"Oh my god," I quickly said after it stopped for a moment.

"Yeah, that seemed like a big one," Michelle said, and another one began.

When we arrived at the birth center, Sarah, the nurse, waved me into the main building.

"My water broke before we left!" I shouted. "Like fifteen minutes ago!" In the doorway of the bedroom and connecting bathroom area they had set up for a birthing room, I tore off the bottom half of my clothes, wet with amniotic fluid, along with my shirt and bra. "Get me in the tub!" I shouted.

Autumn turned the water on as I climbed in, completely naked and not caring at all. I got into the same position I birthed Emilia in: facing the edge of the tub, with my knees on the floor and my elbows pressed down on the edge. The pain at that point was so bad I could hardly keep myself from screaming. I also really needed to poop.

"I need to go to the bathroom!" I yelled for the second or third time. "Please!" The tub had filled most of the way.

"You can't or you'll have this baby on the toilet," Sarah said. A familiar pain that midwives call "The Ring of Fire" began, and I knew my baby's head must be crowning. I wasn't ready. We'd just gotten here. Emilia and Jess weren't even there yet. Then something else felt odd, or out of place.

"Oh my god," I said. "Am I pooping?!"

"It's okay!" Autumn said. Michelle would later tell me Sarah had the job of fishing my turds out with a small net, similar to the ones you use to catch the dead goldfish your kid won at the county fair.

As Emilia arrived with Jess, I yelled so loud I saw ripples in the bathwater in front of my face. It must have been around five in the morning by then. Emilia opted to go outside, saying the yelling was too loud, as I screamed through another contraction.

"Just take the baby out!" I yelled in desperation. "Take her out!"

"Stephanie, you have to push," Autumn said.

"I don't want to push. I'll poop!"

"Here," said Sarah, "make this noise." She proceeded to make a comical grunting noise like she was trying to take a major dump.

"No!" I yelled. "It hurts! Please just take her out." I started to wail.

"Stephanie, you have to push."

"I can't! I can't. Just take her out!"

At some point, my body took over and I had no choice. I made those grunting noises, reached down between my legs with my right hand, and caught my daughter coming out of me. By the time I turned over to sit down in the tub, Sarah had a towel to cover her with. I held her tightly to my chest, her head centimeters from my nose. She smelled like raw steak.

The presence of her body on mine brought a peace I hadn't felt for a long time. Just as Jess had predicted, this small human was the antithesis of anxiety.

Everyone sat still around us, Emilia on the edge of the tub next to me, gazing down at her little sister for the first time. Finally, Sarah asked Michelle if she wanted to cut the cord. I couldn't take my eyes off this new human, who seemed like she could go right back to sleep. Then I started to feel a deep cramping.

"I'm having another contraction," I said, knowing that meant I had to birth the placenta.

"Okay, we need to get you out of the tub and onto the bed," Sarah said.

Someone took the baby from me while another helped me step out of the tub and I felt a towel wrap around my shoulders.

"Be careful walking," Sarah said.

By the time I got to the bed and tried to recline on the pillows behind me through another, lighter contraction, the placenta was on its way out. Jess and Emilia sat in a chair together, and I saw my oldest daughter holding my newest one. I tried to take in the scene. Suddenly the midwife and nurse were moving faster than I'd ever seen them go. I looked down and saw a gush of blood come out of me. My eyes got big and I asked what was happening.

Sarah shouted for someone to grab the phone. "Get ready to call 911!" With only a second's notice, Autumn gave me a shot in the arm.

Then Sarah apologized and shoved huge suppositories right into my rectum while everyone in the room watched. While she did that, her other hand pressed down on my still-swollen stomach. It hurt like hell and I yelled out in pain. "I'm sorry we have to do this, Stephanie," she said. "Looks like we have a small hemorrhage happening. We just gave you medicine to stop the bleeding but I need to push your uterus down so it stops contracting." She looked at me and we briefly made eye contact before she placed two hands on either side of my stomach and grunted as she pressed. The pain grew so intense I made a noise that was between a yell and quaking sobs. She did it two more times.

"Please stop," I begged and sobbed at the same time. "Please. Please just stop doing this to me."

Emilia sat in the chair next to the bed, holding her newborn sister, who'd come into the world with a forty-minute warning, and watched as a nurse and a midwife switched out bright red absorbent pads, sopping up the blood with towels. All while they fretted over whether or not to call an ambulance. This had happened to my mom when she gave birth to my little brother, and there was so much blood my dad had fainted.

Sarah stopped her grunting and pressing into my stomach.

The bleeding stopped. I turned to look over at Emilia, whose face had a look of terror for a second or two, then she smiled at me. She looked down at her new little sister for a moment before the midwife came to gently pick her up so I could cradle her in my arms again. It took some effort to lift myself up so the nurse could change the absorbent pads under me and get me situated.

"Why don't you hold her a bit before we weigh and measure her," Autumn said.

"It'll help your uterus calm down, too," Sarah added before she made a "phew" sound.

I nodded and reached out my arms, still not minding that I had absolutely no clothes on. Coraline's face turned toward my chest, and I unwrapped the towels enough to hold her naked newborn body against mine.

I looked up and saw that Sarah and Autumn had stopped cleaning up the bloody mess I'd just created.

"She's really beautiful," Autumn said.

I sniffed and Sarah handed me a tissue. "She has absolutely no hair!" I laughed as I wiped my nose. Her eyes hadn't fully opened, but I saw when I first held her in the tub that they were that murky newborn blue. "I wonder what color her eyes will be." I picked up her hand to examine her fingers, noticing the long nails I'd have to cut soon.

"She has really light features," said Sarah. "My guess would be blue."

I looked over at Jess, who gave me a smile and a nod. How did she know?

Coraline started to nudge her face into my chest in an attempt to latch on to nurse. "I guess we can try this now, huh?" I fought to remember how to grab my boob in a way that gave her the best chance to get her mouth connected to me in the right way. Coraline proved not to need much assistance and I involuntarily gasped. "Oh! I forgot how weird this feels!"

Both Sarah and Autumn leaned forward and nodded in approval. Sarah said she would put my clothes in the wash and dry them for me, and Autumn said she had to get herself cleaned up before her first client came in. After a little while, Sarah came back and said she hated to take Coraline from me, but they needed to measure and weigh her.

She put Coraline in a blanket and suspended her from a scale with a hook on the end. "My goodness!" she exclaimed. "Eight pounds, fifteen ounces!" She lowered my baby back onto the bed while everyone gasped and murmured. "If she'd been any smaller you would have had her on the way here."

I glanced over at Michelle and told everyone about my water breaking in her truck and how bad the contractions were by the time we arrived. Sarah smiled as she listened, busy with measuring Coraline's head circumference and body length. Michelle laughed and said she would run home and get me something to eat.

Sarah left for a few minutes, then returned and used a special black pad to mark my baby's footprints onto a sheet. I saw that it had *Congratulations* printed on the top and Coraline's weight, length, and the day and time she was born. The time they had printed was 5:16 a.m. I looked up at the clock. Two hours ago.

My cousin Jen showed up with a bag I had forgotten, filled with some baby clothes, diapers, and blankets. She paused to get a look at Coraline before she asked if there was anything else she could do to help.

"Um," I said. "Could you maybe get Emilia home and changed into different clothes and give her something to eat and take her to camp?"

Jen nodded. "Absolutely," she said. "Where is camp?"

"I can give you directions," Jess said, and smiled at Emilia. They were still sitting together in a chair. "I used to work there."

"Does that sound all right?" I asked Emilia, who nodded. Her eyes still had a stunned look to them.

My clothes had had enough time to go through the washer and dryer. Michelle brought me some fruit and toast with peanut butter. Jen left with Emilia to take her to day camp. Michelle went to class. Sarah, Autumn, and even Julie came in to check on me a few times and chatted a bit with Jess. I didn't hear much of what they said.

Once I was on my feet and walking around and had used the toilet successfully, they told me I could go home. Jess went to the truck to grab the car seat while I got Coraline dressed. "All the newborn-sized clothes are already a bit too small," I said with a laugh when she returned. I put my newborn daughter in the car seat. "She really is so calm, it's crazy." We gathered up our things and straightened up the room a little, then went out to the office to tell everyone goodbye. I had only been there for five hours.

"I'll see you tomorrow at your house," Sarah said. "But use the twenty-four-hour line if anything comes up."

Jess helped me load the car seat into my truck in the backseat on the driver's side. I struggled to get myself into the passenger seat. "I don't know if I can do this," I said, and she ran in to see if they had a step stool. Then Jess drove me home, helped me inside, patted me on the shoulder, put on her helmet, and rode away on her bike.

I stood in our living area, staring down at this human who'd been inside my body just hours before. Coraline stretched her fingers in her sleep, then moved her mouth as if she were nursing. I knew I only had minutes to try to get situated, but everything was already set up as much as it could be. I was in for a long, sleepless few days. Coraline's eyes opened and she looked up in my direction. Her hands went up to her face, which grew full with a look of discomfort.

"Well," I said with a sigh. "Here we go."

# Acknowledgments

At speaking engagements, people often ask what motivated me to write my first book, *Maid*. The answer is both lofty and painfully basic. On the one hand, I wanted to dismantle stigmas surrounding single moms, especially those who parent under the poverty line. On the other hand, I needed the money. The prospect of publishing a book wasn't just the answer to a lifelong dream—it was the discovery of a life raft on a sinking ship. With my book advance, I had the financial security I'd severely lacked as a mother, and no longer had to worry about how I would pay rent and feed my kids—my two biggest concerns as a low-income parent.

I never could have imagined the glorious ripples of change that would follow.

I'm grateful to all the readers of *Maid* and for their passionate response to its publication. I'm also grateful to those who discovered my story via the series on which it was based. After the Netflix series debuted, the National Domestic Violence Hotline received the most calls in a month in the history of their organization. Additionally, more people were inspired to volunteer, donate, and not only listen to but believe victims. Parents recognized how difficult it was for their adult children to parent alone, and that their circumstances were not their fault. Mothers watched the series with their daughters and finally encouraged them to accept support in leaving abusive relationships. What began with a cracking open turned into a space that others filled with compassion.

For years I have felt a responsibility to my readers, particularly those who suffered from abuse and food and housing insecurity, to continue the story that—so far—I've only partly told.

This is the book I have always wanted to write. It focuses on my senior year of college—my hungriest year—when my stomach and brain lived in a constant state of anger and lightheadedness.

Throughout that lonely year, I longed to read or see a story like mine. I searched for it. I needed it desperately. Now, when I speak to audiences, I quote Hannah Gadsby: "What I would have done to have heard a story like mine." This is what moves me forward. It gets me up in the morning, gets my suitcase packed, and gets me on the plane to fly far away from my family to speak to rooms full of strangers—something I was definitely not born to do. And even though writing *is* what I was born to do, at forty-four years of age I'm only beginning to feel a little less like an imposter, and a little more like I belong.

All of this is to say that I believe your story is important. I want to see it in the light of day, occupying spaces where people might read it. I want people to know about your struggles. I want people to know how impossible life feels at times. It's fucking hard, and it's not your fault that it's hard. This book won't change the circumstances of class and poverty in higher education, certainly not all on its own. But it's my dream for this book to amplify the experience of those of us who fought our way through, and those of us who were beaten down so hard that we had to make the heartbreaking decision to stop fighting. (And maybe, in the future, more of the privileged among us will join us in that fight.) Thank you, as ever, for inspiring me and so many others who walk beside you. I see you. You are not alone.

While *Maid* was raised by single moms, *Class* was fostered by Sulky Bitches. Through a fucking pandemic, countless illnesses, sleepless nights, sharting, and tears of frustration, anger, anxiety and sadness, we have supported each other and thrived because of that. Thank you, Erin Khar, for starting a Not Writing Club with me in 2021. As our little group grew and evolved into the Sulky Bitches Writing Club, you have hosted weekly Zooms, been my co-parent in a chaotic WhatsApp chat, and have been one of the most dependable humans I know. My gratitude for your friendship is endless. To the Sulkies: Y'all are fierce motherfuckers. I can't wait to see what's in store for each of you.

To Karie Fugett: You carried me through grief—the kind that made me scream, destroy precious things, and spend countless hours sobbing on my bathroom floor. Through all of it, you selflessly sat with me in that space for the worst year of my life and beyond. Without you, I wouldn't have survived four miscarriages in 2020. I wouldn't know what true friendship is. I definitely wouldn't have been able to write this fucking book. I also wouldn't be the proud caretaker of a marimo moss ball. My gratefulness for the universe convincing you to slide into my DMs is eternal. Thank you.

To Neil Gaiman: I stand in utmost gratitude for your friendship, for sending the most amazing texts in the whole world, and offering your time, mentorship, and some of the best advice I've ever received. Thank you, too, for creating a name that fits my beautiful daughter perfectly.

To Micaela Williams, the backbone of "Team Stephanie," for being with me every baby step of the way in writing and shaping this story, and for creating remarkable TikToks, newsletters, posts, stories, and content to tell the world about its existence. Your future is bright, bestie, just you wait. Thank you especially to Amanda Adams and Erika Peterman, the OG team members, for your years of support since the very beginnings when *Maid* was still just an Advance Reader Copy. Thank you all for keeping this ship afloat.

Thank you to my speaker's bureau, Lyceum, and to Hannah Scott, Kate Gannon-Sprinkel, Miriam Feurle, and everyone behind the scenes for being my biggest advocates and support system as I fly all over the country. Thank you for showing up for me like a family would. To Mollie Glick: You have shown me what a true literary agent should be. You are a force, and I'm grateful to know you (and am still kind of amazed that I'm your client). To Julia Cheiffetz, for being the first person ever to tell me "You can write whatever the fuck you want!" and for your unwavering faith and patience through four deadline extensions. And buckets of appreciation to Peternelle van Arsdale, who diligently worked with me to polish my dirty first draft and make it truly shine the way it deserves. You surely saved my mental health from complete collapse. Thank you.

To my she-shed builders: Logan DeBoer, Liz Hamilton, Andrea and Foster McCaffrey, Jeff Soulia, and Zooey Zephyr, thank you for giving up your weekend to help us create the structure that would become this cozy nook in the corner of my yard. Your work not only went on to receive a perfect score on "Room Rater," but is priceless simply because you all showed up and believed in me.

For that, I thank you. Again, I am so, so sorry about all the dog shit in the yard.

To Debra Magpie Earling, Katie Kane, Kelley, Ashby Kinch, Walter Kirn, Reed, Robert Stubblefield, countless other professors, classmates, and friends who sat with me during my years at U of M: Each and every one of you had a part in getting this book published—many because you supported me; others because you fueled my fire. I'm eternally grateful for that.

To the "Stephanie Army," made up of those who have supported me along the way: you have all shared posts, fought off trolls, bought my book, showed up at events, become my Twitter family, and encouraged me to change my inner narrative, to take up space, and to be strong (Christine D'Ercole and #hardCORE, I'm looking at you). All of you reminded me on a daily basis that what I do (yes, including the exercise) matters. You are the reason why I have the ability to advocate, speak up, continue to write, and, well, do my job. Thank you for joining me in the fight.

To Bodhi, Juneau, and Keats, for sitting at my feet or on the she-shed's porch while I write, and somehow knowing when I needed that the most.

To Orion, for fulfilling my dreams.

To Frank Gonzales, aka "Cyber Dad," for being so proud of me that I can feel it beyond your years. I know you would have loved this book, too, but only after I redacted the sex scenes.

To Timothy, my tall, dark, and handsome "Hot Viking" husband extraordinaire: Thank you for swiping right, for jumping into our life together feetfirst, for getting me through my first book tour, for taking care of our kids, dogs, plants, fish, vehicles, and house when I'm gone, and for bringing me coffee every morning that I'm home. Thank you, most of all, for selflessly adopting Coraline immediately after we were married, and for continuing to be the loving father both of my children have always deserved. I've basically been working on this book since we got married. Know that I was able to finish it because of the endless heaps of love you give and your impressive amount of stubbornness and commitment to see it through. I love you, sweetheart, and always will. Can't wait to snuggle.

To my sweet Emilia Story: Thank you for your endless empathy, your impeccable example of strength and determination, and growing up into one of the most amazing humans I know. I deeply appreciate your texts (especially when I'm away for work), and for playing Wordle with me long after it was cool. I stand in awe of you daily, and love you so, so much. Thank you for living this with me, for *surviving* it with me, and tolerating me writing about it. Twice. I can't say it'll be the last time. I apologize in advance.

To Coraline: Oh my goodness I love you more than life itself. You are a wonder, a beautiful soul, and the brightest light. Our true sunshine from the moment you were born. Thank you for finding us. My life was complete when I held you for the first time.

# About the Author

STEPHANIE LAND is the author of *Maid: Hard Work, Low Pay, and a Mother's Will to Survive* and inspiration for the Netflix series *Maid*. Her work has been featured in the *New York Times*, the *Guardian*, the *Atlantic*, and many other outlets. She focuses on social and economic justice and parenting under the poverty line. Find her @stepville or at stepville.com.